16

PATRICK PEARSE

The 16LIVES Series

£15 00

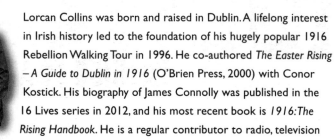

LORCAN COLLINS – SERIES EDITOR

Lorcan Collins was born and raised in Dublin. A lifelong interest in Irish history led to the foundation of his hugely popular 1916 Rebellion Walking Tour in 1996. He co-authored *The Easter Rising – A Guide to Dublin in 1916* (O'Brien Press, 2000) with Conor Kostick. His biography of James Connolly was published in the 16 Lives series in 2012, and his most recent book is *1916: The Rising Handbook*. He is a regular contributor to radio, television and historical journals. 16 Lives is Lorcan's concept, and he is co-editor of the series.

DR RUÁN O'DONNELL – SERIES EDITOR AND AUTHOR OF 16LIVES: PATRICK PEARSE

Dr Ruán O'Donnell is a senior lecturer at the University of Limerick. A graduate of UCD and the Australian National University, O'Donnell has published extensively on Irish Republicanism. His titles include *Robert Emmet and the Rising of 1803*; *The Impact of the 1916 Rising* (editor); *Special Category: The IRA in English Prisons, 1968–1978* and *1978–1985*; and *The O'Brien Pocket History of the Irish Famine*. He is a director of the Irish Manuscripts Commission and a frequent contributor to the national and international media on the subject of Irish revolutionary history.

16LIVES

PATRICK PEARSE

[signature]

Ruán O'Donnell

THE O'BRIEN PRESS
DUBLIN

First published 2016 by
The O'Brien Press Ltd,
12 Terenure Road East, Rathgar, Dublin 6, D06 HD27, Ireland.
Tel: +353 1 4923333; Fax: +353 1 4922777
E-mail: books@obrien.ie. Website: www.obrien.ie
The O'Brien Press is a member of Publishing Ireland.

ISBN: 978-1-84717-262-4

8 7 6 5 4 3 2 1
20 19 18 17 16

All quotations, in English and Irish, have been reproduced with original spelling and punctuation.

Printed and bound by CPI Group (UK) Ltd, Croydon, CR0 4YY
The paper used in this book is produced using pulp from managed forests.

PICTURE CREDITS

The author and publisher thank the following for permission to use photographs and
illustrative material:

Front cover and back cover: portraits of Patrick Pearse courtesy of the Pearse
Museum, Dublin. **Inside front:** O'Donovan Rossa funeral photograph courtesy of the
National Library of Ireland.

Photo section 1: p1 (both), p2 (both), p3 (both), p4 (bottom), p8 (top) courtesy of the
Pearse Museum, Dublin; p4 (top) courtesy of TopFoto; p5 (bottom) and pp6–7 courtesy
of the National Library of Ireland; p8 (bottom) courtesy of the Kilmainham Gaol
Collection.

Photo section 2: p1, p2, p4, p5 (both) and p7 courtesy of Lorcan Collins; p3 (top left)
courtesy of Tom Stokes; p3 (top right and bottom left) courtesy of the National Library
of Ireland; p6 (top, 17PC-1A54-24f), p6 (bottom, 17PC-1A54-24b), p8 (top, 17PC-
1B14-19) and p8 (bottom, 17PD-1A12-01) courtesy of the Kilmainham Gaol Collection.

DEDICATION

In memory of Al O'Donnell (1943–2015)

ACKNOWLEDGEMENTS

I wish to acknowledge the encouragement of Criostóir de Baróid, Mary Elizebeth Bartholomew, Ken Bergin, Rory and Patsy Buckley, Lorcan Collins, Tony Coughlan, Finbar Cullen, Jim Cullen, Dan Dennehy, Eamon Dillon, Eoin Dougan, Rita Edwards, Seamus Fitzpatrick, Jeff Leddin, Marcas and Leonora McCoinnaigh, Sean McKillen, Ger Maher, Patrick Miller, Dermot Moore, Mary Holt Moore, Brian Murphy, Róisín Ní Ghairbhí, Michael O'Brien, Dick O'Carroll, Labhras O Donnaile, Deasun O Loingain, Seamus O'Mathuna, Owen Rodgers, Charlene Vizzacherro, and Mary Webb (RIP). Thanks also to Maeve, Ruairi, Fiachra, Cormac and Saoirse O'Donnell.

16LIVES Timeline

1845–51. The Great Hunger in Ireland. One million people die and over the next decades millions more emigrate.

1858, 17 March. The Irish Republican Brotherhood, or Fenians, are formed with the express intention of overthrowing British rule in Ireland by whatever means necessary.

1867, February and March. Fenian Uprising.

1870, May. Home Rule movement founded by Isaac Butt, who had previously campaigned for amnesty for Fenian prisoners.

1879–81. The Land War. Violent agrarian agitation against English landlords.

1884, 1 November. The Gaelic Athletic Association founded – immediately infiltrated by the Irish Republican Brotherhood (IRB).

1893, 31 July. Gaelic League founded by Douglas Hyde and Eoin MacNeill. The Gaelic Revival, a period of Irish nationalism, pride in the language, history, culture and sport.

1900, September. Cumann na nGaedheal (Irish Council) founded by Arthur Griffith.

1905–07. Cumann na nGaedheal, the Dungannon Clubs and the National Council are amalgamated to form Sinn Féin (We Ourselves).

1909, August. Countess Markievicz and Bulmer Hobson organise nationalist youths into Na Fianna Éireann (Warriors of Ireland), a kind of boy scout brigade.

1912, April. Asquith introduces the Third Home Rule Bill to the British Parliament. Passed by the Commons and rejected by the Lords, the Bill would have to become law due to the Parliament Act. Home Rule expected to be introduced for Ireland by autumn 1914.

1913, January. Sir Edward Carson and James Craig set up Ulster Volunteer Force (UVF) with the intention of defending Ulster against Home Rule.

1913. Jim Larkin, founder of the Irish Transport and General Workers' Union (ITGWU) calls for a workers' strike for better pay and conditions.

1913, 31 August. Jim Larkin speaks at a banned rally on Sackville (O'Connell) Street; Bloody Sunday.

1913, 23 November. James Connolly, Jack White and Jim Larkin establish the Irish Citizen Army (ICA) in order to protect strikers.

1913, 25 November. The Irish Volunteers are founded in Dublin to 'secure the rights and liberties common to all the people of Ireland'.

1914, 20 March. Resignations of British officers force British government not to use British Army to enforce Home Rule, an event known as the 'Curragh Mutiny'.

1914, 2 April. In Dublin, Agnes O'Farrelly, Mary MacSwiney, Countess Markievicz and others establish Cumann na mBan as a women's volunteer force dedicated to establishing Irish freedom and assisting the Irish Volunteers.

1914, 24 April. A shipment of 25,000 rifles and 3 million rounds of ammunition is landed at Larne for the UVF.

1914, 26 July. Irish Volunteers unload a shipment of 900 rifles and 45,000 rounds of ammunition shipped from Germany aboard Erskine Childers' yacht, the *Asgard*. British troops fire on crowd on Bachelor's Walk, Dublin. Three citizens are killed.

1914, 4 August. Britain declares war on Germany. Home Rule for Ireland shelved for the duration of the First World War.

1914, 9 September. Meeting held at Gaelic League headquarters between IRB and other extreme republicans. Initial decision made to stage an uprising while Britain is at war.

1914, September. 170,000 leave the Volunteers and form the National Volunteers or Redmondites. Only 11,000 remain as the Irish Volunteers under Eoin MacNeill.

1915, May–September. Military Council of the IRB is formed.

1915, 1 August. Pearse gives fiery oration at the funeral of Jeremiah O'Donovan Rossa.

1916, 19–22 January. James Connolly joins the IRB Military Council, thus ensuring that the ICA shall be involved in the Rising. Rising date confirmed for Easter.

1916, 20 April, 4.15 p.m. The *Aud* arrives at Tralee Bay, laden with 20,000 German rifles for the Rising. Captain Karl Spindler waits in vain for a signal from shore.

1916, 21 April, 2.15 a.m. Roger Casement and his two companions go ashore from *U-19* and land on Banna Strand in Kerry. Casement is arrested at McKenna's Fort.

6.30 p.m. The *Aud* is captured by the British Navy and forced to sail towards Cork harbour.

1916, 22 April, 9.30 a.m. The *Aud* is scuttled by its captain off Daunt Rock.

10 p.m. Eoin MacNeill as Chief-of-Staff of the Irish Volunteers issues the countermanding order in Dublin to try to stop the Rising.

1916, 23 April, 9 a.m., Easter Sunday. The Military Council of the IRB meets to discuss the situation, since MacNeill has placed an advertisement in a Sunday newspaper halting all Volunteer operations. The Rising is put on hold for twenty-four hours. Hundreds of copies of the Proclamation of the Irish Republic are printed in Liberty Hall.

1916, 24 April, 12 noon, Easter Monday. The Rising begins in Dublin.

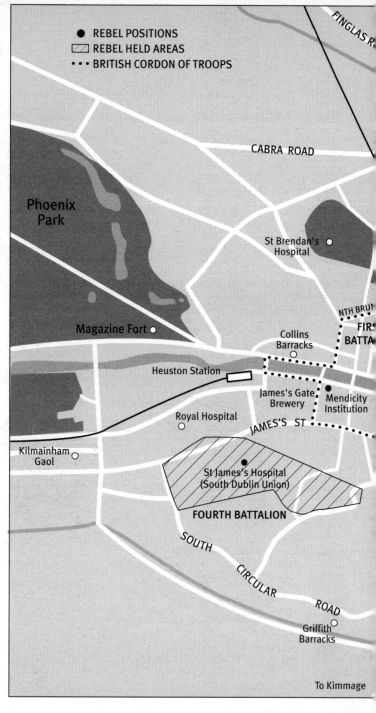

16 LIVES MAP

REBEL POSITIONS
REBEL HELD AREAS
BRITISH CORDON OF TROOPS

FINGLAS R

CABRA ROAD

Phoenix Park

St Brendan's Hospital

NTH BRUN

FIRST BATTA

Magazine Fort

Collins Barracks

Heuston Station

James's Gate Brewery

Mendicity Institution

Royal Hospital

JAMES'S ST

Kilmainham Gaol

St James's Hospital (South Dublin Union)

FOURTH BATTALION

SOUTH CIRCULAR ROAD

Griffith Barracks

To Kimmage

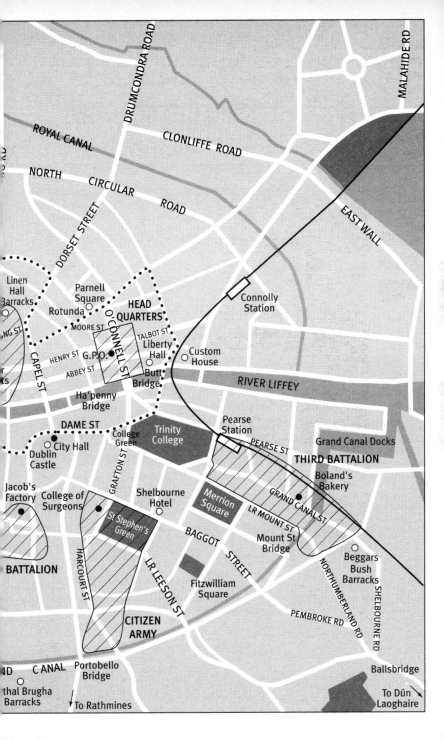

16LIVES – Series Introduction

This book is part of a series called 16 LIVES, conceived with the objective of recording for posterity the lives of the sixteen men who were executed after the 1916 Easter Rising. Who were these people and what drove them to commit themselves to violent revolution?

The rank and file as well as the leadership were all from diverse backgrounds. Some were privileged and some had no material wealth. Some were highly educated writers, poets or teachers and others had little formal schooling. Their common desire, to set Ireland on the road to national freedom, united them under the one banner of the army of the Irish Republic. They occupied key buildings in Dublin and around Ireland for one week before they were forced to surrender. The leaders were singled out for harsh treatment, and all sixteen men were executed for their role in the Rising.

Meticulously researched yet written in an accessible fashion, the 16 LIVES biographies can be read as individual volumes but together they make a highly collectible series.

Lorcan Collins & Dr Ruán O'Donnell,
16 Lives Series Editors

CONTENTS

Chapter 1

• • • • •

The Young Pearse

Patrick Henry Pearse was born on 11 November 1879 into a family of English, probably Anglo-Norman, stock and pre-modern Gaelic Irish heritage. His father James was born in London in 1839 and lived for many years in Birmingham where he worked as a stone-carver. The boom in church-building and Gothic decoration brought James Pearse to Dublin, and, by the early 1860s, he was a foreman for Charles Harrison at 178 Great Brunswick Street. From 1864, he sculpted for Earley & Powells of 1 Camden Street.

He had married Emily Fox in Birmingham the previous year. Mary Emily was born in 1864 and James Vincent in 1866. Agnes Maud followed in 1869. Both Agnes and her sister Catherine, who was born in 1871, died in early childhood. Such tragedies contributed to an inharmonious marriage, which ended with the death in 1876 of Emily from a spinal infection. She was just thirty years of age.[1]

A short time later, on 24 October 1877, James married Margaret Brady in the Church of St Agatha, North William

Street, Dublin, and they set up home at 27 Great Brunswick Street, modern-day Pearse Street. James operated his stone-cutting business from this address. Great Brunswick Street was a major thoroughfare leading to College Green and fashionable Grafton Street, with easy access to O'Connell Bridge and the north side of the river Liffey. They faced the substantial campus of Trinity College Dublin and were adjacent to Tara Street Fire Brigade Station.

James's second family produced daughter Margaret ('Maggie') in 1878, Patrick in 1879, William in 1881 and Mary Brigid in 1884. Living conditions were far from salubrious but were vastly superior to the city's notorious tenements where tuberculosis (TB) wreaked havoc.

Margaret Brady's extended clan had farming interests, which provided the city-born Pearse children with a modicum of rural exposure. Contact with their great-aunt Margaret was especially significant. In 1913, Pearse wrote:

I had heard in childhood of the Fenians from one who, although a woman, had shared their hopes and disappointment. The names of Stephens and O'Donovan Rossa were familiar to me, and they seemed to me the most gallant of all names; names which should be put into songs and sung proudly to tramping music. Indeed my mother (although she was not old enough to remember the Fenians) used to sing of them in words learned, I daresay, from that other who had known them; one of her songs had the lines 'Because he was O'Donovan Rossa, and a son of Grainne Mhaol.'[2]

Pearse's maternal grandfather, Patrick, had left the Nobber district of Co. Meath in the 1840s to escape the worst years of the Great Irish Famine and had settled in Dublin city. A supporter of the radical Young Ireland movement in 1848, he was sworn into the Irish Republican Brotherhood (IRB, aka 'Fenians'), who, from 1858, revived the revolutionary agenda.[3]

Pearse recalled a visiting ballad singer performing 'Bold Robert Emmet' and other favourites in the republican repertoire, songs that moved him to explore the locality after dark, hoping to find 'armed men wheeling and marching'. Upon finding none, he sadly declared to his grandfather that 'the Fenians are all dead'.

Certainly, the family into which Patrick Pearse was born was steeped in Irish cultural inheritance, a tradition of political engagement and a sense of the diaspora.[4] At least two Bradys had fought as United Irishmen during the 1798 Rebellion, one of whom was reputedly interred in the 'Croppies Grave' on the Tara Hill battle site. Walter Brady, Pearse's great-grandfather, survived the bloody summer and qualified for the Amnesty Act that enabled the vast bulk of combatants to resume private life. Pearse's maternal grand-uncle, James Savage, was a veteran of the American Civil War

of 1860–5 in which approximately 200,000 Irish-born soldiers participated. It is unknown whether Savage was one of
the tens of thousands who simultaneously joined the Fenian
Brotherhood, sister organisation of the IRB, who were reor-
ganised as Clan na Gael. When facing execution in 1916,
Pearse claimed, 'when I was a child of ten I went down on
my bare knees by my bedside one night and promised God
that I would devote my life to an effort to free my country. I
have kept that promise.'[5]

James Pearse thrived as an independent ecclesiastical
sculptor and occasional partner of Edmund Sharp in the late
1870s and 1880s. The firm produced altars, pulpits, railings
and expensive features for churches the length and breadth
of the country. A healthy volume of contracts brought prosperity, and in 1884 the family relocated to a house at 3 Newbridge Avenue in the coastal suburb of Sandymount.[6]

Not only a respected craftsman and an independent
thinker, James Pearse was also a man versed in English literature. His library included books on the plight of Native
Americans, history, legal tracts, language primers and modern
classics. Significantly, he possessed republican tendencies and
admired Charles Bradlaugh, a radical polemicist with the
Freethought Publishing Company. In 1886, James published
a pro-Home Rule pamphlet in which he stressed his English ancestry to underline the innate justice of the proposed
devolution of local government to Dublin.[7] Raised in a

household where aesthetic, philosophical and cultural values were prized, Pearse cherished his 'freedom-loving' parents from 'two traditions' who 'worked in me and fused together by a certain fire proper to myself ... made me the strange thing I am'.[8]

In 1891, Pearse was sent to the Christian Brothers on Westland Row, where the robust, practical education posed no challenge to the highly intelligent youth. The school was convenient and one of a select few that taught Irish as part of the curriculum, providing Pearse with an untypically strong grounding for a Dubliner, which he later exploited with considerable effect.[9] Pearse mused that the people he presumed to be 'gallant and kingly' were unknown to his schoolmaster in Westland Row.[10]

By 1900, Pearse possessed a BA in Irish, English and French from University College Dublin (UCD) and a BL from Trinity College Dublin (TCD). His prowess in Irish ensured a temporary teaching position in UCD as well as work as an external examiner in Irish history at Clongowes College, Co. Kildare.[11]

In September of that year, James Pearse died while on a visit to Birmingham. An *Irish Times* obituary reported that the funeral was held in St Andrew's Church, Westland Row, and that James Pearse was a man who 'rapidly rose to the foremost place amongst the ecclesiastical sculptors of the Three Kingdoms. Essentially a Gothic artist, his works may be seen in practically every church of importance through-out the country, forming beautiful and enduring memorials to the skill of his chisel.'[12]

It fell to Patrick to administer the estate of his father, who died intestate.[13] Although still twenty-one, and a self-described 'law student', Pearse was listed as 'Head of Family' in the Census taken on 31 March 1901.[14] He was called to the Bar in Dublin later that year. The family address was 39 Marlborough Road, Ranelagh, in October 1903.[15] Building on the status accorded their father, the cultural, educational, artistic, legal and political accomplishments of Patrick and Willie Pearse were frequently charted in the mainstream print media.[16]

In 1896, at the age of sixteen, Pearse had formalised his commitment to promoting the national language by joining the Gaelic League (Conradh na Gaeilge). At its inception in 1893, Douglas Hyde strove to situate the project firmly in the cultural domain; however, politically active members, not least an invisible cadre of IRB men, intended a more ambitious programme. The Gaelic League, as with the Fenian-inspired Gaelic Athletic Association (GAA), went from strength to strength as rising membership yielded a national organisation unconnected to the State.

Although by no means precocious, Pearse was tenacious and ambitious and applied himself with vigour to all matters dear to his heart. As early as 1897, the teenager averred in an address to Irish-language revivalists that 'The Gael' was fated to a 'destiny more glorious than that of Rome … to become the saviour of idealism in modern intellectual and social life'.[17] The juvenilia of Pearse, like that of his heroes Tone and Emmet, was not primarily significant for its thematic content but rather for its very existence. Such writings manifested a spirit of engagement and proved, in retrospect, harbingers of later evolutions.

The actions of Pearse in maturity demonstrated that he believed himself to be part of new generation of citizens and not mere subjects, as they were classified by an alien crown. In the late 1890s, it was eminently possible for a youth to be enthused by the glories of romantic nationalism while simultaneously striving to champion cultural values in the present. Restoring Irish to day-to-day life was a minority interest entailing a rejection of Anglocentric norms, with all the obvious political implications. The unelected House of Lords had frozen Ireland, England, Scotland and Wales in a proto-democratic phase in which the aristocratic 'Victorian' Establishment directed 'national' discourse. A minority of men and no women possessed the right to elect the House of Commons in London.

Pearse and his schoolfriend Eamonn O'Neill were the driving force behind the New Ireland Literary Society (NILS) formed on 1 December 1896 in the Star and Garter Hotel, D'Olier Street.[18] On 20 December 1897, Pearse wrote to Eoin MacNeill, Professor of Irish at St Patrick's College, Drumcondra, inviting him to deliver the weekly lecture on 18 January 1898. MacNeill lectured in Molesworth Hall on 'Ossianic Gaelic Poetry' in the presence of eminent antiquarian Dr George Sigerson.[19] Pearse held MacNeill in high regard, as evidenced by his dissolution of the NILS at the older man's suggestion in order to bolster membership of the Gaelic League.

Ireland was by no means unique in having intimately connected worlds of culture and politics, but the lack of a national parliament motivated young men like Pearse to combine the strands. Diligence was rewarded by advancement to the League's Executive Committee in 1898.[20] Pearse adapted lectures given to the jettisoned NILS for publication as *Three Essays on Gaelic Topics*. Always mindful of maximising impact, this title provided his first bid for a literary afterlife.[21]

At the 1899 Pan-Celtic Congress in Cardiff, Pearse made a strong impression on James Mullin, an ex-Fenian and occasional critic of Gaelic League policy, who regarded the 'young' Pearse as 'an idealist with his head in the clouds' and an obsessive faith in the 'cult of the Irish language'. Mullin mistook Pearse as apolitical, later admitting his error of judgement.[22]

Seamus Ua Caomhanaigh joined the Gaelic League in 1899 and moved in the ambit of Brian O'Higgins.[23] Ambitious and bright, he transferred to the Wednesday gatherings of the Ard Craobh in 24 Upper O'Connell Street: 'At these meetings I met and became well known to a number of people whose names will live forever in Irish history: P. H. Pearse, Douglas Hyde, Agnes O'Farrelly, Father [P. S.] Dineen and Bill Rooney.'[24] Young IRB activist Seán T. O'Kelly was a leading member, as was Eamonn O'Neill, 'a close associate of Padraig Pearse'.[25] This was the most prominent forum of the Gaelic League.[26]

On 25 January 1903, Pearse participated in an event to support the mission of Fr Mathew Memorial Hall on Church Street where the declining Temperance Movement organised social events, Irish classes and educational lectures for teetotallers. The Church-backed mission attracted prominent personalities such as Lord Emly and the future Archbishop of Melbourne, Daniel Mannix. When Mannix moved a vote of thanks to those who had lectured over the course of the year, Pearse seconded the resolution.[27]

He was also active in the Catholic Graduates and Undergraduates Association and was part of the ruling committee that criticised Westminster for 'the utterly inadequate provision for University Education in Ireland'.[28] The Committee, as with the League, comprised members of both genders and received national media coverage. Such dynamism was rewarded in March 1903 by his appointment as Editor of the League's weekly organ *An Claidheamh Soluis*.[29] Pearse received an annual salary of approximately £200 per annum for his editorial duties and attained considerable reach in national affairs by virtue of the fact that the paper catered to Irish-speakers as well as monoglot supporters of the language movement.[30]

In 1903, Pearse visited Connemara to improve his Irish in the company of close League friend and teacher Mary Hayden.[31] There was no suggestion of romantic interest, and Pearse in adulthood was not known to have formed a lasting relationship of this nature with anyone.

In April, Pearse acted as examiner in Rosmuc, Co. Galway, for a group of young men seeking Gaelic League certification in Irish-language instruction. They studied Séamus Ua Dubhghaill's *Tadhg Gabha* in detail and awaited with trepidation the arrival of the important visitor from Dublin:

> He was a young, dapper and handsome man, pale-faced and studious, with a high forehead and a thick head of black hair. He was a very timid person with that shyness that is the preserve of a loner. A silent, reserved type, he preferred listening to speaking, and he had a squint in one eye [the right], which only seemed to add to his dapper appearance … Being examined by a person as renowned as Pearse left me in a bit of a daze.[32]

The standard of Irish used by Pearse, Hyde and MacNeill, as well as the language-policy stance taken by *An Claidheamh*

Soluis, was challenged by J. J. O'Kelly ('Scellig') and other Munster-dialect proponents. Seán T. O'Kelly believed their bitterness stemmed in no small part from Pearse's assumption of control of the main League title, a position coveted by Cathal Brugha of the Keating Branch of the Gaelic League.[33]

O'Kelly recalled that 'P. H. Pearse was very prominent in the Central Branch and never went outside it. As the Americans say, he was not a good mixer.'[34] Yet the rise of Pearse was hailed by many. Denis F. Madden, a young solicitor's clerk in Fermoy, Co. Cork, recalled a lecture Pearse delivered in the Assembly Rooms in 1904, chaired by 'patriot priest' Fr Kennedy:

> Pearse's lecture was something entirely new to me. I had been listening to the eloquence of [William] O'Brien and the others including John Redmond, for a long time before this. Here was something different. His delivery was perfect and what he spoke was original. It was on the language revival. When his finished his address, Father Kennedy, a very able man, praised it. He said: 'sparkling as it was with genius and with wit'.[35]

In November 1904, *An Claidheamh Soluis* carried an article by Pearse about his recent visit to Ballyvourney, Co. Donegal, where he re-encountered Dr Domhnall Ó Loingsigh. They had met at a Celtic Conference in Paris in 1900 and on other occasions in Ireland. Pearse cycled to Donegal from Cork City via Macroom, where he was reunited with the charismatic Ó Loingsigh, a man who had financed the construction of a public hall. In a telling appreciation, Pearse remarked, 'During his time in Ballyvourney he has encouraged young and old to hold fast to their priceless linguistic traditions and the recent rise of Ballyvourney is the most striking example in the history of the language revival movement of the influence of a personality over a community.'[36]

Eager to research language instruction, Pearse took advantage of his fluency in French to visit Belgium in 1905, where the 'direct method' of imparting skills through realistic scenarios impressed him greatly. In 1906, he adopted the ephemeral *nom de plume* 'Colm O Conaire' to write *Poll an Piobaire*, an early attempt at an adventure story appealing to Ireland's youth in their historic language.[37]

As the first decade of the new century progressed, Pearse's editorials gradually engendered a separatist outlook that deviated from purely culturally motivated colleagues. From the vantage of 1914, he claimed, 'I here protest that it was not philology, not folklore, not literature, we went into the Gaelic League to serve but Ireland a Nation.'[38] While the nominally neutral outlook of the League was then under stress from the Home Rule crisis, the organisation was regarded in 1902 as having 'progressed' from its 'anti-Irish and West-British' conservative stance during the 'Rebellion' centenary celebrations in 1898. The infusion of new blood exemplified by Pearse was part of the journey Arthur Griffith contended was necessary 'if the [language] movement is to keep in full sympathy with the country'.[39]

Other voices in the mainstream did not embrace the strengthening timbre of self-determination under the Crown, let alone sovereign independence outside the UK. D. P. Moran, Editor of *The Leader*, who ultimately expressed regret to Sinn Féin's Seán T. O'Kelly for vituperating in his newspaper those who fomented the 1916 Rising, probably always represented a larger national sentiment than the militant strand cultivated by Griffith and Pearse.[40] O'Kelly later acknowledged the 'propaganda work of people like Dr Douglas Hyde, John [aka Eoin] MacNeill, Pádraig Pearse, and the other early pioneers of the language movement' in bringing people into the orbit of the political 'Irish-Ireland' organisations.[41]

The Dublin District Committee of the Gaelic League hosted a meeting at the Rotunda, Parnell Street, on 25 February 1905, in which Pearse, Hyde, Edward Martyn and Alderman Walter L. Cole lectured on primary education in Ireland. John Redmond represented the Irish Parliamentary Party (IPP). Organisers claimed the Treasury operated a 'starvation policy' towards education in Ireland.[42]

This front-line advocacy was repeated on 29 March when Pearse delivered a lecture entitled 'The Irish University

Question: Wanted, a Policy' in the Hall of the Catholic Commercial Club. The event was arranged by the Catholic Graduates and Undergraduates Association in which he had been prominent for years. Attendees including MacNeill, John Dillon, Charles O'Connor KC, Tom Kettle and Lord Louth.[43] In the absence of what he regarded as a genuine national university and the poor prospect of Home Rule enabling significant short-term progress, Pearse addressed the debate regarding reforming Dublin University (TCD). His tone was strident and pointed. Having noted his objection to the historically anti-Catholic ethos of TCD, he argued that it should 'come into touch with Ireland' by overhauling its governance, rescinding sectarian policies and adding chairs in modern Irish language and literature, old Irish and Celtic philology, as well as Irish history and archaeology:

They had a University which catered more or less adequately for that portion of the British garrison which could not afford to go to Oxford or Cambridge. In addition to that West British University they had another, the Royal, which was intangible and ghost-like … They wanted an intellectual headquarters for Irish Ireland – an Irish National University safeguarding the scruples of Catholics, but whose doors would be open to all. They demanded University Education, not because they were British subjects, but because they were an Irish nation.[44]

The Gaelic League brought Pearse into court to practise as a barrister, a profession he had not pursued since being called to the Bar in 1901. On 16 May 1905, he defended Donegal's Niall Mac Giolla Bhríde, who had been prosecuted on 11 March for writing his name in Irish on his cart, an offence, as the words were 'illegible' in English. This mild act of defiance in a region where Irish pre-dated English by millennia was in accord with a League drive to restore the language to common usage.[45]

During the High Court appeal, Pearse acted as Junior Counsel under Dr P. S. Walsh and T. M. Healy KC, MP. He was 'instructed' by P. M. Gallagher and shared a trait with Mac Giolla Bhríde in that both published poetry in Irish and English. While the defence failed to exonerate their client, it was held that Pearse's contribution in asserting the legitimacy of Irish was well made, albeit irrelevant vis-à-vis the legislation. Piaras Béaslaí recalled that Pearse had 'distinguished himself as a patriot rather than a lawyer'.[46]

He may well have prospered in a legal career: Pearse was wry and articulate when fending off the prosecutor and evoked laughter by suggesting that the logic of the law dictated 'if an unfortunate Italian came over with the name Giovanni Giacomo his name should read John James'.[47] When upholding the conviction on 18 May, the Lord Chief Justice conceded that the case had been 'most elaborately and interestingly argued by Mr Walsh and Mr Pearse'.[48]

Pearse also appeared in defence of Domhnall Ua Buachalla, founder of the Maynooth Gaelic League branch in Kildare, who had used Irish on his shopfront, stationery and dray. Prosecuted in Celbridge in December 1905, Ua Buachalla refused to pay the fine when threatened with distraint and imprisonment. On 13 February 1906, Pearse opened the defence for Ua Buachalla's second trial, held in Dublin at the King's Bench Division No. 1. He told Lord Chief Justice Andrews and Justice Wright that a legal 'point' had not been resolved in earlier proceedings as the lettering in question had been rendered in Roman script and was arguably 'legible' despite being in Irish. The decision to uphold the Mac Giolla Bhríde precedent dictated that the case was unwinnable, but ancillary benefits accrued.[49]

Attempts to force the issue out of court by means of seizing Ua Buachalla's property, as well as boycotting by pro-Imperial elements, failed due to the resolution of the sympathetic community. Auctioned forfeited goods were purchased at ultra-low prices by collusive friends and returned to their owner. Acts of private solidarity included Pearse's attendance at a Maynooth League fund-raising 'concert' where Éamonn Ceannt played the Irish warpipes.[50]

Pressing the widely reported matter in *An Claidheamh Soluis*, Pearse wrote:

The language movement has won yet another victory in the British courts of law. That is to say, it has forced a British tribunal to pronounce the Irish language illegal … However gracious a British viceroy or even a British monarch, we of the Gaelic League are rebels and law-breakers; our organisation has an illegal propaganda; the meetings of the Coiste Gnótha are liable at any moment to be broken in on by soldiery. So says the law … Tá breall ar an dlighe, adeirmid-ne [The law is defective, we say].[51]

Conradh na Gaeilge published *Íosagán agus Sgéalta Eile* by Pearse in 1907, a compact book of ten stories in vernacular Irish regarding life in the west of Ireland. Noted artist Beatrice Elvery, who befriended Willie Pearse in the School of Art, Kildare Street, illustrated the volume.[52] Pearse's *Bodach an Chóta Lachtna*, published by the Gaelic League in January 1907, drew upon manuscripts in the Royal Irish Academy to generate a fresh Irish-language story from the Ossianic Cycle featuring the Fianna.[53] Pearse's revision of 'Oro, Sé do Bheatha 'Bhaile' reworked a popular Irish-language ballad that hailed the Scottish 'Bonny Prince' Charles Stuart as poised to assist self-determination at the head of liberating allies from France and Spain. Pearse, however, in the spirit of self-reliance championed by republicans, exchanged external Jacobite agency for that of the equally figurative yet native leadership of Connacht's celebrated 'pirate queen', Granuaile.

Deliverance from imperial thrall by resort to arms remained a constant theme.[54]

Pearse had a special affinity with the Rosmuc district of Connemara, which he visited frequently on Gaelic League as well as personal business from 1903. Colm O Gaora, who wrote the influential memoir *Mise* in 1943, appreciated that his exposure to native speakers and intermittent periods of immersion in their routines provided Pearse with vital inspiration for his writings in Irish and English.

He acquired a lakeside cottage, An Turlach, at Inbhear outside Rosmuc for holidays and was respected for his unfeigned egalitarianism:

> he didn't hold himself aloof from the people. You would always find him down in the cabins of the poor people, speaking Irish and learning the history and lore of the Irish-speaking areas at their firesides … The local gentry and their flunkeys thought Pearse an eccentric. Why an educated man such as him was more interested in the needs and culture of the rustic poor rather than spending his time with the 'higher-ups' of society was a mystery to them.[55]

O Gaora sighted him in 1908, strolling alone on a rural road:

[w]alking at a steady pace at one moment and then slowing down again the next, like somebody who was debating some big question in his mind. As I cycled past him, we began to chat and I told him about the fund raising efforts we were involved in for the hall. He promptly gave me a gold sovereign as a donation ... That man was none other than Patrick Pearse ... He must have decided on a spontaneous visit.[56]

The two became friends, with the Dubliner acting as cultural and political mentor to the gifted writer. Already from a Fenian family, O Gaora joined the IRB in Galway soon after. The O Gaoras brought Patrick and Willie Pearse sailing in the *Naomh Pádraig* and engaged in free-ranging discussions on the future of Ireland. The subject of Home Rule arose on one occasion when the Pearses and O Gaoras were deep in discussion. Colm O Gaora recalled vividly: 'the consensus was that any acceptance of Home Rule would prove a sell out and a waste of time'.[57]

Countering the march of Anglicisation into Irish-speaking areas took many forms for Pearse and extended to screening a film at Turloughbeg schoolhouse using equipment sourced in Dublin. The devoted O Gaora compiled an account of the evening for *An Claidheamh Soluis*. He remembered that people walked ten miles to see a film about the rich history and culture of our own country and people … Pearse was an animated figure that night and his speech was the best that I ever heard from him … The English gentry never held another party on their estates for the locals after that, a fact which really irritated their lackeys.[58]

Dr Philip Murphy, who founded a League branch in 1900 in his native Carrick-on-Suir, was one of many Tipperary-men who first encountered Pearse through the language revival. Pearse stayed with Murphy when he was invited to open the annual feis and to deliver a number of lectures to League adherents. Murphy was a schoolfriend of The O'Rahilly at Clongowes Wood College and in 1914 became a founder member of the Irish Volunteers in the sector.[59]

In 1908, bilingual advertisements placed in the *Freeman's Journal* and the *Irish Independent* announced that the 'Irish Ireland boarding and day school for Catholic boys' would commence on 7 September in Cullenswood House, Oakley Road, Rathmines, a 'spacious schoolhouse and grounds'.[60] Pearse was listed as Head Master and Thomas MacDonagh as Second Master. MacDonagh, who was also Pearse's colleague in the Gaelic League, had previously worked in Rockwell College in Cashel, Co. Tipperary, as well as in St Colman's College in Fermoy.

The concept of the college, however, required unusual specificity, notwithstanding the transparent assertion of an 'Irish-Ireland' agenda:

> Apart from its distinctively National standpoint, St Enda's School will adopt several new and important principles in educational aim and method. Features of its system will be the Direct Method teaching of modern languages and bilingual instruction in all other branches. It will devote special attention and 'modern' subjects generally. While aiming at producing scholars, St Enda's will aim in the first place at producing strong, noble and useful men. The domestic arrangements will be in charge of an experienced lady …
> For prospectus apply to Pádraic Mac Piarais (P. H. Pearse), Cuil Crannac, Cill Muire Caippgin (Leeson Park), Baile Ata Cliat (Dublin).[61]

The assertive advertisement was a manifesto for the transformation of the curriculum and modes of instruction as part of an overt socio-political mission. Rather than imposing full immersion in the Irish language and insisting that GAA be played to the exclusion of all 'garrison' games, youths were to receive lessons in different languages and to participate in sporting codes that reflected the hybrid culture of modern Ireland. They would be equipped with a skill set in which deep appreciation of Gaelic society impeded neither third-level education nor the professional environment, where the language of the imperialist coloniser remained essential.

Pearse contributed an important section of pedagogy in *An Macaomh* entitled 'By Way of Comment' in which he downplayed 'high and patriotic motives' in founding the school and promoted the ambition of helping 'as many boys as possible to become good men'. His definition of 'good', however, necessitated 'Irish learning as its basis and fundament'.[62]

The highly qualified staff included Thomas MacDonnell, J. P. Henry and T. P. O'Nolan, who possessed extensive teaching experience.[63] The credibility of the school was quickly established, reinforcing Pearse's authority within the Gaelic League and as a national-level commentator on education affairs and on the Irish language. From the vantage of 1914 New York, where he was raising funds for the school, and when there were seventy students thriving on campus in St Enda's, Pearse recalled the situation in 1908:

The curriculum in the secondary schools and colleges in Ireland was of such a character that the students who attended them were becoming imitation English. To put briefly, St Enda's was started for the purpose of saving the mind of Ireland from becoming completely denationalised ... Ireland's ancient civilisation and culture, the lives of her great men, the ideals they cherished, fought and died for were things unknown to the students of those institutions … St Enda's programme from the start has been thoroughly Irish and its example has had its effect upon other Irish school and colleges of the same class. … St Enda's was founded by me in 1908 with the object of providing for Irish boys a secondary education which, while modern in the best sense, should be wholly Irish in complexion and bilingual in method.

Apart from its Irish standpoint, our College is distinguished from other secondary schools and colleges in Ireland by the appeal which its ideals make to the imagination of its pupils, by its objection to the 'cramming' system, its via voce teaching of modern languages, its broad literary programme, its courses in manual training, and, in short, its linking of the practical with the ideal at every stage of its work. We are convinced that we are training useful citizens for a free Ireland.[64]

In the early days, students were handpicked. Maurice Fraher from Waterford was among the first boarders. Pearse knew his father, Dan Fraher, who was a native Irish speaker, from GAA and 'broad Irish connections'.[65] According to Maurice Fraher's brother-in-law, Pax Whelan of Dungarvan, Co. Waterford, Maurice had been 'sought out by Pádraic Pearse'.[66] A relationship blossomed between the families.

Eamon Bulfin was ostensibly 'the second boy' to join.[67]

His father, 'Señor William Bulfin' of Buenos Aires, hailed from Birr, Co. Offaly, and was Editor of the English-language Irish-Argentinean paper *The Southern Cross*. A republican, he supported Griffith and raised money for the faltering *Sinn Féin* title prior to his death in 1910.[68] Frank de Burca (aka Burke) was the son of a doctor, Fenian and IRB organiser who lived in London, Belfast and Kilkenny.[69]

Joe Buckley was recruited when Pearse wrote to his father, Domhnall Ua Buachalla, his 'constant friend', urging enrolment. The Maynooth militant was promised that his son would join 'a great band of young Irish people'.[70] Another overseas student, Des Ryan, was born in England to Irishman W. P. Ryan, editor of pro-Sinn Féin newspaper *The Irish Nation*. W. P. was well known in League circles. Following graduation, Des stayed on as a teacher and also worked as Pearse's secretary. He drew upon this close contact in his loyal publications.[71]

Pupils from committed political dynasties of this kind were far from the norm in Dublin, and they entered an educational project tailored for the cultivation of nascent republican leaders. Pearse prided himself that 'many prominent Irishmen have sent us their sons to be educated. We have pupils from almost every county in Ireland, and the children of exiles have come to us from places as distant as Seattle and Buenos Aires.'[72]

Nationalist media were intrigued. A lengthy review of plays performed in a temporary theatre built by staff and students in the garden was carried in the *Freeman's Journal* of 22 April 1909. The boys had assisted their teachers in manufacturing props and uniforms. Douglas Hyde's *An Naomh ar Iarraidh* and Standish O'Grady's *The Coming of Fionn* were staged to a level of praise indicative of revelation:

> It is not easy to overestimate the educational and nationalising influences of such plays on the youthful mind, and the staff of Sgoil Éanna appear to be fully alive to the importance of Irish plays in moulding character and as agencies in the intellectual development of their pupils, who, in turn, seem to take the very keenest and most intelligent interest in their work, judging from the manner in which the plays were produced.[73]

Pearse's 'famous boy-players' were honoured on 9 April 1910 by being given access to the Abbey Theatre for a Saturday-night performance. Hyde's reprised *An Naomh ar Iarraidh* preceded Pearse's *Íosagán*, a dramatisation of his 'miracle' Irish-language short story. It was claimed that 'in "Íosagán" he has raised the standard of revolt against the folk form, which he says, has hitherto prevailed'.[74] In keeping with the promotion of bilingualism, Pádraic Colum's *The Destruction of the Hostel* and Standish O'Grady's *The Coming of Fionn* rounded out the bill.[75]

Back in St Enda's, the school theatre's cast numbered 100, ensuring that all with a remote interest in production and performance could participate. Their annual ceilidh on 17 February 1910 had featured Alice Milligan's *Last Feast of the Fianna* and a reading by Thomas MacDonagh of his unpublished play *Metempsychosis*.[76]

Plaudits flowed arising from Pearse's steering the students to produce the journal *An Macaomh* in June 1909. The *Western People* reported

> its coming is a surprise to us all. Just twelve months ago many laughed at the idea of ever starting a secondary school where Irish should be the vernacular. Others thought Pádraic Mac Piarais was starting too soon, and they feared the result. Very few indeed did not expect failure. Success then is a surprise to most of us, but more especially the success betokened by the issue at the end of the first scholastic year of a magazine that other colleges could not attempt twenty years after their foundation.[77]

The formation of the Éire Óg branch (Croabh Éanna) of the Gaelic League from the student body was an additional strand of activist incubation.[78]

The opening of a new study hall in St Enda's was celebrated in October 1909 by a visit by Douglas Hyde, Agnes O'Farrelly and Colonel Maurice Moore, as well as by

Scottish Gaelic-speaker Major Cameron, who was research-
ing League methods. In a moving scene, 100 boys cheered
the entrance of the dignitaries.[79]

The white-hot energy driving Pearse revealed his immense
character and selfless purpose. By 1910, he had surpassed all
contemporaries in terms of concrete achievement of short-
term goals and multifaceted engagement on several fronts
with strategic importance for generating an Irish Ireland.

In April, the press covered Pearse's view on the Board of
Studies policy on the status of Irish within the National University. The key question was whether matriculation should
require knowledge of Irish, a major issue as it was deemed
that if it were discounted as a prerequisite for university
entrance in what became UCD the standard of language
instruction was in danger of falling.[80]

That same year, St Enda's moved to the more spacious
Hermitage estate in Rathfarnham, south Co. Dublin, free-
ing Cullenswood for use as a girl's boarding school. Scoil Íde
(St Ita's College) was managed by Gertrude Bloomer, but it
did not prosper and closed in 1912.[81] Teacher Louise Gavan
Duffy recalled, 'Pearse had no money to keep it going; any
money he had he wanted it for St Enda's ... Pupils melted
away.'[82]

'The Hermitage' was leased on 15 July 1910 and absorbed
funds released by the winding up of the Pearse family's
sculpture business.[83] Donegal writer and historian Seamus

McManus was 'one of the most generous supporters of Pearse'.[84] He had underwritten Griffith's *United Irishman* and its successor title, *Sinn Féin*, which came into being after a libel action was brought against the *United Irishman* by a Limerick cleric.[85]

Seán T. O'Kelly worked closely with Pearse in the Gaelic League and grasped the budgetary pitfalls of the far-sighted project: 'Pearse, from the time he founded the school, was always in financial difficulties. How he managed to drag along I often wondered.'[86] As a minor investor, O'Kelly was invited to a 1910 meeting of creditors in Westmoreland Street. Teetering 'on the verge of bankruptcy', the college survived for the simple reason that sympathetic contributors endorsed its long-term mission.

Rathmines businessman Thomas O'Connor, who had £1,000 irredeemably advanced, confided in O'Kelly:

> I think Pearse is doing magnificent work with this school of his. It is the type of school that was very badly needed. Most … are hotbeds of 'West-Britonism'. They encourage their boys to play foreign games; they do little or nothing to teach them Irish history … Pearse deserves the support of every true Irishman.[87]

The College outlived the 1910 conclave that could have justifiably foreclosed the venture on financial grounds. Debts were voided or rescheduled with extra funds provided 'as best they could'.[88]

Margaret McGarry of the Ard Craobh of the Gaelic League was a confidante of Pearse. Her daughter Maeve recalled,

> Pearse used to come to the house, when he got into difficulties with the school. I saw him cry one day on account of his financial distress. She used to help him with money, as she had the greatest sympathy with him and she thought St Enda's the most important undertaking of the time.[89]

Maeve's brother Milo was transferred from the well-established St Mary's College to St Enda's in due course.[90]

Another trusted friend was Kitty O'Doherty (née Gibbons), member of Cumann na mBan, whose IRB husband also joined the Irish Volunteers, 2nd Battalion:

> I was a friend of Pearse and also knew Pádraig Colum. I used to go boating with Pearse and I met others at Gaelic League outings and aeridheachta. I was intimate with Pearse and interested in his experiment at Cullenswood and St Enda's. He was a dreamer, but unfortunately never had the money to bring his dreams to fruition.[91]

Financial disaster, however, seemed a perennial threat, and a January 1912 attempt to put matters on a firm footing ensured a mere reprieve.[92] As St Enda's demanded more and more attention, Pearse employed Seán Mac Giollarnáth to assist in the production of *An Claidheamh Soluis*, and The O'Rahilly also helped with the management of the newspaper.[93]

Dick Humphreys joined the school shortly after its relocation from Ranelagh to Rathfarnham in 1910. Humphreys was brother to the future National Vice President of Cumann na mBan, Sheila Humphreys. Their aunt, Aine Rahilly, habitually called to Liberty Hall to collect *Workers' Republic* and subscribed to *United Irishman*, *Sinn Féin* and *Irish Freedom*, and the writings of Pearse were familiar to the family from *An Claidheamh Soluis*.[94] Humphreys' diary entries are infused with a sense of the eclectic educational, social and political pursuits possible in a suburban estate within reach of the capital:

> 18th January 1912: Nearly all the boys went out to the Panto. I went down to the Lady of the Lake, had a good time, came up and read at the fire in the linen room till eleven o'clock.
>
> 21st January 1912: Had no out match, played hurling with [Eamon] Bulfin. Dwyers were up practising.
>
> 23rd January 1912: Rode home and settled in alright. Was stopped by a bobby coming home for having no lamp, name and address taken, but nothing happened.

25th January 1912: Mr. Pearse told some of the boys to get
   rifles.

27th January 1912: Had a hurling match, rode home in the
   evening, took a dive from the cycle into the mud. Got
   the rifle with Michael at Truelocks.

28th January 1912: Played a hurling match in Ringsend
   against Fontenoys; was late for first half. Won by 7–2 to
   nil.

29th January 1912: Tried the rifle. Mr. Pearse cleaned it
   afterwards. […]

1st February 1912: Went down to Confession after tea,
   walked back slowly as it was a lovely night and as I didn't
   know my Euclid.

2nd February 1912: The hurling and football cups and
   medals were given out by Mr. Pearse in the study hall;
   had a living picture performance afterwards. […]

10th February 1912: Mr Pearse started boxing. Saw some
   good fun between Fred O'Doherty and Clarke. I was
   made master of games.[95]

   The O'Rahilly, the Humphreys' uncle, visited St Enda's
on 23 February 1912 to lecture on the subject of the 1798
Rebellion.[96] The Rathfarnham district had been a stronghold
of the United Irishmen. Town Major Henry Charles Sirr, the
man who arrested Lord Edward FitzGerald in June 1798,
had lived in Cullenswood, Ranelagh. Sirr also frequented

the Hermitage to search for documents retained by Sarah Curran, who lived there, which were used to prosecute her fiancé, Robert Emmet. Anne Devlin had been half-hanged in July 1803 for refusing to divulge information on the mysterious 'Ellis' (Emmet) of nearby Butterfield Lane.[97]

The boys of St Enda's were too young to recall the effusion of fervour unleashed by the United Irishmen commemorations in 1898 and 1903, but many of their elders held dear such memories of past vigour.[98]

Humphreys made a succint diary entry for 29 February 1912: 'Mr Pearse went away.' Absence was a frequent occurrence and one that the pupils, who were encouraged to view the world in terms of participation as well as intellectual preparation, training and aesthetic appreciation, took in their stride.

Some professed awareness of the nature of their headmaster's life beyond St Enda's. Humphreys noted on 14 March 1912, 'Mr Pearse had to go out about his new paper so he gave us [a] half day. We played a great hurling match.'

Humphreys joined Na Fianna Éireann while a student at St Enda's and, later, the 3rd Battalion of the Irish Volunteers.[99] Such actions were approved by Pearse, who, in July 1909, carried the advertisement in *An Claidheamh Soluis* that announced the formation of Na Fianna Éireann in 34 Lower Camden Street the following month.[100] Michael Lonergan became the IRB military commander of the youth organisation under the nominal 'civilian' direction of Markievicz.[101]

Eamon Bulfin, a graduate of St Enda's, science student at UCD and member of the IRB, was the main recruiter of students living in the school.[102] Bulfin said that Pearse

> was a great admirer of the Fianna, and he believed that every man should know how to use a rifle. In his talks to his students, he always stressed the fact that every generation of Irishman should have a rising in arms. He stressed it in such a way that you felt impelled to believe that he did actually believe that there should be some attempt, especially when the Volunteers were formed [in November 1913].[103]

In April 1913, Fianna Éireann members gave a public display of drilling and camping at the annual St Enda's fête.[104]

None other than Major John MacBride presented 'a grand lecture on the Irish Brigade in [South] Africa' in March 1912.[105] The commander of the pro-Boer Transvaal Irish Brigade might not have been a conventional role model, although staff at St Enda's clearly believed otherwise.

Two years later, Seán MacBride, Major John MacBride's son, was brought to St Enda's aged ten to enrol as a student. In his memoir, he recalled the essence of his lengthy one-on-one interview in the 'great Palladian mansion': 'Pearse interviewed me, as one would expect a schoolmaster should, about my level of education in France where, of course, things were different, there being a great deal more Latin. He never once mentioned politics.'[106] Pearse would not have required assurances of a compatible worldview from a boy of his background.[107]

Pearse permitted past pupils to continue to live in an upper storey at their alma mater if pursuing further studies in Dublin. This armed elite of a political elite had the privacy necessary to assemble bombs on campus under the direction of their former science teacher.

Chapter 2

• • • • •

Republican Politics

Pearse was a regular at meetings of the Wolfe Tone Committee (aka Club), which, as Des Ryan knew, was 'a cover for the IRB'.[1] He had closely studied Theobald Wolfe Tone, founding father of Irish republicanism. As Ryan observed, 'he carried Tone's *Autobiography* around with the unfailing care some ministers would appear to carry their Bibles, and knew it as literally'.[2] At a meeting on 28 December 1910, Sean Gall's lecture 'On the Eve of '98' struck a raw nerve with Pearse. Ryan watched amazed as his mentor attacked the meeting:

> He said they were always talking and doing nothing and that if he could get hold of 100 men who meant what they said he'd guarantee to take Dublin Castle ... P. J. Devlin was quite riled by Pearse's speech and he answered him very brusquely ... Pearse muttered to me, 'I am the only revolutionary in this room.' Anyway, Devlin was sorry afterwards and sent an apology to Pearse. That was his outlook and he

used to say that there was too much talk; that there ought to be a definite policy of using any Home Rule parliament that came and then in ten years there would be a really republican movement. He added, however, that the movement would always end in force.[3]

Pearse very rarely disclosed militant views in public and even within the bastion of St Enda's 'only spoke in these terms to the senior pupils'.[4] This public emotive outburst of a reserved man suggested an additional quotient of frustration or perceived provocation was in play.

The stultifying moderation of the Gaelic League had vexed Pearse to the point of distraction. Behind closed doors in 1907–8 he attempted to instil a sense of urgency into the business of an Ard Craobh 'too busy with resolutions to think of revolution'.[5] In 1910, Pearse expressed the private opinion that the 'old Fenians … had run to seed or were doting and used to talk in public houses'.[6] This was a common perception of the ageing generation who had not been forced into exile by virtue of being on the run, escaped prisoners or clandestine militants.

The unspeakable kernel of truth, that the IRB was being mismanaged, was then under active review by internal reorganisation steered by the combined efforts of Tom Clarke, Seán MacDiarmada, Denis McCullough, Bulmer Hobson, Pat McCartan and Diarmuid Lynch.[7] Significantly, several senior Fenians linked to the dominant John Devoy/Joe McGarrity Clan na Gael network had recently returned to Ireland from Philadelphia and New York.

Pat McCartan returned to Ireland from the USA in 1905, and both Lynch and Clarke made the journey in 1907. Together with MacDiarmada and McCullough, who also had strong American connections, and in alliance with Hobson, they assumed control of the IRB.[8]

Posing as a repatriated ex-Fenian shopkeeper in Dublin, a city in which he had never resided for an extended period, Clarke soon ran the IRB Supreme Council. As Treasurer, he worked intimately with Hobson, McCartan, Lynch, McCullough and a small pool of men au fait with the utter seriousness of John Devoy, Joe McGarrity and John T. Keating (the Clan na Gael Revolutionary Directory) to invigorate revolution in Ireland in the medium term. More than anyone, Clarke was responsible for the fast-tracking of Pearse to influence in a streamlined, reinvigorated and effective IRB command.[9]

McCartan's familiarity with 'methods and procedure' of Clan na Gael meetings in the USA instilled in him a sense of frustration at what he regarded as the excessive caution of the IRB leadership. Irritated by the practice of making 'loyal' resolutions at public meetings, he prepared the ground for a more republican environment at the forthcoming March 1911 commemoration of the anniversary of Robert Emmet's birth, held in the Rotunda.[10] In the February edition of the IRB-run journal, *Irish Freedom*, McCartan declared that no such resolutions would be proposed at events held by the Wolfe Tone Committee. Unpublished was the key fact that the committee was actually 'the public organisation under which the IRB held any public function'.[11]

The selection of Pearse, a man who idolised Emmet, as the main orator was apposite, particularly for a night chaired by the militant Major MacBride. Thomas Barry, inducted into the IRB in London in 1905 by veteran Dr Mark Ryan, believed that 'Clarke got Pearse to address a meeting of the Wolfe Tone Memorial Committee at the Rotunda. That was the first time Pearse came before the public and he was brought out by Tom Clarke and the IRB.'[12]

Pearse's stirring words electrified McCartan, who was seated beside Countess Constance Markievicz: 'The part of his speech that caught me was when he said Dublin would have to do some great act to atone for the disgrace for not producing a man that would dash his head against a stone wall in an attempt to rescue Robert Emmet.'[13]

Emboldened by Pearse's vehemence, and with his words 'ringing in his ears', McCartan proposed a resolution condemning 'loyal' addresses. He was seconded by a quick-thinking Clarke, who gauged the mood and occasion and who, for all intents and purposes, broke cover by doing so. This raised questions regarding IRB policy that hastened

McCartan's advancement to the Supreme Council and bolstered the position of the already well-established Clarke.[14]

In an embarrassing revelation of interim dissension within a secret organisation, two versions of *Irish Freedom* issued from oppositional editorial staffs in March 1911. The Clarke–McCartan axis won the day in a struggle in which Pearse had played, probably unwittingly, the role of catalyst. When the crisis deepened, McCartan's link to McGarrity proved decisive inside the IRB.[15]

According to de Burca, Pearse believed that his politicised speeches 'should have attracted the IRB to him' and waited, perhaps impatiently, for their approach.[16] Impressed by his range of talents, McCartan had indeed broached the question of bringing Pearse into the republican movement after his performance in the Rotunda. Clarke revealed that the Supreme Council had considered the matter before deciding that the Dubliner was 'more useful outside than inside the organisation'.[17] McCartan inferred that Fred Allen and Sean 'Jack' O'Hanlon (other leading IRB men) were nervous of Pearse's quiet charisma.

The IRB upper leadership was in a period of transition that witnessed the retirement of Allen and O'Hanlon and the coalescence in 1911–12 of Clarke, McCullough and P. S. O'Hegarty. In late 1914, McCartan joined the inner circle. He remarked that Pearse 'must have come into the organisation quite soon after [c. December 1911] … Seán T. O'Kelly

… approached him on the subject and discussed it with him and got his agreement to join.'[18] O'Kelly had entered the IRB in 1899 and was one of the most active recruiters in Leinster.[19]

Aine Ceannt recalled that whereas Arthur Griffith's small Sinn Féin party had kept its powder dry when the Third Home Rule Bill they regarded as doomed passed the House of Commons in April 1912, the party hosted an ad-hoc grouping named the United National Societies Committee at their offices in 6 Harcourt Street. Éamonn Ceannt, Sean Fitzgibbon, Seán MacDiarmada and The O'Rahilly were prominent, and Pearse was attracted to their public meetings to arrange anti-royalist demonstrations.

This, in the inexpert opinion of Aine Ceannt, 'was the first time that Pearse … took any interest in Irish affairs outside the Gaelic League'.[20] Frustrated by the law, the principal event was a defiant pilgrimage to the grave of Wolfe Tone in Bodenstown, Co. Kildare, although a further protest assembled in Foster Place which resulted in the arrest of Helena Moloney.[21]

In the early 1910s, the *Gaelic American*, the muscular republican weekly organ of Clan na Gael, began to reprint articles from *Irish Freedom* and *An Claidhamh Soluis*, many of which were penned by Pearse.[22] Devoy promoted cultural affirmation, nationwide organisation and fund-raising appeals, assistance acknowledged in the 1916 Proclamation as that provided by 'the exiled children in America'. Contact was maintained by various means, including IRB courier Tommy O'Connor, a seaman in the employ of Clarke.[23]

Captain Ruaidhri Henderson of the Command Training Depot, Cathal Brugha Barracks, compiled a dossier in 1945 for the Historical Exhibition, Military Tattoo, which recognised the potency of Fenianism:

> The IRB – aided morally and materially by the Clan na Gael in America – never ceased to be a vital force in maintaining and propagating the ideal of Republicanism. The permanent establishment of the Irish Republic sovereign and independent, remained its constant aim; its influence was unceasingly directed against each and every move that tended to any lesser conception of Ireland's political goal.[24]

A notice was placed in *Irish Freedom*, inviting interested parties to attend a meeting in the Moira Hotel on 2 March 1912. The keynote of Pearse's address to those who assembled was that 'a rifle should be made as familiar to the hands of an Irishman as a hurley'.[25] It was plain to Peadar Kearney that 'those present were growing uneasy as the evening advanced when it dawned on them that Pearse was determined to carry out his policy'.[26] They adjourned before any decision was taken on whether to operate either in public or private. The proposed organisation was never reconvened.[27]

Pearse's personal initiative and evident militancy were akin to raising a green flag in front of an evaluating IRB. He subsequently published a polished version of his overture in *An Claidheamh Soluis*.[28]

Peadar Kearney reported on the Moira Hotel gathering to Clarke, who formed the view that Pearse and some of his associates should be brought into the IRB. Éamonn Ceannt, Thomas MacDonagh, Pádraic Ó Conaire and Cathal O'Shannon were all intelligent, nationally minded men of organisational and literary talent. Pearse, when probed by the IRB, most probably Seán T. O'Kelly, expressed interest in joining the 'Boys' Circle' of the IRB, of which Con Colbert was centre.[29] This was more generally known as the 'Fianna Circle' within the IRB as it constituted the main branch for those with dual membership.[30] Liam Mellows and Eamon Martin, full-time Fianna Éireann organisers recruited by Clarke, belonged to this coterie.[31] When Colbert visited St Enda's to conduct drill practice for the students, Des Ryan and others secretly recruited from Na Fianna Éireann into the IRB 'disappeared at certain times', much to the perplexity of their headmaster.[32]

Contemporaries dispute the precise timing of Pearse joining the IRB, but what is known is that once he was privy, by virtue of membership, to the reason behind his students' erratic behaviour, he was apparently 'very much amused', probably pleased that St Enda's patriotic *raison d'être* had exceeded his expectations in regenerating the republican ideal.[33]

From the IRB's point of view, Pearse's range of skills marked him as a real asset and the most suitable proxy for Clarke. Once instated as the de-facto public-relations officer of the IRB, Pearse's hitherto personal drive to inspire short-term action was effectively underwritten, and he gained significant political backing, albeit secretly.

On 31 March, Pearse participated in a massive pro-Home Rule rally in Dublin that attracted 100,000. John Redmond, Joe Devlin and Laurence 'Larry' Kettle of the IPP were also present. Several platforms were erected on Sackville Street, and Pearse shared that occupied by Joe Devlin at the Middle Abbey Street junction.[34]

Seán T. O'Kelly was present and recalled that

Pearse was invited as a representative of the Irish-Ireland movement ... He spoke in Irish and English, and many Irish-Irelanders and not a few supporters of the Independence movement went to that platform to hear what Pearse would have to say in favour of Home Rule ... Pearse was much criticised by many of his enthusiastic friends and supporters of the language movement and in the independence or republican movement for consenting to speak from a Home Rule platform, and to associate himself with the Irish Parliamentary Party. He, however, vigorously defended his action, and any time I was present … when the speech was under discussion and he was the subject of attack, I noticed that he was very well able to defend himself and his action.[35]

In his speech, Pearse issued a thinly veiled threat, which was all but ignored by mainstream print media:

Let us unite and win a good Act from the British … I think it can be done. But if we are tricked this time there is a party in Ireland – and I am one of them – that will advise the Gael to have no counsel or dealings with the Gall [i.e. the British Government] for ever again but to answer them henceforward with a strong hand and the sword's edge. Let the Gall understand that if we cheated once more there will be red war in Ireland.[36]

It was not irrelevant that his speech was delivered in the company of Joe Devlin, *bête noir* of republicans.[37] Devlin virtually had a private army in the guise of Ancient Order of Hibernians (Board of Erin) (AOH-BOE) and rivalled the United Irish League, in which he was also a prime mover, for influence within the IPP.

Various groups connected with the IRB stood out in clear relief from the IPP juggernaut by persisting to advocate for the attainment of the Republic. The imminence of Home

Rule engendered such debates with new potency. The resources of Clan na Gael, channelled through IRB Treasurer Tom Clarke, provided vital capital, and men like Pearse were recruited.

Offstage, Pearse admired the contributions of Michael Davitt and Charles Stewart Parnell and saw Home Rule as an incremental advance towards the revolution he then believed was on the cards. This pragmatism was typical of Gaelic League outlook prior to the IRB infusion that resulted in more explicit final-status terms. Pearse retained a good personal relationship with John Dillon, the potential IPP leader bested for primacy by John Redmond.[38]

Min Ryan appreciated that Pearse and 'even Griffith [in Sinn Féin] stepped on the soft pedal to give' Redmond 'a chance … They would accept anything for the sake of advancing the idea of freedom.'[39] IRB man Mortimer O'Connell reflected that

[Pearse's] sole reason for appearing on the same platform with John Redmond in 1914 at a meeting to boost the Home Rule Bill was that he was convinced that without unity the language and culture of the nation would be lost, and in this he saw a means of saving the spirit of the nation. If Home Rule came into force we would be in a position to save the language.[40]

Des Ryan noted that Pearse 'advocated the expediency of a measure of Home Rule as it would give a national centre, and control our education'.[41] Speaking to Irish-language supporters at Monkstown Farm in July 1911, Pearse had averred, 'If Home Rule came the education question would right itself. One of the first acts of a Home Rule Parliament would be to sweep away the National Board [of Education] ... but Home Rule might not come as soon as they desired.'[42] Pearse also endorsed in general terms the 'Irish Council Bill' which contained useful 'educational proposals'.[43] By his presence in Sackville Street, Pearse blurred the lines between those who rejected the compromise of Home Rule while demanding the Republic. If moderate in tone regarding the language question, he was ahead of the radical curve turning in his favour.

Ryan recalled that 'Hobson was sounding us about Pearse' over an extended period and eventually swore him in 'between July and December 1913'. According to Ryan, 'Pearse had been previously blackballed' by Clarke and Béaslaí as they mistakenly deemed him to be 'too moderate' and hostile towards the IRB. This assessment derived from Pearse's outburst at the Wolfe Tone Committee in December 1910 and his fleeting association with the reformist IPP leadership, which the IRB disdained.

Such problematic instances, as Clarke ascertained from Kearney et al., did not correspond with Pearse's real and favourable attitude towards revolutionary politics.[44] A column by Pearse in the June 1913 issue of the IRB's *Irish Freedom* asserted that 'This generation of Irishmen will be called upon in the near future to make a very passionate assertion of nationality.'[45] Pearse founded the seditious *An Barr Buadh* (*The Trumpet of Victory*) on 16 March 1912, and it attracted contributions from Éamonn Ceannt and Thomas MacDonagh among others.

Pearse's journalism facilitated dialogue between the IRB and the socialist republicans who were destined to fight by his side in 1916. In October 1913, when the 'Lockout' trade-union dispute was crippling the city, he wrote:

> My instinct is with the landless man against the lord of lands, and with the breadless man against the master of millions. I may be wrong, but I do hold it a most terrible sin that there should be landless men in this island of waste yet fertile valleys, and that there should be breadless men in this city where great fortunes are made and enjoyed.[46]

The IRB judged that the response of Empire loyalists and Irish unionists to the passage of the Home Rule Bill in April 1912 had set the stage for the creation of a mass nationalist movement. When, in January 1913, powerful elements opposed to the devolution of limited power to an elected Dublin forum founded the 'Ulster Volunteer Force', the IRB appreciated that no credible moral or enforceable legal proviso could inhibit nationalist emulation. The prospect of marshalling a militia from the approximately 80 per cent of the Irish nation who supported Home Rule was irresistible to organised republicans in New York, Philadelphia and Dublin.

Seán T. O'Kelly was aware that 'certain members' of the Supreme Council of the IRB were disposed to act 'immediately after the establishment of the Ulster Volunteers'.[47] The decision to found the public organisation had been made secretly in October 1913 by the IRB Supreme Council following discussion with select advanced nationalists. Eleven IRB members and associates met privately by invitation in Wynn's Hotel, Lower Abbey Street, on 11 November 1913 to plan the launch of a theoretically independent, armed, nationalist body.[48] Pearse convened in Wynn's with Eoin MacNeill, Seán MacDiarmada, Seamus Deakin, Piaras Béaslaí, Sean Fitzgibbon, W. J. Ryan, Joe Campbell and The O'Rahilly.[49] Hobson believed himself too well known as an 'extreme nationalist' to attend.[50]

The IRB leaders in Dublin took great care to see that control of the Irish Volunteers was kept in the right hands in every area where the organisation existed or had contacts, and their men were instructed to be active in organising and controlling local forces.[51] Hobson, who had also been lobbied by Casement, facilitated this process by permitting the 'Provisional Committee of the Irish Volunteers' to use his office at 12 D'Olier Street.

Clarke wanted 'reliable' and 'safe men' in the vanguard, persons not automatically associated with the IRB or Sinn Féin yet within their sphere of influence.[52] MacNeill's academic profile qualified him to be the designated Chief of Staff, and he was invited to submit his pro-Volunteer essay to *An Claidheamh Soluis* – for publication in English so that its reach was maximised.

An important article by Pearse which had been published in the same title was sent to the *Gaelic American* and was reprinted on 29 November under the title 'Volunteering Spreading in Ireland':

A thing that stands demonstrable is that Nationhood is not achieved otherwise than in arms ... I am glad that the North has 'begun'. I am glad that the Orangemen have armed for it is a goodly thing to see arms in Irish hands. I should like to see the AOH armed. I should like to see the Transport Workers armed. I should like to see any and every body of Irish citizens armed. We must accustom ourselves to the sight of arms, to the use of arms. We may make mistakes in the beginning and shoot the wrong people; but bloodshed is a cleansing and a sanctifying thing, and the nation which regards it as the final horror has lost its manhood. There are many things more horrible than bloodshed; and slavery is one of them.[53]

'P. H. Pearse of St Enda's College' became primarily associated in the USA with the origins of the Irish Volunteers.[54] When Pearse embarked for America, it was in his exalted new capacity as a member of the executive of the paramilitary Irish Volunteers. Such high office in the most extensive private armed Irish organisation since the United Irishmen would have been inconceivable without IRB sponsorship.

The cautious IRB leadership had cultivated Pearse, a man whose outward demeanour often confused those who did not know him well, for some time. Mortimer O'Connell noted that 'some people found it very difficult to get on with Pearse. He was a difficult man to understand. I only met him once or twice and I must say I was immensely taken by him.'[55]

Clan na Gael followed proceedings from New York. A letter from Hobson was printed in Devoy's *Gaelic American* on 14 November, informing readers that 'in the course of a few days it is expected that a National Volunteer Corps will be started in Dublin … several private conferences have already been held … it is expected that the movement will spread to many parts of Ireland'.[56] By then, MacNeill, aided by The O'Rahilly, MacDiarmada, Béaslaí and Hobson, had prepared the ground.[57] On 21 November 1913, the *Freeman's Journal* reported that invitations had been issued, instructing delegates to assemble at 8 p.m. on the 25th, in the Rotunda Concert Hall, 'to commence the enrolment'.[58]

The name Óglaigh na hÉireann revealed revolutionary inspiration in an ostensibly moderate pro-Home Rule
initiative. The 'Irish Republican Army' (IRA) had been the
nom de guerre of the Fenians since May 1866 when they
invaded Canada from Buffalo, New York. The peacetime
term, 'Irish Volunteers', had been raised within the Fenian
leadership in 1861 and was widely used by Irish-American
militias in the early twentieth century.[59] In 1782, the original Volunteers, a national armed body raised in Ireland for
policing duties during the American War of Independence,
met in the Rotunda to profess political views akin to the
pro-democracy revolutionary US Patriots. The commonly
held misconception that Dublin's sabre-rattling Volunteers
had 'won for Ireland a free Parliament' was encouraging for
those deprived of any such forum.[60]

Two days before the meeting, a 'huge procession' marched
from St Stephen's Green to Glasnevin Cemetery to honour
the 1867 Manchester Martyrs.[61] Thousands were drawn to
the capital, scores of whom were earmarked for induction
into the Volunteers. Tom Clarke was the common denominator in the two events, a fact that was thinly concealed by
his use of the 'Old Guard Benevolent Union' and 'Wolfe
Tone Monument Association' cover and his 41 Parnell
Square address.[62]

On 25 November 1913, a dangerously large capacity
audience packed into the Rotunda, with numbers massed in

the Concert Hall (later Gate Theatre) and Gardens. Around 7,000 thronged to the event. Other than some heckling in the Rink when Irish Transport and General Workers' Union members objected to Larry Kettle's ties to a business with 'locked-out' workers, matters proceeded without dissent. This was indicative of the depth of nationalist grievance and the concomitant desire to bind the alliance into a potent armed force.[63]

Among those who took to the stage were Richard 'Dick' O'Carroll, Secretary of the Dublin Bricklayers Union.[64] O'Carroll opposed child labour and specifically the exploitation of youths hired out for domestic service from the South Dublin Union.[65] M. J. Judge of the AOH-BOE, Seán T. O'Kelly and Seán MacDiarmada addressed overflow meetings in the Concert Hall and Gardens.[66]

Westmeath republican Tom Malone was in attendance in the crowd. Sworn into Na Fianna Éireann by Liam Mellows at the age of fifteen, he had opened fire on Dalystown Royal Irish Constabulary (RIC) Barracks in 1911 to keep 'them busy investigating for a week' while land agitation proceeded.[67] The Malone family had experienced eviction during the Famine era and were committed to rectifying Ireland's inequitable land-tenure system as part of the mission to achieve the Republic. Malone was with Mellows at the Rotunda and conversed with MacDiarmada, 'who was well known in our house'.[68] Pearse was an unfamiliar until the two met that evening: 'I knew of him only as a writer in Irish, and one who ran a most unusual private school at Rathfarnham.'[69]

Frank de Burca was an IRB steward on the night: 'Pearse was for us the chief speaker at that meeting.'[70] The *Gaelic American* reported the speech:

> This movement did not spring from any differences of opinion that divided Irishmen today. It had its root in what all Irishman shared in common, the sentiment of love for Ireland. For all who loved Ireland there would, [Pearse] hoped, be a place in the Irish Volunteers ... They were all agreed that it was for Ireland herself to say how much freedom she wanted and not for the Empire to tell them how much she should get. Ireland armed would, at any rate, make a better bargain with the Empire than Ireland unarmed.[71]

Des Ryan spoke to Pearse afterwards: 'he said to me, "We started a Rising tonight".'[72]

Hobson claimed to have initiated Pearse into the IRB in December 1913 ahead of his planned lecture tour in America: 'when these arrangements were made, and in view of the fact that Pearse would almost certainly have been brought into the IRB at a very early date I swore him in'.[73] Pearse travelled to New York in February 1914; therefore, the coincidence of Hobson's and Ryan's witness statements indicate a probable oath-taking in December 1913. Furthermore, Diarmuid Lynch, Divisional Centre for Munster and a Supreme Council member from 1911, recalled chairing a 'general meeting' of the IRB command structure at 41 Parnell Street 'early in December 1913' where Pearse was 'occupying a seat in the rear of the [Foresters] Hall'. The purpose of the meeting was to 'emphasise the duty of IRB men to cooperate to the fullest extent in the formation of Irish Volunteer Companies and of choosing IRB men as officers where possible'.[74]

Pearse joined the Fintan Lalor Circle, which was headed by MacDiarmada and which met at 41 Parnell Square.[75] Charles Donnelly recalled that 'Seamus O'Connor was secretary [and] Pádraig Pearse was a member'.[76] The Bartholomew Teeling Circle, attended by Seán T. O'Kelly and Diarmuid Lynch, convened in the same venue.[77]

Significant republicans were headhunted for important roles in the newly established Irish Volunteers. Seamus O'Connor, a member of the Volunteer Executive, invited Gaelic League/Celtic Literary Society stalwart Seamus Ua Caomhanaigh to act as Secretary of the 'Defence of Ireland Fund' out of which the arms were to be purchased. Ua Caomhanaigh reported to Michael O'Hanrahan. Another Gaelic League activist, Liam O'Carroll, was a third-generation IRB member and founder member of A Company, 1st Battalion.[78]

Not all efforts to extend the Volunteer organisation were successful. Pearse used a Manchester Martyrs

commemoration run by the Young Ireland Society of Charleville, Co. Cork, to seek enlistment, with unpromising
results. IRB members attended, including Michael Motherway, but the requisite popular response was conspicuously
absent. Motherway attributed the setback to the strength of
William O'Brien's IPP followers in the locality and the vigilance of party rivals who supported John Redmond. It was
not until spring 1914 that the first Irish Volunteer unit was
formed under AOH auspices aided by Thomas MacDonagh.
Dialogue between various elements, not least Corconian J. J.
Walsh of the Ancient Order of Hibernians (Irish-American
Alliance) (AOH-IAA) and the unseen IRB, secured eventual
O'Brienite/Redmondite cooperation.

Pearse and his associates had initially misjudged the deeper
complexities of regional factionalism. Appeals to counter the
Ulster Volunteer Force (UVF) and uphold the Home Rule
project were at first insufficient to guarantee IPP voter allegiance.[79] Casement and MacNeill encountered similar problems in Cork City Hall on 13 December 1913, despite the
joint efforts of J. J. Walsh, Liam de Róiste, Tomás Mac Curtain and Terence MacSwiney.[80]

Although an IRB revolutionary, Pearse appreciated
the importance of moving through more moderate envi-
ronments. He reputedly suggested the formation of 'Bua-
chaillí na hÉireann' in which the sons of Irish Volunteers
could enlist. This, in the eyes of Aine Ceannt, signalled an

acceptance that the Fianna Éireann cadre shaped by the IRB primarily attracted recruits from 'the most extreme families'. Kathleen Clarke, Kerry Reddin and Fionán Lynch backed the project. A meeting in a national school in Dublin's Sheriff Street was addressed by Pearse, after which it became clear that Liam Mellows held a minority position on the Fianna Éireann executive in supporting what was regarded as a rival endeavour. The idea was abandoned.[81]

On 16 December 1913, the Provisional Committee of the Irish Volunteers issued an appeal in Dublin addressed to 'Irish people at home and abroad'. Printed in full in the *Gaelic American* of 7 February 1914, Devoy promoted the Irish Volunteer Fund for which Denis Spellissy acted as Treasurer.[82]

Even though he was a founding member of the Irish Volunteer Executive, Pearse was obliged to undergo basic training. Michael Lonergan, a senior member of Na Fianna Éireann and junior member of the IRB, imparted the rudiments of drilling at 41 Parnell Square: 'I was the first man in Ireland who taught Pádraig Pearse to "form fours." When admitted to the Volunteers he was assigned to my company … as were many of his students.'[83]

Pearse was elected Captain of E Company of the 4th Battalion (aka the Rathfarnham Company/Pearse's Own) and regarded as 'the original O/C [Officer Commanding]'.[84] The unit was reviewed on 7 June 1914 when Pearse asserted in Ballyboden that 'they would arm in spite of the

Government. Some of them were armed already.'[85] Former students Eamon Bulfin, John 'The Yank' Kilgallon, Des Ryan, Brian Joyce, Con and Eunan McGinley, Joe Buckley, Joseph Sweeney and Frank de Burca joined, as did Peter 'Sla' Slattery, the St Enda's science master. Several were members of the IRB's 'Fianna Circle'.[86]

Slattery delivered extracurricular lectures on 'military subjects' and, from late 1915, supervised bombmaking on school premises.[87] When available, Pearse led E Company on Sunday exercises, which including route marches, orienteering and paramilitary training on the fringes of the Dublin Mountains.[88] They used the Old Mill on Whitechurch Road for parades. Charles Donnelly recalled:

> When the Volunteers were formed in 1913, we were instructed by the IRB to join Volunteer companies in our own areas. This was to ensure that there would be IRB members in almost all the companies formed. I joined the Rathfarnham Company. Liam Clarke, who was also a member of the IRB, was one of the principal organisers of this company. Pádraig Pearse was a member from the start and eventually was elected company captain. Michael Boland was 1st Lieutenant and Liam Clarke 2nd Lieutenant.[89]

By 1916, Bulfin was the operational unit leader, owing to the much wider commitments of Pearse.[90]

Familiarity with Rosmuc underpinned Pearse's dynamic role in raising Volunteer companies in the locality, as well as in nearby Carraroe and Garmna Island. He had introduced Liam Mellows to the district and fostered the expansion of Na Fianna Éireann there. Colm O Gaora, one of the founding Rosmuc Volunteers, took the IRB oath from MacDiarmada at the Galway Oireachtas and was enthused by the response of his contemporaries to the new public movement:

> We raw recruits lined up in our new and spruce uniforms … At the end of each night's drilling routines, Pearse made a point of speaking to all of us before we went home and I will never forget his fiery idealism and enthusiasm that was written in his features. In addition to our various drilling and weapons routines, Pearse also oversaw three hours of athletics for us each week. We were all intensely loyal to him and gave it our all … only three members of our company went to the other side when the IRA split during the Civil War.[91]

Pearse and M. J. Judge were the 'principal speakers' on 6 January 1914 when the Gorey Company of the Wexford Volunteers was formed in the old town hall. The event was presided over by Seán Etchingham, Chair of Gorey Sinn

Féin and Captain of the new unit. James Gleeson recalled: 'So many people turned up at the meeting that the hall was packed and a large crowd had to remain outside. Pearse addressed the meeting in the hall and explained the objects of the Volunteers. He also addressed the crowd outside from one of the windows. About sixty joined.'[92]

The account furnished to the *Gaelic American* claimed that 'Mr P. H. Pearse, headmaster of St Enda's School, County Dublin, was especially good.' He was quoted as stating that the new organisation was 'drilling and arming. Beyond this we have no programme.'[93] An IRB member since 1906 and a private in A Company, Wexford Battalion, Bob Brennan knew that the secret revolutionary group 'was responsible for the organisation of the I[rish] V[olunteers] in Wexford' and achieved its subtle influence by 'insuring that the officers were members of IRB'.[94]

The Limerick Volunteers were raised on 26 January 1914 in the Athenaeum. Again Pearse played a leading role, along with Casement and local man Michael O'Callaghan. John Daly's contribution was hailed as that of 'the old Fenian'.[95] Redmondites predominated in North Munster's main city, and members of the Wolfe Tone Club, Na Fianna Éireann and the controlling IRB were tasked with getting 'themselves selected to represent trade unions and such bodies'.[96]

In January 1914, the editor of the *Enniscorthy Echo*, William Sears, established the *Irish Volunteer* newspaper, to address issues relevant to the nascent organisation. Wexford journalist and IRB man Larry de Lacy was appointed editor. Bulmer Hobson was dissatisfied with the secondary commercial and political outlook of the nationally distributed weekly. In November 1914, when Sears relinquished his interest, Hobson recapitalised the paper with a £100 grant from Volunteer finances and instated a willing MacNeill as nominal editor.

Although MacNeill contributed diligently to the 'Notes' section, J. J. O'Connell and Eimar O'Duffy provided much of the copy, working with Hobson.[97] The *Irish Volunteer* gifted Pearse with an invaluable vehicle to assist his senior role in the organisation. His competency and energy were evident to all, including those at the helm of the IRB and Clan na Gael.

When Pearse travelled to the USA in early 1914, he had two missions. The foregrounded task was raising money for St Enda's, which was going to have no long-term future if it continued to rely on fees paid by its relatively small enrolment. With £6,000 invested but debts of £2,000, the school was threatened with closure within twelve months. In October 1913, Pearse pressed parents to pay outstanding fees, claiming, 'I have heavy expenses always at this time of year and this year they are heavier than ever.'[98]

The quasi-political nature of the school probably deterred Ireland's middle-income population, although this special aspect was appreciated by ideological allies. Reaching these

potential sponsors in person seemed advisable, and a significant public appeal, the first of its kind, was carried in the
Gaelic American of 7 March 1914.[99] This was the main public
legacy of the US tour as it resulted in the establishment of
a subscription fund, promoted by Devoy. At all times, Pearse
stressed the socio-political mission of St Enda's: 'our work is
radical; it strikes at the root of Anglicisation. Infinitely the
most vital duty of the hour here is to train the young in an
Irish way for the service of Ireland.'[100]

The second purpose of the tour was to finance the 'Equipment Fund' of the Irish Volunteers: 'Devoy and the Clan and
Irish organisations generally' were indispensable.[101] Pearse's
numerous speeches concerned not pedagogy but Ireland's
political future, and the imbalance evidently 'worried Pearse
very much', resulting in a perception of 'a kind of conflict
between sacrificing the school for his Volunteer principles
and ideals'.[102]

Hobson canvassed Devoy, McGarrity, John Quinn and
Judge Martin J. Keogh of the New York State Supreme
Court to compile a draft itinerary for Pearse's visit.[103] Des
Ryan was familiar with the preparatory stages and knew that
when Pearse sailed from Cobh on 8 February, it was, perhaps
unknown to Hobson, with 'introductions from Clarke and
MacDermott recommending' the bearer.[104]

On 22 February 1914, Pearse made his New York speaking debut in the form of a report on 'educational conditions

in Ireland' at a rally organised by the United Irish-American Societies in the Irish American Athletic Club, 159 East 69th Street, Manhattan. Among the influential board members present were Tom Tuite, Major Thomas Nolan and Denis Spellissy (Chair of the Education Committee).

That evening, he attended a Clan na Gael function to mark George Washington's birthday, at Cavanagh's on West 23rd Street and Eighth Avenue. Judge C. F. Collins of the Court of General Sessions and lawyer John J. McTigue delivered short addresses before their unannounced Irish guest received a 'very hearty reception' for his overview of the political situation in Ireland.[105] Pearse made a strong impression.[106]

Pearse attended a gathering in Brooklyn on 28 February, where he delivered a lecture entitled 'Present Day Conditions in Ireland', speaking after New York State Governor Martin H. Glynn, who had formerly been the main attraction. Clan na Gael acclaimed Pearse as 'author of the excellent series of articles entitled "From a Hermitage" in *Irish Freedom*', and his memorable orations in Bodenstown in 1913 and the Rotunda in 1911 were referenced. He was credited with being 'one of the staunchest workers who have led the fight for the revival of the Irish language'.[107]

A major event in Irish-American centres was the commemoration of the birth of Robert Emmet, and Governor Glynn was engaged to give the 'principal oration' in the Brooklyn Academy of Music.[108] A capacity crowd of 2,500 braved the worst snowstorm to engulf Brooklyn since 1888. County Clerk Charles S. Devoy chaired proceedings in which Governor Glynn extolled Emmet energetically.[109] By no means upstaged, Pearse addressed the gathering in Irish before switching to English. His anecdotes riveted those present, especially when he claimed to work in a room in St Enda's where 'Robert Emmet is said often to have sat'. He continued: 'in our garden is a vine which they call "Emmet's vine" and from which he is said to have plucked grapes … Half a mile from us across the fields is Butterfield House where Emmet lived during the days preceding the [1803] Rising.' He related that a friend had met an elderly woman who witnessed dogs lapping blood from under the platform used for hanging and decollating the hero on 21 September 1803, a visceral image of past revolutionary commitment.

Moving on to the Irish Volunteers and the immediate future, Pearse reportedly excited the 'greatest enthusiasm' from the floor with reports of their progress in twenty counties.[110] Having dismissed Home Rule as an acceptable 'final settlement', he claimed:

When one looks at the movements that are stirring both above the surface and beneath the surface in men's minds at home, that the fact [is] that the new generation is reaffirming the Fenian faith, the faith of Emmet. … What one may call the Westminster phase is passing; the national moving is swinging once again into its proper channel. A new junction has been made with the past: into the movement that has never wholly died since [18]67 have come the young men of the Gaelic League … Ireland is once more organising, once more learning the noble trade of arms. In our towns and country places Volunteer companies are springing up … I cannot speak for the Volunteers; I am not authorised to say when they will use their arms or where or how. I can speak only for myself; and it is strictly a personal perception … I say that before this generation has passed the Volunteers will draw the sword of Ireland.[111]

This placated those conversant with the disturbing reports about the IPP being sounded out on the temporary exclusion of part of Ulster from Home Rule arrangements.

Clan na Gael staged an evening at the Aeolian Hall, West 43rd Street and Fifth Avenue, on 8 March 1914, which was supposed to be presided over by New Jersey Supreme Court Judge James F. Minturn.[112] In a clear effort to increase attendance, the *Gaelic American* claimed that Pearse was 'a speaker of rare ability and without resorting to the tricks of the orator, his words never fail to make a deep impression on his audience'.[113] Extensive reports of proceedings were produced in the *Gaelic American* of 14 March 1914, which pictured Pearse, alone of all participants, on the front page.[114]

Another special guest that night was Bulmer Hobson, who had not informed Pearse of his intention to follow him to the USA within two weeks. His visit concerned the clandestine business of Roger Casement, but he may also have been disconcerted by Pearse's sudden exaltation.[115] Hobson recalled that Pearse was 'surprised when I turned up'. He closed an overtly Fenian speech with the words, 'Our cause, the National Cause, the cause of establishing in Ireland an independent Republic, will go on unaffected by anything that England may do until we have the flag of a free Republic flying over the capital of a free Ireland.'[116] Pearse followed with an equally assertive address in which he stated 'the time has not yet come to talk of peace' with 'England' and claimed 'Irishmen who promise Irish loyalty to England are wrong.'[117] Having castigated British imperialism and those envisioning Home Rule as a 'final settlement', Pearse lauded the virtues of the Irish Volunteers and the rising generation:

I can speak for … some of the young men that are attending the National University, for my own pupils at St Enda's College, for the boys of the Fianna Éireann. To the grey haired men whom I see on this platform, to John Devoy and Ricard Burke, I bring this message from Ireland; that their work of forty years ago was not without its harvest, that there are young men and little boys in Ireland today who remember what they taught and who, with God's blessing, will one day take – or make – an opportunity of putting their teaching into practise [sic].[118]

The warmth of the reception was such that Pearse decided to extend his sojourn in the USA. Although he was buoyed by the acclaim for his political oratory, the need to devote time to fund-raising for St Enda's was also clearly a factor. He spoke in New Rochelle, New York, on 22 March, to aid 'the poor of the parish of the Blessed Sacrament'. The following night he was in the major Irish hub of Philadelphia, Pennsylvania, where he spoke on 'Ireland Today' and 'Irish Education'. Other topics offered to potential hosts were 'The Heroic Literature of Early Ireland', 'Wolfe Tone and [17]98', 'John Mitchel and [18]48', 'The Irish Volunteers, 1778–1914', 'The Fight of the Language' and 'An Ideal in Education'.[119] Pearse worked out of Devoy's offices in William Street, Manhattan, where he corresponded with Denis Spellissy and others on *Gaelic American* stationery.[120]

Accounts of the new 'St Enda's College Building Fund' were published in the *Gaelic American* on 21 March 1914. Heading the donors was Judge Martin J. Keogh, National Treasurer of the Gaelic League, followed by John Delahunty, James Butler, William Grace and John W. Goff, who each subscribed $100. Clan na Gael clubs, including the Shamrock, Inisfail and Napper Tandy, advanced sums of $45–65, while the Owen Roe Club managed $10. Prominent Irish

Americans such as Dr Thomas Addis Emmet, Cornelius F. Collins and Jeremiah O'Leary all provided $25, with donations as low as $1 faithfully recorded. Judges, lawyers, politicians and Fenians of the past and present united to aid St Enda's.[121] Contributions came from far and wide, including from the substantial Irish community of Butte, Montana.[122] John O'Malley, the Clan na Gael leader in St Louis, Missouri, broadened the geographic reach of the appeal with a small donation.[123]

The initiative was boosted by a St Patrick's Day letter to the editor of the *Gaelic American* by leading Irish-American activist John Kenny, who declared himself gratified that 'the Irishmen of New York appreciate the work which [Pearse] is doing and are according him a generous support ... He is engaged in a work not alone of general education but in a work of necessity in the cause of Ireland.'[124] Further endorsement came from Seumas MacManus, who declared Pearse to be 'the leading educationalist in Ireland', attempting 'not merely to educate the youth ... but also to educate the educators'.[125] In a lengthy tribute, MacManus claimed:

Pearse gave up salary and ease and assumed a burden of work and worry, debts and most harassing care, which would quickly crush or disillusion and dispirit many of the best ... [He] has during the past few years suffered a martyrdom rather than resign the great work so well begun

… while persisting, all alone, in pushing his ideals against what almost seemed the venom of the Fates. Enough it is to say that he as suffered and sacrificed as few realise in pursuing his very great, idealistic and patriotic work … After the establishing of the Gaelic League itself, I consider the successful establishing of Pádraic Pearse's school one of the most hopeful things our forward marching country has known in the last quarter of a century.[126]

Pearse secured an introduction to Joe McGarrity, whom he met when he lectured in Philadelphia on 23 March. The Tyrone man was impressed and, while focused on bankrolling the revolutionary effort, he also made a donation of $100 to the St Enda's Building Fund.

Pearse, conflicted to some degree by obligations to the financial welfare of the Gaelic League, St Enda's and the Irish Volunteers, lectured on 12 April on the relatively mild subject of Irish literature. Using Cuchulain and Fenian lore as his foundation, he contended that 'the great spiritual force of that literature' in Ireland marked it apart from other 'ancient' equivalents in Europe.[127]

The fund was gifted the proceeds from the annual 'opening games' of the GAA season at Celtic Park, Queens, 19 April.[128] The 'St Enda's Field Day' was organised by a committee working out of the Irish American Athletic Club. Pearse, it was noted, was President of the Leinster Schools

League in which St Enda's had been the 'pioneer' when expanding Gaelic competitions across the country. 'Cavan' and 'Kildare' met in the football match while 'Kilkenny' and 'Cork' battled for hurling honours. Gold medals were provided by Hopkins & Hopkins of Dublin.[129] Attendees in Celtic Park were reminded that St Enda's was the 'only Irish Nationalist College'.[130]

The occasion was deemed a success on the basis of turnout but was disrupted when a 'few coarse hoodlums' approached the entrance and 'made a scene'. Bizarrely, a team claiming to represent 'Kildare' gained entry, but they were not the side recognised by the organisers. After an evaluation of the tense situation, the interlopers were permitted to play 'Cavan' in lieu of the formal team.[131] The presence of the First Regiment, Irish Volunteers, guarded against a potentially embarrassing fracas if matters were not resolved. The unit's board of officers received a 'lengthy communication' of acknowledgement from a gratified and no doubt relieved Pearse.

Ties between the New York Volunteers and the Irish Volunteers were represented in the person of Dublin's Captain Michael Lonergan, who attended a drilling session. Lonergan, an officer in Na Fianna Éireann from its inception, had recently immigrated to the USA. With the aid of John Kenny, a supporter of Pearse, he founded 'The Fianna League of America' in the late summer which replicated the role of Na Fianna Éireann in Ireland.[132] It was Lonergan, a young

IRB man, who in late 1913 had instructed Pearse in marching drills.[133]

The Irish-American Association of Wilmington, Delaware, hosted Pearse's talk on 'Irish Nationality'. He drew what the *Gaelic American* regarded as a 'representative' crowd. Back in New York, Brooklyn's American Irish Society hosted him for 'The Saving of a Nation' on 2 May at 529 Vanderbilt Avenue.[134] In an address described as 'eloquent and scholarly', Pearse outlined the history of the independence movement in Ireland and encouraged supporters within the audience with a message of renewal: 'The spirit of Fenianism was again animating Ireland, and the Irish Volunteers, as well as the Fianna Éireann, were developing the present generation to work for nationhood.'[135] His final appearance was on 6 May at the Harlem Gaelic Society, where he spoke on the subject of 'The Gaelic West'.[136] Pearse was frequently interrupted by applause as he discussed life in Connaught.[137]

He departed New York on 7 May by which time the St Enda's fund held $2,090.75.[138] Updated totals published on 9 May noted the surge to $3,289.25, primarily due to a $1,000 injection from the Irish American Club of Philadelphia, a city with an estimated 100,000 Irish-born residents. The $2.50 deposited by Tom Tuite was notable for the unreferenced yet appreciated prestige of its contributor, a veteran of the 1867 Rising who worked for Dr Thomas Addis Emmet. Other celebrity contributors included philanthropist John

Quinn, Judge Daniel F. Cohalan and Judge John C. McGuire of Brooklyn.[139]

The formation, on 1 June 1914, of the American Provisional Committee of the Irish National Volunteers was the fruit of intensive public and private agitation by Pearse, Hobson, Lynch, Ashe and others. Chaired by McGarrity, its purpose was to 'raise funds to arm and equip Ireland's National Army of Defence'. Many of the main players were personally acquainted with Pearse, including Spellissy (Treasurer), Nolan, Devoy and Kenny. The Fenian guiding hand was evidenced by the prominence of J. T. Keating in Chicago, Captain John T. Ryan in Buffalo and Edward Hawkins in Detroit, and the AOH openly backed the venture in several states.[140]

In August 1915, Pearse wrote to Judge Cohalan from St Enda's to say he was 'looking forward to meeting' him again in New York.[141] Events in Ireland dictated that this did not transpire.

Chapter 3

• • • • •

Prelude to Insurrection

Back in Dublin, Pearse spoke at a gathering to commemorate the 1014 battle of Clontarf. O'Kelly recalled that Pearse 'had just returned from New York … that was the first time I saw the military side of his character. The spirit of the meeting was all that could be desired … I daresay it was Pearse proposed John MacNeill as visible head of the Volunteers.'[1]

Due to his sojourn in America, Pearse had missed an important event on 9 April when all four Dublin battalions mobilised before moving to take up positions around the capital.[2] Such demonstrations were viewed in hindsight as dry runs for a *coup d'état*. At a Volunteer meeting in Jenkinstown, Co. Louth, on 24 May, Pearse moved from discussing history to explicitly contemporary concerns: 'Ireland demanded Home Rule not for three-quarters of the country, but for the whole country.' He declared that he 'was amongst those who believed that Ireland could not attain to any real or true measure of freedom within the British Empire …

It was for Irishmen to say how much freedom they wanted and not for England to say how much she would give.'[3] This was a rebuke to the IPP for entertaining debates in London about the temporary partition of part of Ulster from the devolution due within months. Recollections of his US tour underlined Pearse's increasing public militancy:

> The last words spoken to him by one of the most promi-
> nent Irishmen in the United States, just before he came on
> board a fortnight ago, were, 'Let the men at home show that
> they are in earnest: let them show that they are men and the
> help of Irish-America will not be wanting for them.'[4]

Republicans in the USA viewed the raising of the UVF, Edward Carson's 'Army of the North', as a challenge and an opportunity.[5] Reports of the subsequent progress of the Irish Volunteers were extensive, and the question of its military potential a major concern.[6] This became urgent in April 1914 when the UVF imported major consignments of arms from Germany and provided incentive to the vast majority of the population who broadly supported Home Rule.

By the spring of 1914, any efforts by the IRB and Sinn Féin to conceal the extent of their grip on the Irish Volunteer command were unconvincing. The IPP was unnerved by both the membership and the geographic extent.[7] Redmond progressed a bold plan to gain control of or neutralise the body by demanding the right to nominate twenty-five IPP members to the Provisional Committee. This was, he understood, the equivalent of 50 per cent of its complement and, for all intents and purposes, a voting majority.

This gauntlet was thrown down to the consternation of republicans. Hobson argued that maintaining unity at a time when the organisation was still acquiring armament left them with 'no alternative'.[8] Casement and MacNeill were persuaded, but Hobson was the only IRB man on the Committee to acquiesce to Redmond's demands. Clarke was stunned by Hobson's actions, and the man from Belfast promptly 'resigned' as Leinster Centre while remaining Chair of the Dublin Centres Board.[9]

Redmond's power play divided the Volunteer Executive and drove a wedge between several of its most important IRB members. Pearse, according to Des Ryan, was 'quite prepared ... to fight Redmond on the nominee question but was relieved when it was decided to give way to Redmond for the moment. He later blamed Hobson for the admission of the nominees, and their relations were not so friendly from that time.'[10] Even so, Pearse, MacDiarmada, Béaslaí, Ceannt, Colbert, Fitzgibbon, Martin and Judge voted against the ultimatum, and, on 18 June 1914, they urged all parties to 'persist in their efforts to make the Irish Volunteers an efficient, armed, National Defence Force'.[11]

Pearse was unable to attend the dissenting gathering in Wynn's Hotel but telephoned Fitzgibbon to state that he would 'act in common with whatever action the Committee took' while making a 'strong plea that there should be no recrimination in the way of upbraiding by the majority of our colleagues who had taken a different course and opposed us'.[12]

The IPP nominees contained a strong AOH–BOE group, not least Joe Devlin, who was certain to assert the primacy of constitutionalism.[13] Seamus Ua Caomhanaigh was sufficiently well positioned to ascertain salient details of the Provisional Committee's deliberations behind closed doors. His role in managing sensitive accounts dedicated to the purchase of firearms and munitions gave him a level of insight that was not commensurate with his formally modest rank. He knew, for instance, about the visceral confrontations between members of the expanded executive:

It was easy to judge from general talk in the office following [the] meeting that there was a good deal of friction between our people and the Redmondites. I heard of a number of incidents, one in which J. D. Nugent attempted to assault Pearse. O'Rahilly, I was told, took out his gun, placed it before him on the table and said to Nugent 'If you dare raise your hand again to Mr Pearse that gun will talk to you, not I.' That kept Nugent quiet for the remainder.[14]

Nugent, from Keady, Co. Armagh, was Secretary of the
AOH-BOE and wielded considerable influence on the IPP
and particular wards of Dublin City Corporation.[15] Joseph
Plunkett told his sister Geraldine that 'at one of the meetings of the Provisional Committee, Pearse slapped John D.
Nugent's face, because he suggested that Pearse had manoeu-
vred the accounts. Joe was delighted.'[16]

In the aftermath, Devoy fired Hobson, and he was also
dropped from the Supreme Council of the IRB in Dublin.
Pearse believed that Devoy had been harsh, but it was to his
advantage as he then received greater press coverage in the
USA than before. His speech to the Tralee Irish Volunteers
on 28 June 1914 was published in New York on 18 July.
The account noted that 530 Volunteers and members of Na
Fianna Éireann marched from the drill hall (aka 'the Rink')
to the sportsfield, led by the Strand Street Band. Commandant Ned Leen and Fr Charles Brennan were present when
Pearse delivered another 'spirited' address. Stressing common
cause in a body that might contain 'Parliamentarians, Sinn
Féiners or Total Separatists', he declared:

Let there be no mistake … it is for Irish freedom that the
Irish Volunteers are springing to arms. The Volunteers were
the most important men in Ireland today and counted
more in the present political crisis and in the future history
of Ireland than all the political parties, all the politicians and

all the newspapers combined, and it was no exaggeration to say that the issue of the present crisis depended upon the Irish Volunteers. The future of Ireland was in the hands of the Volunteers to be moulded as they saw fit ... When they would have completed the organisation of the Volunteer force [by] the arming of that force ... it would be simply impossible for English politicians to force upon us any solution of the Irish question which they did not wish to accept. He did not suggest that the Irish Volunteers were going to meet the British army in the field. It would not come to that, please God, but what they meant was that with the Volunteers behind them, they would be able to drive a better bargain with the British nation ... Once they got arms they would stick to them and not haul down their colours at the bidding of anyone.[17]

Discerning listeners would have noted Pearse's opposition to unacceptable 'solutions', a reference to Partition and his failure to discount the possibility that the Volunteers could face the British military in arms.

Committed Redmondites could not abide ambiguity and implicit threats, factors that contributed to factionalisation in several sectors. In Cork in early July, the recently expanded Bantry unit was 'segregated ... one acknowledging the leadership of Mr. Redmond' while the other adhered to the 'original policy – non-political and non-sectarian'.[18]

Shortly before August 1914, Joseph Murray, a member of the IRB and the Dublin 1st Battalion, suggested to Pearse that the Volunteeers use national route marches throughout the country with a view to raiding as many of Ireland's 1,700 RIC barracks as possible for firearms. This daring plan was debated by the Supreme Council of the IRB, the only body likely to greenlight such a gambit, and was only narrowly rejected. Clarke informed Murray that a 'resolution in favour … was defeated by his casting vote as Chairman'.[19] His reasoning was that Britain 'was bound to be beaten in the [coming] war as she had never been up against a first-class power before, and that we would get our freedom without any fight'.[20] Provocative mass raids, therefore, were unjustifiable. Pearse, however, was intrigued and asked Murray if he 'had any other scheme'.[21]

Ambitious plans to equip the Volunteers were already in train. In an operation of great complexity, 1,500 firearms were imported from the Continent using money advanced by Alice Stopford Green's social circle in London, backed by a grant from Devoy. Darrell Figgis, The O'Rahilly and Roger Casement played significant roles in arranging the landing of the rifles at Howth on 26 July and at Kilcoole, Co. Wicklow, on 1–2 August.

After a testing voyage from the North Sea, Erskine Childers piloted the *Asgard* into Howth, where waiting republicans spirited the weapons to safety. A stand-off with the RIC on the road to Dublin passed off without serious injury, but soldiers of the King's Own Scottish Borderers overreacted to crowd hostility on Bachelor's Walk, mortally wounding four. The second batch of rifles reached Kilcoole the following week on Conor O'Brien's *Chotah*. Minor setbacks in transportation were overcome, resulting in a stunning feat at a time when the authorities were vigilant.[22]

Although not directly involved, Pearse rushed home from Rosmuc after Howth.[23] Cars used to move the weaponry from Kilcoole were hidden in the grounds of St Enda's, including one that conveyed Cathal Brugha and City Engineer Michael J. Buckley, the brother of Domhnall Ua Buachalla.[24] Pearse reported on the triumph to McGarrity but downplayed the significance of the quantity of weapons landed:

It is obvious that before we can intervene, or even pretend to intervene, in the crisis to any purpose we must have arms. Hence the one great duty of the hour, the duty which overshadows every other duty, is to get guns and ammunition into the country. It is up to the American Committee to act at once and on a large scale … Every penny you can command must be expended now and the goods sent to us with as little delay as possible. A supreme moment for Ireland may be at hand.[25]

One of the most salient aspects of the Howth and Kil-
coole operations was the disproportionate presence of the
IRB and Na Fianna Éireann. Brugha, Mellows, Fitzgibbon,
Hobson, O'Kelly and others worked to plans laid by Clarke,
MacDiarmada, The O'Rahilly and Casement.[26] A high per-
centage of the Volunteers led to Howth Harbour by Cathal
Brugha were IRB members, as were those entrusted with
moving and storing the war material, such as Sean Tobin.
Whereas MacNeill was not privy to the location of dumps,
Joseph Plunkett had a major site under his control. Plunkett
had evidently joined the IRB in early August 1914 having
been in the midst of key figures for some years.[27]

Ua Caomhanaigh had 'the pleasure of telling off J. D.
Nugent' on the day following Howth:

> The Redmondites were anxious to get control of the guns
> to send them north where, they said, they would be most
> needed. In the course of my talk I told him what he and
> his [Board of Erin] Hibernians wanted was to get the arms
> away from us so that they would never be used.[28]

Moving limited stocks of weaponry to Ulster was by no
means irrational given the vitriolic tenor of undemocratic,
sectarian regional governance and the seeming collective
paralysis of the judiciary, RIC and British Army garrisons to
enforce the common law of Great Britain and Ireland. Yet

Redmondite Volunteers and their IPP masters had dissembled on the threat to Ireland's ultimate sovereignty posed by the bizarre option of partitioning an island nation. Such weakness was anathema to the more stringently ideological Irish Volunteers and their IRB backbone aided by Clan na Gael.

Events vindicated Ua Caomhanaigh's darkest suspicions. When the vexed matter was live in Dublin, in early August, he hailed the decision of Liam Mellows to place a sentry at the Irish Volunteers Kildare Street office. Sean Dolan, a young protégé of Casement, guarded Volunteers headquarters with two revolvers and a glinting Bowie knife. Redmondite Larry Kettle was among those prevented entry by Dolan, notwithstanding his right of access as an Honorary Secretary.[29]

Britain's declaration of war on Germany on 4 August 1914 altered the strategic equation, particularly when London confounded Berlin by honouring the Entente Cordiale and dispatching the Expeditionary Force to France. With the cream of Britain's professional army entrenched in France and Belgium, the capacity of Westminster to bind Ireland to the distracted Empire became uncertain. The shelving of all non-essential legislation, not least the contested Home Rule Act, kicked to touch the question of Ireland's independence as a 'small nation'.

Hostilities, however, stimulated discussion of concerted revolutionary action. Seán T. O'Kelly observed, 'In IRB

Left: Willie, Patrick, Maggie and Mary Brigid Pearse. **Below:** The Pearses on a family outing, pictured by the railings of Trinity College.

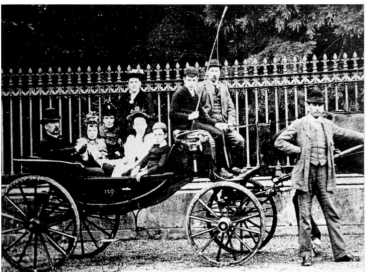

Patrick Pearse (second row from back, first on the left) and other representatives of the Gaelic League at a Celtic conference in Paris in 1900. Next to him is Eoin MacNeill. Douglas Hyde is in the second row from front, right of middle, with walking stick. Michael O'Hanrahan is seated at the front, second from right.

Pearse was called to the Bar in 1901.

The Pearse cottage in Rosmuc, Co. Galway.

Willie (back row, first on left) and Patrick (back row, middle) with friends on a Gaelic League outing to Omeath in 1905.

Left: Patrick and Willie deep in conversation at an event in St. Enda's.

Right: The body of Jeremiah O'Donovan Rossa lying in state at City Hall, Dublin, in August 1915.

Left: In Volunteer uniform, Patrick Pearse addresses a recruiting meeting in Dublin, 1915.

Pearse (right of centre, holding cap, next
to John MacBride) prepares to deliver
his oration at the graveside of Jeremiah
O'Donovan Rossa in August 1915.

The exterior and gardens of St Enda's in Rathfarnham.

circles there was more activity than ever immediately war was declared.'[30] The Wexford Circle met in Bob Brennan's home, where, in early 1914, Hobson had announced, 'war between Germany and England was practically certain and that when it occurred we would certainly have a Rising'.[31] Tom Clarke confirmed this shortly afterwards to Brennan and other members of the Leinster Council gathered at 41 Parnell Square.[32]

Pearse had ruminated along similar lines and told Des Ryan, 'the only time you can rise is in a time similar to the Boer War when there were few troops in the country and the enemy was otherwise engaged'.[33] Pearse was, in fact, tormented with the consequences of neglecting opportunity: 'What would the people think of us after all our talk and promises if we said, "Well, after all the British are too strong and we don't feel like fighting them." The people would just laugh at us and our movements would collapse.'[34] Hobson's estrangement from the Supreme Council deliberations in June 1914 due to his toleration of the Redmondites, as well as his antipathy towards many of the Military Council from May 1915, undermined his retrospective analysis of the Rising.[35] While Pearse admired MacNeill and respected Hobson's motives, he held that 'neither of them was revolutionary'.[36]

Pearse attended the 9 September 1914 meeting at 25 Rutland Square where the Supreme Council of the IRB elicited the views of theoretically unaligned republican, socialist and labour leaders. Convened as the short-lived 'Volunteer Advisory Committee', Pearse advocated anti-conscription and counter-famine measures.[37] The late-September gathering of the IRB Supreme Council finalised what had been merely discussed over the past year: 'before the war finished, the Council should take war action'.[38]

On 20 September 1914, at Woodenbridge, Co. Wicklow, John Redmond pledged the participation of the Irish Volunteers in the Imperial forces. The bulk of the original (pre-June 1914) Volunteer Executive met four days later in 41 Kildare Street and claimed, 'Mr Redmond is no longer entitled through his nominees to any place in the administration and guidance of the Irish Volunteers organisation.'[39] Accordingly, estranged Redmondites established the 'National Volunteers'. Its headquarters were at 44 Parnell Square, on the same Georgian terrace used night and day by their adversaries.[40]

The schism deepened in October, and, while most Redmondites did not follow their leader into the military, they did withdraw from assertive nationalism. Approximately 10 per cent of the 181,000 remained under MacNeill.

The split entailed hard choices in Charleville, Co. Cork: either to join the 'National Volunteers, or continue to serve with the Irish Volunteers under P. H. Pearse who were opposed to the British'.[41] Most voted 'against Pearse' in what was an IPP stronghold, although the militants regrouped in

January 1915 when encouraged by a circular from 'Pearse and the Committee in Dublin'.[42]

Recognition of militant subsections extended to incorporation of free-standing cadres, including Sean Boylan's 'Volunteer Unit', a corps of thirty in Dunboyne, Co. Meath. Boylan coalesced with the MacNeillites on the basis of ideological confluence. A man with strong GAA connections whose ancestors had fought in 1798 and 1867, he was fast-tracked to prominence:

> I was appointed by P. H. Pearse to look after the Meath area on the General Council of the Irish Vol[unteer]s which met once monthly at No. 2 Dawson St[reet]. The General Council consisted of Eoin MacNeill (President), Pearse, Plunkett, MacDonagh, Ceannt, Sean McDermott, Bulmer Hobson and a representative from each county.[43]

Boylan and leading Meath Volunteers subsequently joined the IRB, forming the new 'Dunboyne Circle'.[44]

Membership of Dublin's B Company 3rd Battalion plummeted, a winnowing that revealed something of the relative ideological commitment of key figures. Charlie Murphy, founding Second Lieutenant, declined re-election at company level and instead joined MacNeill's headquarters.[45] In E Company, 4th Battalion, Pearse was left with just thirty men out of the original 200.

A concerned Liam Managhan, from Ballylanders, Co. Limerick, called to Pearse 'to see how things were' and found him in company with William Sears: 'I asked Pearse about the situation, and he said: "Dublin is solid with us." He exhorted me to do my best about the measures for organisation.'[46] The city was by no means a stronghold, and the once rare IRB/Volunteer duality, distilled by defections and retirements, became a key factor in future plans in the four provinces.

The division of Pearse's E Company, 4th Battalion, occurred during a parade held in the Old Mill, Whitechurch Road. Adjutant Frank Sheridan spoke in Pearse's absence. Sheridan 'explained that Redmond wanted us to fight for England and that Pearse wanted us to fight for Ireland in Ireland'.[47] Crucially, Sheridan, Boland and Clarke remained as officers, as did the silent IRB men (including Donnelly). Twelve followers were connected to St Enda's, marking the company as exceptionally bonded to Pearse.

Joe McGarrity wrote to McCartan, stating that he was 'confused' by the split.[48] McCartan believed that Casement could explain the situation, but when Clarke objected to investing such authority in his hands, it was MacDiarmada who travelled to the USA. Meetings in Philadelphia and New York with Devoy, Casement and McCartan enabled in-depth discussion.

Casement's stock had risen, thanks to his role in the arms importations, and he was working on a series of articles, later published as *Ireland, Germany and the Freedom on the Seas*.[49] The pamphlet was secretly printed in Wexford by the IRB-controlled *Enniscorthy Echo*, and copies were brought from Larry de Lacy's house to St Enda's after a dramatic night drive through the Wicklow and Dublin mountains.[50]

Casement's ambition to bind Imperial Germany to Ireland's independence deepened in the neutral USA, and he sought endorsement for raising a brigade from Irish soldiers in German captivity. Having concluded the business at hand, McCartan returned to Ireland bearing £2,000 in gold for the IRB and a gift of McGarrity to Pearse of £700 in gold for St Enda's. He arrived into Derry with Thomas Ashe, who had also been in the USA on Gaelic League and IRB affairs.[51]

The first Volunteer convention after the split was held in the Abbey Theatre on 25 October 1914. Extant members of the original executive were reappointed, and delegates were told that Clan na Gael was behind their minority faction, a by-product of their unmentioned IRB status.[52] Michael Staines was in charge of the security arrangements at the convention. He inspected the credentials of all attendees and delayed the entry of the ticketless Pearse, whom he knew well from the Gaelic League and the Volunteers. Only when The O'Rahilly confirmed Pearse's identity did Staines relent. Such zealousness impressed Pearse, who, within the year, selected him for special duties.[53]

Those privy to Pearse's discreet activism knew that he was in earnest regarding military preparations. According to Donnelly, 'Pearse always emphasised that we were to guard our arms with our lives.'[54] From early 1915, Donnelly delivered secret dispatches to Éamonn Ceannt in Larkfield, Kimmage, after every 'parade'. Pearse stressed that Donnelly was 'not to allow' the messages 'fall into the hands of the police' and routinely examined his .38 revolver to reinforce his seriousness.[55]

Pearse's prominence in extra-parliamentary politics guaranteed discord with pro-Imperial elements, such as J. P. Mahaffy, the Vice Provost of TCD. On 12 November 1914, Mahaffy forbade the 'Dublin University Gaelic Society' from hosting Pearse on the occasion of the centenary of the birth of Thomas Davis. Feigning ignorance, Mahaffy castigated the invitation to 'a man called Pearse' for the 17 November anniversary owing to his anti-recruitment statements in the *Irish Volunteer*.

Charles Power, Correspondence Secretary of the Dublin University Gaelic Society, countered that Pearse's name had been circulated for 'some considerable time past', and he implied surprise at the sudden decision on the propriety of a meeting held to honour one of the remarkably few Protestant republicans commemorated in Dublin. Mahaffy had been expected to chair the commemoration, but, having described Pearse's anti-enlistment stance as 'traitorous' on 11

November, it was evident that this would not come to pass.

When the position of the Vice Provost hardened to the point of prohibition, the indignant Power furnished the correspondence to the *Irish Times* for publication.[56] An editorial on 16 November praised Mahaffy for doing the 'right thing', by which time the Gaelic Society had been abolished by the 'Board of Trinity College'. Pearse was described by the *Irish Times* as 'a Celtic scholar of some distinction. He is also an ardent Sinn Féiner, a member of the original Committee of the National Volunteers and a leader of the anti-recruiting campaign.'[57]

Undeterred, Pearse joined W. B. Yeats, Denis Gwynn and Tom Kettle on 20 November for the Davis commemoration in the Antient Concert Rooms on Great Brunswick Street by the Students National Literary Society.[58] Des Ryan inverted Mahaffy's supercilious disdain in 1919 when he published *A Man Called Pearse* with Maunsel & Company.[59]

After the Rising, an unfounded canard claimed that documentary evidence seized in Dublin regarding 'the setting up of an Irish Republic' earmarked Pearse, 'Commander of the Republican Army', for the coveted Provostship of TCD. Character assassination followed that of the firing squad.[60]

On 25 November, the Irish Volunteers Central Executive appointed a military committee, charged with nominating a general headquarters (GHQ) staff. This was endorsed by the General Council on 6 December. MacNeill was Chief of Staff,

with Pearse Director of Organisation. Plunkett was in charge
of 'Military Operations', MacDonagh 'Training', and The
O'Rahilly was 'Director of Arms'. Hobson became Quartermaster General. Other 'Directors' were added in the following twelve months: Ceannt (Communications), O'Connell
(Inspection) and non-GHQ member Sean Fitzgibbon
(Recruiting).[61] Pearse, meanwhile, steadily advanced into the
heart of the IRB. This dual authority yielded immense influence in the lead-up and course of the 1916 Rising.

Richard Connolly, newly appointed delegate of the
London IRB, attended his first meeting of the Supreme
Council in Clontarf in January 1915. Clarke made it clear
that he 'would never allow the occasion of the war to pass
without having a fight'.[62] MacDiarmada privately argued
that 'before the Americans came into the war they would
have a tussle, that they would have a better chance of sympathy'.[63] Communications with the USA 'would be broken' if
America committed itself, and this was crucial given that 'the
only hope of any German assistance [for the IRB/Irish Vol-
unteers] … would come through Devoy'.[64]

Pearse was guest of honour at the 14 February 1915 annual
Gaelic League feis in Waterford. East Waterford was a stronghold of Redmondism, and the small Irish Volunteer body in
the river-port city were jeered on their marches by the larger
tendency. The Gaelic League provided a comparatively neutral space for cultural nationalists and republicans to mingle.

Thomas Cleary, son of a Fenian and scion of a family that suffered eviction and transportation within living memory, found the occasion memorable:

[A] very large crowd assembled to hear Pearse. This great man told his listeners to love and cherish the Irish language: 'Love your country and support the national movement of the Gaelic League for the time is not far off when you may be called on to defend your language and your country.'[65]

The Irish National Foresters Hall, constructed at the rear of 41 Parnell Square, provided a convenient location for drilling once colonised by the IRB. Na Fianna Éireann organisers, such as Con Colbert and Seán Heuston, graduated from their early days training in Camden Street to weekly sessions at the inner north-side base. The main building was the venue for the Wolfe Tone Committee, another IRB front controlled by Tom Clarke which interacted with the public by means of hosting weekly literary and historical evenings.[66] MacDiarmada's Fintan Lalor IRB Circle also met on the premises. Nearby 25 Parnell Square was the headquarters of the Gaelic League where Irish-speaking nationalists, republicans and an occasional culturally minded pro-Empire unionist mixed promiscuously in the 1910s.[67] Volunteers of the 1st Battalion drilled in both addresses, as well as in St Colmcille Hall in Blackhall Street.[68]

Simon Donnelly recalled exercises in Easter 1915, during which the 2nd Battalion 'occupied' Stepaside on the fringe of the Dublin Mountains while the 3rd and 4th 'attacked' from the high ground: 'I remember seeing Pádraig Pearse that day with a contented and happy smile on his face as he saw the lines of armed men descending the mountain.'[69]

IRB officials grasped that these manoeuvres, which were happening nationwide, provided an ideal opportunity to redirect followers from route marching, orienteering and parades further along the path to an actual insurrection.

If appropriately disposed urban and regional commandants were in place, men who were either members of the IRB or judged amenable to its plans could deal a heavy blow without the formal endorsement of the broader headquarters.[70] MacNeill was by no means disrespected, but from the outset, in the Rotunda in November 1913, his function was only ever that of a front man. Clarke, having anointed Pearse to a higher degree, was not prepared to risk confrontation on his revolutionary plans with a relative moderate.

Alec McCabe, a student in St Patrick's Training College, Drumcondra, and member of Sinn Féin, joined the Sligo Volunteers in December 1913 and was shortly afterwards inducted into the IRB. He organised for both groups in the Sligo sector. Diarmuid Lynch advanced him to the Supreme Council, and he was instated as Divisional Centre for Connaught at Clontarf Town Hall in May 1915. He recalled: 'P. H. Pearse was co-opted a member. A Military Committee was established at this meeting consisting of Pearse, Ceannt and Plunkett. The purpose of this committee was to look after military organisation. I understood the appointments were to be in the nature of a Military staff.'[71]

Lynch knew that from November 1914 an 'advisory committee' within the IRB had generated plans for fighting in the Dublin sector, but that Clarke dispensed with their suggestions and, 'shortly thereafter, Pearse, Plunkett and Ceannt cooperated in drafting plans for an Insurrection'.[72] This presaged their formal appointment in Clontarf as the embryonic 'Military Committee' in May 1915.[73] The IRB Military Council secreted within the Executive of the Irish Volunteers was essentially the creation of Clarke and MacDiarmada. Dublin commandants and other senior officers rotated the chair for the Wednesday meetings of the Central Executive of the Irish Volunteers. MacDonagh chaired the session of 12 May 1915 and Pearse that of 19 May.[74]

On 5 June 1915, the *Irish Volunteer* carried reports about the 'Whitsuntide rallies' around the country, with particular reference to the fractious parade in Limerick. An occasion engineered to honour Patrick Pearse and Robert Monteith, the march was, at best, a qualified success.[75]

'Oro, Sé do Bheatha 'Bhaile' was the marching song of the Limerick City Volunteers, whom Pearse regarded as among 'the best we have'.[76] According to the *Irish Volunteer*, 'the march evidently impressed very favourably the citizens of Limerick, the vast majority of whom were plainly sympathetic. Hostile demonstrators chronicled in the newspapers were confined to a single quarter of the city, and to a section of the people.[77]

As the marchers approached Limerick city centre from Mungret Lane and Broad Street, some women, who had relatives in the Royal Munster Fusiliers that took heavy casualties at Gallipoli in April 1915, misinterpreted the event as a pro-German rally.[78] Unseen by the 'shrieking women' of garrison families, local republican Michael Brennan joined Pearse, MacDiarmada, Clarke, MacDonagh and MacSwiney in John Daly's Barrington Street home.[79] Kevin McCabe, IRB and F Company, 1st Battalion (Dublin), was 'cursed and stoned by the "separation" women and prayed for by others. One woman held a crucifix over us through an upper window.'[80]

Matters deteriorated when the visitors attempted to leave for Dublin. At the train station, fully armed Volunteers from Limerick, Dublin and Cork brigades were under RIC oversight.[81] Priests from the Redemptorist Order urged angry elements to refrain from provocative actions that might incite 'bloodshed'. This was prudent, as protesters could not have known that the Volunteers were under 'strict orders that we should not injure anybody'.[82]

While a murderous overreaction like Bachelor's Walk was never in prospect, self-defence was otherwise assured given the exceptionally 'staunch' character of companies present. Dan Breen was among those prepared to shoot assailants as a last resort. 'Ruffled and weary', Tom Clarke quipped to father-in-law, John Daly, 'I've always wondered why King William couldn't take Limerick [in 1691]. I know now.'[83]

In 1915, the Irish Publicity League released the 'Tracts of the Times' series, written by leading Volunteers. MacNeill's *Shall Ireland Be Divided?* was self-explanatory, as was Griffith's contentious *When the Government Publishes Sedition*. With 23,000 copies sold in the series, forthcoming contributions from Pearse, Hobson and Desmond FitzGerald were eagerly awaited. Such publications were mutually supportive, and Herbert Pim, who wrote *Ascendancy While You Wait* under the pseudonym 'A. Newman', carried a 'Books for Irishmen' advertisement promoting Pearse's *How Does She Stand?* and *From a Hermitage*, both available from Whelan & Son, National Booksellers, 17 Upper Ormond Quay. The intended readership was indicated by the insert from John Lawler & Son of 2 Fownes Street, which sold American .22 rifles and ammunition as well as Irish-manufactured military paraphernalia.[84] Another new title from 12 D'Olier Street, Arthur Griffith's pro-Sinn Féin *Nationality*, asserted that James Connolly's the *Workers' Republic* and *The Reconquest of Ireland* were 'necessary things for every Irish Volunteer'.[85]

A spirit of reciprocation and tentative alliance was in the air. Circulation of *From a Hermitage*, which contained articles by Pearse that had first appeared in *Irish Freedom* and *An Claidheamh Soluis* in June and November 1913, raised his profile among the radical constituency that mounted the 1916 Rising.[86] James Connolly expressed approval on the front page of the *Workers' Republic*:

> Pearse passes his opinion upon things concerning Ireland and the Irish. We find ourselves in agreement with most of the things he says on that matter and are surprised to find him so wisely sympathetic on the struggles of the workers with whom we are most closely identified.[87]

Dublin Metropolitan Police (DMP) Superintendent Owen Brien was responsible for collating surveillance reports from undercover Crime Branch agents into daily dossiers that were delivered to the Dublin Castle hierarchy. Various undersecretaries viewed and forwarded the digests, generally within twenty-four hours, to ensure that all branches of the administration were familiar with the 'movements of Dublin extremists'. All known republican, socialist, labour, suffragist and pacifist activists domiciled in the capital were routinely and closely watched. The DMP did not, however, divine the precise nature of the interrelationships between the overlapping cadres, nor the relative subversive authority of particular individuals.

On the basis of the close observation, the shop kept by Tom Clarke at 75 Parnell Street proved a hotbed of intrigue in the summer of 1915. During the period 31 May to 6 June, visitors included Eoin MacNeill and Seán T. O'Kelly (31 May); Major John MacBride, Thomas MacDonagh and J. J. Walsh (1 June); Arthur Griffith (2 June); Con Colbert and Piaras Béaslaí (3 June); Sean Fitzgibbon (5 June); and Charlie Wyse Power and Terence MacSwiney (6 June). In the space of a week, six of the fourteen men executed in the city by the British military in May 1916 assembled in two Dublin addresses, as did The O'Rahilly, who was killed in action. Having already met with leading Fianna Éireann activists at midday on 10 June, Clarke received a second delegation after 10 p.m. A police agent diligently recorded: 'Countess Markievicz in conversation with Clarke for over half an hour.'[88]

During the same period, Volunteer Headquarters, editorial hub of MacNeill's *Irish Volunteer*, attracted those in Hobson's orbit. Noted visitors included Patrick Ryan, Michael O'Hanrahan and J. J. O'Connell (1 June); Thomas MacDonagh, Éamonn Ceannt, Piaras Béaslaí and Con Colbert (2 June); and The O'Rahilly (5 June).[89]

The unilateral threat to progressive politics posed by draconian legislation did nothing to diminish the increasingly intimate personal connections between the upper echelons of the IRB, Irish Citizen Army (ICA), Gaelic League, Irish Volunteers, Hibernian Rifles and Cumann na mBan. Other leading figures moved inconspicuously in their midst. These included Pearse, who met IRB associates singly in St Enda's, a security-conscious distancing from open affairs that intrigued those unaware of his high status. Writer James Stephens, a supporter of Sinn Féin, never saw this dimension of Pearse and found him 'less magnetic' than other leaders of his acquaintance. On the basis of posthumous revelations, he conceded, 'yet it was to him and around him they clung … He had a power; men who came into intimate contact with him began to act differently to their own desires and interests.'[90]

Militancy, bordering on provocation, was increasingly in evidence. The benign Francis Sheehy-Skeffington moved with purposeful alacrity from the dock to a prison hunger strike in order to press his claim to emancipation. Within seven days he had secured release using an ancient Irish mode of generating psychological and moral pressure. Whereas the suffrage movement, of which he was a noted supporter, resorted to short fasts on occasion, pressing a full-blown threatened strike to the death was a distinctly Irish republican tactic in the 1910s. IRB/IRA leader Thomas Ashe was the first such fatality of the century in September 1917. On 26 July 1915 Pearse wrote to commend Sheehy-Skeffington to McGarrity in Philadelphia: 'he is anxious to get engagements as a lecturer in the United States. His opinions on recent happenings should be welcome to Irish-American audiences.'[91]

On 2 June, Seán MacDiarmada and Sean Milroy stood trial at the Northern Police Court, charged under the Defence of the Realm Act for making anti-conscription speeches in Beresford Place, Dublin.[92] MacDiarmada received a four-month term of imprisonment, and Milroy was given three months by Resident Magistrate Mahony, at which he asserted, 'you have the power to send me to jail, but you have no power to make me a criminal'.[93]

Well-wishers at the trial included James Connolly, Piaras Béaslaí, Éamonn Ceannt and Liam Mellows. At 7.30 p.m. on the day of the sentencing, 9 June, Pearse joined Patrick Ryan, Béaslaí and Hobson for a meeting at Volunteers head-quarters. Meanwhile, Thomas MacDonagh led thirty-six unarmed Volunteers from Rutland Square towards Glas-nevin in a further test of Dublin Castle's resolve to use the Defence of the Realm Act.[94]

Detectives of G Division watched on 19 June as Clarke, Arthur Griffith and Diarmuid Lynch convened in Clarke's shop on Parnell Street. Lynch, a Corkonian and a naturalised US citizen, had been very prominent in the Philo-Celtic Society of New York and in the Gaelic League in the early 1900s. He assumed high-level IRB duties after MacDiar-mada was jailed.

The following day, 20 June, marked the annual republican pilgrimage to the grave of Wolfe Tone in Bodenstown near Sallins, Co. Kildare. Two trains conveyed 1,500 supporters from Kingsbridge to Sallins – Pearse, Lynch, Connolly and Clarke among them. It was observed that contingents from the Irish Volunteers, the ICA and Na Fianna Éireann worked in harmony and that at least seventy men were openly armed. A Dublin Castle official annotated the report: 'Sinn Féin, Irish Volunteers, Labour, Citizen Army'.[95]

Connolly's *Workers' Republic* commented on the event: 'The arrangements were in the hands of [the] Wolfe Tone Association, with the Irish Volunteers and the Citizen Army co-operating and was carried out without a hitch of any kind.'[96] Éamonn Ceannt directed 'military arrangements', with Michael Mallin controlling the ICA:

> The Guard of Honour was provided by an equal number of armed men from the Irish Volunteers and the Citizen Army. The latter body also deposited a Memorial Wreath upon the grave … On the arrival home at Kingsbridge the united bodies marched together to Blackhall Place, where they were dismissed … The whole commemoration was an inspiration to all concerned. Not the least inspiring feature of which was the appearance at the graveside, full of fight and faith as ever, of our friend Tom Clarke.[97]

Convergence of militants and mutually sympathetic reports of political activities boded ill for the British writ in Ireland.

The flurry of interaction observed by Dublin Castle ranged from socialising, intelligence-gathering, consultation on illegal activities and the formation of the 'Military Committee' of the IRB in May 1915. The new subcommittee, also known as the 'Military Council', was built around a kernel of Pearse, Plunkett and Ceannt, IRB men with high Volunteer ranks deriving from their revolutionary potential as assessed by the Executive of the Supreme Council in November 1913.

The inherently powerful duo of Clarke and MacDiarmada were added as ex-officio members. In January 1916, various factors combined to suggest the co-option by invitation of James Connolly of the ICA. Thomas MacDonagh joined shortly before the Rising to complete the seven-man Military Council, who, in the guise of the Provisional Government, declared the Irish Republic on 24 April 1916.[98] They operated in the shadows without the knowledge of Eoin MacNeill whose own deliberations with the Volunteer Executive did not extend to military planning.[99]

The shift in gear was discernible in articles carried by the *Irish Volunteer* on 26 June 1915, which presented the first in a series of templates suggested by Pearse for exercises by which 'a limited number of men and a limited time' could practise actions in the field. The opening instalment provided a rubric for an attack and defence of the fictional 'Byrne's Farmhouse'.[100] A separate feature on 'Victories of Irregular Troops' examined the battle of Bang Bo in Tonkin

(China) in 1885. Acknowledging the dubious value of battlefield practices that had confounded overconfident French invaders in Asia, J. J. O'Connell observed, 'to some extent the procedure would be similar to the successive employment of hedges in Ireland'.[101] If exotic, the juxtaposition of such tactical variants anticipated those used with great effect by the IRA in 1916 and 1919–21.

While Hobson, MacNeill and O'Connell favoured 'guerrilla tactics suited to the Irish terrain', prominent men, including Pearse and Connolly, lectured on street fighting and static defence in 1915–16 in the knowledge that such factors were also critical to the prospects of a modern *coup d'état*.[102]

MacDiarmada met dual IRB/Gaelic League leaders ahead of the 1915 Ard Fheis to 'put the Gaelic League in line with the Nationalist forces in Ireland that sought for separation from Ireland'.[103] As a result, the Ard Fheis, held in July in Dundalk, witnessed the final transition of the organisation into an IRB-controlled entity.

In June, Clarke had briefed associates on a proposed change to the League Constitution, which amended Rule 2 to bind the organisation to 'realising the ideal of a Gaelic speaking and independent Irish nation, free from all subjection to foreign influences'.[104] This bundled an ostensibly cultural language project with the self-determination of small nations – the stated agenda of republicans. Hyde's faction secured the deletion of the explicitly republican clause but lost a rearguard action to maintain a semblance of political detachment.[105] A second problem was Hyde's opposition to the IRB tactic of appointing imprisoned republicans to the ruling body of the Gaelic League, not least MacDiarmada. When a second IRB nominee was elected to the leadership, Hyde 'swept his papers from the rostrum and left' the forum ahead of resigning.[106] Hyde had been outmanoeuvred by the IRB grip on delegates and stepped aside as president to be succeeded by MacNeill.[107]

Pearse had vied with Hyde for years and in August 1913 penned an 'open letter' to him, which was carried by *Irish Freedom*. In November 1913, Pearse asserted, 'I have come to the conclusion that the Gaelic League, as the Gaelic League, is a spent force ... Whenever Dr Hyde, at a meeting at which I have had a chance of speaking after him, has produced his dove of peace, I have always been careful to produce my sword.'[108] This played on the translation of *An Claidheamh Soluis* ('The sword of light') but was absolutely cogent. A possibly irreconcilable question of strategic direction loomed, although ongoing functional cooperation was evidenced by Hyde's generous comments at St Enda's summer fête in June 1914.[109]

The death of Jeremiah O'Donovan Rossa in Staten Island, New York, on 25 June 1915, deprived Fenianism of a hero. Those familiar with his experiences of confinement knew that his resistance to starvation, isolation, rule of silence and abuse jettisoned physical well-being in order to maintain sanity.

After prolonged decline, his care was underwritten by a dedicated Clan na Gael 'fund'. Established by John Devoy and the enterprising Mary J. O'Donovan Rossa, this revived the old Fenian's celebrity to its greatest height since the dynamitard and amnesty campaigns of the 1860s to 1880s.[110] Contributions flowed steadily from Clan na Gael camps including the Robert Emmet Club of Rochester, New York; the Phil Sheridan Club of Buffalo, New York; the Knights of the Red Branch, San Francisco, California; the Robert Emmet Literary Society of Portland, Oregon; the Samuel McAllister Club of Philadelphia and the Emmet Club of Butte, Montana.[111]

After his death, the management of O'Donovan Rossa's remains provided an opportunity for those devoted to his life's work. The IRB Supreme Council learned of his terminal phase and decided, pending family acquiesence, 'to have the funeral immediately [in Ireland] in order to get a boost up for the organisation'.[112] Pearse, Griffith, William O'Leary Curtis, C. J. Kickham and James Dodd met with Clarke in 75 Parnell Square on 1 July 1915, where they held a thirty-minute discussion.[113]

Pearse was the sole liaison between the 1915 grouping and Volunteer leadership that met under MacNeill on 3 July in Dawson Street.[114] The DMP divined that the willingness shown by Mary J. O'Donovan Rossa to permit a Dublin burial was significant in view of the triumphant burial in the same 'republican' plot of Terence Bellew McManus in 1861. McManus had also died in exile in the USA. Such demonstrations were indicative of the organisational acumen of Fenianism and intended to be interpreted as such by all observers.[115] The 3 July edition of *Ná Bac Leis*, Pearse's Irish-language side project, devoted half its front page to lamenting 'Ó Donabáin An Rossa'.[116]

A steering committee convened at 41 Parnell Square on 9 July 1915. Predictably, Clarke was the first name noted by spies, followed by James O'Connor and Patrick Pearse. Two members of Dublin Trades Council were involved: William O'Brien and Dick O'Carroll. IRB members Con Colbert, Joe McGuinness, Ned Daly and others assumed the challenge of transforming death into hope of final victory.[117] Thomas MacDonagh was entrusted with coordination.[118]

The first task assigned to Pearse was writing the short 'Character Study' of the deceased for the souvenir programme. It commenced in the combative prose style he had developed writing for *Irish Freedom*:

O'Donovan Rossa was not the greatest man of the Fenian generation, but he was its most typical man. He was the man that to the masses of his countrymen then and since stood most starkly and plainly for the Fenian idea ... Rossa was not only 'extreme' but he represented the left wing of the 'extremists'. Not only would he have Ireland free, but he would have Ireland Gaelic. ... He had great intellectual intensity. His mind was like a hot flame. It seared and burned what was base and mean; it bored its way through falsehoods and conventions; it shot upward, unerringly, to truth and principle ... No man, no government, could either break or bend him. Literally he was incapable of compromise.[119]

It was evident that the violent, assertive and clear-sighted qualities discerned by Pearse in his pen portrait were acceptable, if not universally endorsed, by the diverse organising committee. Writing from the Gresham Hotel, Dublin, on 22 July 1915, Rossa's widow proclaimed that her husband had remained 'the same unconquerable Irishman breathing the same unalterable desire for the absolute freedom of his country and its utter separation from England that he breathed in the dock' in 1865.[120]

On 28 July 1915, Requiem Mass was celebrated in St Mary's Pro-Cathedral on Marlborough Street, after which the remains were moved to City Hall to 'lie in state' for three days.[121] Ned Daly commanded the 'military bodies' on a day described by the *Weekly Irish Times* as 'remarkably well organised'.[122] The 'pageant' left City Hall for Glasnevin at 2.40 p.m., 1 August 1915, under the direction of Thomas

MacDonagh. The distraction enabled IRB–controlled Volunteer companies, such as the Laois unit, to transfer 'gelignite and other explosives' to Dublin associates.[123]

Pearse may well have been aware that he was destined to be the first Irish republican leader to be filmed delivering a public oration. At least two cameras were in operation, one in the service of British Pathé news.[124] The second unit was arranged by Irish Americans in New York. Dressed in Irish Volunteer uniform, Pearse delivered one of the most stirring speeches in Irish history, surrounded by the Irish Volunteers, the ICA, the Hibernian Rifles and Na Fianna Éireann. Cumann na mBan attended, as did numerous IRB and Fianna Éireann members in civilian clothes.

From his haven in Rosmuc, kept company by his brother Willie and by Des Ryan, Pearse had prepared what he appreciated would be his most penetrating oration yet. Ryan had many conversations with him during the 'holiday' and claimed 'he was more open in his speech ... than I had ever known him to be'.[125] Pearse's 'panegyric' was carried in full by the *Weekly Irish Times* on 7 August 1914 and therefore reached a much larger readership than through the republican media. Closing a rousing, measured speech, he stated: 'The fools, the fools, the fools! They have left us our Fenian dead and while Ireland holds these graves Ireland unfree shall never be at peace.'[126]

Chapter 4

• • • • •

Momentum

Shortly after the funeral, Des Ryan received a cryptic instruction from Pearse, who had learned of his plan to visit Donegal:

> He told me that if I got a message from him or from his sister or from Éamonn Ceannt asking for a certain book I was to return at once because there would be a fight in Dublin that day … I got no order and Pearse never referred to that again.[1]

In all likelihood, Ryan was being apprised that the Volunteers were going to be ordered to resist suppression or disarmament if Dublin Castle moved against them.[2]

J.J. O'Connell ran three two-week 'camps' over the summer of 1915 in Wicklow, the Galtee Mountains and Athlone, Co. Westmeath. The 'Shannon Camp' in Athlone drew members of 'Pearse's Own' E Company, 4th Battalion. They marched to the 'vicinity of Galway City' for exercises with locals units.

Influential IRB/Volunteers at the Shannon camp included Austin Stack of North Kerry, Terence MacSwiney of Cork City and Pierce McCann of South Tipperary.[3]

On 22 August 1915, Liam de Róiste, Vice-Commandant Sean O'Sullivan and other republicans travelled to Millstreet to attend the feis and to 'accompany' Pearse to Cork City, where he was due to speak in their Sheares Hall headquarters, named after local lawyers executed in Dublin in 1798 as leading United Irishmen.

Having attended the O'Donovan Rossa funeral with fellow Cork Volunteers, de Róiste appreciated that Pearse occupied a position of prominence that meant increased Dublin Castle surveillance. His diary, quoted in his witness statement, recorded:

> He spoke at the Feis and spoke well. He was not expecting to speak at a public meeting in Cork, only to our Óglaigh [i.e. Volunteers]. He has been warned to be very careful (as he is being closely shadowed by the police). This, I presume, is consequent upon his oration at Rossa's funeral ... On [the] return journey [from Millstreet] to Macroom with Pearse, we stopped at Carriganima and also had a talk with some young men of the locality. My conversation with Pearse was chiefly in Irish. I had met him previously at meeting of the Coiste Gnótha of the Gaelic League.[4]

Pearse was 'restrained' but 'good' on the occasion. Fortunately, unlike January 1914, when MacNeill had inadvertently unleashed uproar orchestrated by IPP factions, the meeting was orderly and yielded recruits. Outside Sheares Hall, partially inebriated 'separation women' who had just received their payments resorted to 'vile language' to register their antipathy when 'egged on' by watching soldiers.

The poor reputation of the RIC among republicans was not improved by the fact that they 'left when the disturbance began'.[5] If they wished to enable an unseemly riot by their departure, they must have been disappointed, as the discipline of the Irish Volunteers held firm.

In September 1915, Pearse addressed the Wexford Brigade in the 'Barley Field', Vinegar Hill, where the United Irishmen escaped encirclement on 21 June 1798. The O'Rahilly accompanied him from Dublin. The Gorey Company of Volunteers, captained by Seán Etchingham, had been raised in the presence of Pearse in January 1914 and had retained almost 50 per cent of its complement during the split.[6] Seamus Rafter captained A Company of the Enniscorthy Volunteers, 'most' of whom were IRB members, with Pat Keegan as lieutenant.[7] Tom Stokes of A Company led the singing of 'A Nation Once Again'.[8] Captain W. J. Brennan-Whitmore, leader of the Ferns Company, was also present:

Every member of the [Irish Volunteer] Executive anticipated an eventual rising and was agreed on it, at least, to
this extent: if the British authorities attempted to disarm
the Volunteers they should fight no matter what the consequences. All were agreed on that course. Failing such an
attempt being made some members were against initiating
a rising unless supported by considerable aid in the form
of arms and ammunition from America or Germany or
both … Realising these differences, Pearse sought to make
amends to MacNeill when he said: 'Let no man point the
finger of scorn at Eoin MacNeill.' It was a generous attempt
at the *amende honorable*.[9]

Michael Staines, who was by now attached to 'Pearse's staff'
with the rank of lieutenant, resigned from the Gaelic League
to concentrate on his new responsibilities as Quartermaster for three 1st Battalion companies under The O'Rahilly.
Staines' brother, Humphrey, was employed on the White Star
liner *Baltic* on the Liverpool–New York route and smuggled
revolvers from the USA in batches of twenty. When twelve-
piece cases of shotguns were obtained from Henshaw's,
Staines arranged for well-disposed merchants to accept
delivery until they were collected. His cluster of discreet
contacts included 'Donal Buckley' (Domhnall Ua Buachalla) in Maynooth, Pearse's close associate.[10] Working as much
for the secret Military Council as for the Irish Volunteers,

Staines facilitated the gathering of important intelligence as per the instructions of Pearse and Ceannt. He also equipped St Enda's with a radio aerial, concealed in the college's 'flag staff'.[11]

In Belfast in late September 1915, around 130 armed Volunteers marched from the top of the Falls Road, near their Divis Mountain training grounds, to St Mary's Hall on Bank Street where Pearse, in uniform, spoke with memorable effect.[12] Henry Corr recalled that when Pearse read Robert Emmet's 'Speech from the Dock', he requested that those present 'stand up as we would for the gospel'.[13]

The second annual convention of the Irish Volunteers since the split was held in the Abbey Theatre on 31 October 1915. The Central Committee, presided over by Eoin Mac-Neill, comprised Patrick Pearse, Thomas MacDonagh, Joseph Plunkett, Sean Fitzgibbon, Seán MacDiarmada, Éamonn Ceannt, Liam Mellows, Seamus O'Connor, J. J. O'Connell, The O'Rahilly and Bulmer Hobson (Honorary General Secretary). Liam de Róiste observed the 'strict scrutiny of delegates' credentials' and that 'about 150' men were present from active 'corps only, of some time standing'.[14]

Winter training was inaugurated at the suggestion of Liam Manahan, who contended that rural Volunteers would be less preoccupied with seasonal farming work. Manahan formed the impression that Pearse and Ceannt headed a militant element at variance with another involving Hobson,

Fitzgibbon and others.[15] A more peripheral if equally obser-
vant member, Brennan-Whitmore, detected a strategic rift
during this period between what he later discerned were
the undeclared IRB element, whose 'head and font' on the
executive was 'undoubtedly Patrick Pearse'.[16]

When the broader General Council of the Irish Vol-
unteers was formed, adding regional commanders to the
executive members for monthly meetings, Eamon de Valera
chaired the session in Great Brunswick Street that appointed
Michael Staines to represent Dublin's companies. Already
reporting directly to Pearse, Staines gained further status.
Other 'military' members included Jim Leddin of Limerick,
Tomás Mac Curtain of Cork, Pierce McCann of Tipperary,
Seán Etchingham of Wexford and Larry Lardner of Galway.[17]
Pearse's new title was 'Director of Military Organisation'.[18]

In late 1915, at Volunteers headquarters, officers heard
lectures from Pearse, MacDonagh, Ceannt, MacBride and
Monteith. Dick McKee, Peadar Clancy and other leading
Dublin IRA men during the War of Independence were
present. Connolly lectured on street fighting.[19]

Around that time, Peadar Bracken, Captain of the Tullamore Company of Volunteers in Offaly and an experienced
IRB member, was 'called to Dublin by Pearse to St Enda's'.[20]
Owing to the anti-Redmond stance of local Volunteer
officers, Bracken's unit had lost 50 per cent of its rank-and-
file personnel during the split yet retained the bulk of its

armament, which they supplemented by purchasing modern Lee-Enfield .303 rifles from British soldiers. He was in the process of organising a new brigade area centred on Athlone, which had strategic importance owing to the presence of a major artillery barracks, river communications and railway linkages. Bracken recalled of the St Enda's consultation:

> It was then I was made aware that it was intended to have a Rising soon. Pearse arranged a signal or code with me. As I was a sculptor, it was arranged that he would put an advertisement in the papers for a monument. On receipt of that signal I was to mobilise the Volunteers in the area to hold the line of the Shannon occupying Shannon Bridge and Shannon Harbour, and to connect with the Galway Volunteers under [Liam] Mellows … At this meeting with Pearse I was appointed Officer Commanding the Area.[21]

In a series of one-to-one consultations, Pearse agreed personalised signals with most if not all key Volunteer officers in rural Ireland. Through acumen and energy, Pearse cemented his authority in the Irish Volunteers executive, having progressed steadily towards the inner sanctum of the IRB.

In December 1915, following his release from Belfast's Crumlin Road prison in November after a four-month sentence, Denis McCullough attended a special meeting of the IRB Supreme Council in Dublin. A new IRB executive was due to be selected, and the agenda required the replacement of the outgoing chair, Seamus Deakin. McCullough told MacDiarmada that he intended to propose Pearse for the exalted position and received an unexpected reply:

> He asked me 'for God's sake' to do nothing of the kind, as 'we don't know Pearse well enough, and couldn't control him' – an important factor then. He told me that they – I presumed Tom Clarke and himself, in whom I had absolute trust – would propose a name in due course. When the matter came up, [MacDiarmada] proposed and Tom Clarke seconded my name for the position. I protested that I did not think I was a suitable man for the position.[22]

MacDiarmada was re-elected as Secretary and Clarke as Treasurer. This 'executive' headed a supreme council in which McCullough additionally represented Ulster, Sean Tobin Leinster, Diarmuid Lynch Munster, Alex McCabe the south of England, Dick Connolly the north of England and Joe Gleeson Scotland. The ruling body was completed by 'Pádraig Pearse and Dr. [Pat] McCartan – coopted members'.[23]

As the year drew towards a close, the question of military conscription arose. On 14 December 1915, MacNeill and Pearse addressed a packed Mansion House. Pearse claimed that any man in Ireland who loved the British Empire, let him go and die for it. He said not a word against the recruitment of such a man. But was it to be tolerated that the man who did not believe that the interests of Ireland were bound up with those of the British Empire should be taken against his will?[24]

IRB gunrunners Seamus Reader, Eamon Murray and Alec Carmichael left Glasgow for Belfast and Dublin on 1 January 1916 to deliver contraband and to confer with the leadership.[25] Reader recalled:

Pearse said that he would be presiding at the Central Executive of the Irish Volunteers on the 4th January, 1916, at headquarters, Dawson St, where the business of reorganising and arming the Volunteers would be brought up by Tomás MacDonagh. He said that the Central Council of the Irish Volunteers would be meeting at 12 noon on the Sunday of January 16th, 1916, and he would like, if it were possible, Capt Joe Robinson and Pat McCullum or Tomás O Baun of Glasgow to be present and there they would discuss other matters concerning Irish Volunteers with E. O'Neill [i.e. MacNeill], Bulmer Hobson and The O'Rahilly.[26]

Reader briefed James Connolly on Scotland when they met in Connolly's lodgings at the Markievicz home on

Leinster Road, on 17 January 1916. Connolly was upbeat about the prospect of receiving armaments from unionised dockworkers, seamen and cattle drovers on the Glasgow–Dublin route. The inconvenient arrival home of Countess Markievicz with Michael Mallin terminated the secret conversation. Reader believed that Connolly

> had been in conference with Pearse and MacDermott, that they had discussed with him the reports of the Volunteer, Cumann na mBan and Fianna Éireann Conventions, held in 1915, and that there was a feeling, among the young minds in Dublin, that the older men were going to let them down. I thought that the points he was stressing to Mallin and the Countess were that there was a change in the IRB Military Council, or about to be, and that he, Pearse and MacDermott were the Council that would formulate for action.[27]

Diarmuid Lynch confirmed that 'secret instructions of I[rish] V[olunteer] Com[mandan]ts (IRB men)' were issued by Pearse 'early in January 1916 at St Enda's'.[28] Lynch was required to 'convey these orally to the Cork, Kerry, Limerick and Galway Commandants. He outlined the positions which these Brigades were to occupy on the Volunteer manoeuvres which had been decided on the Easter weekend'.[29] This preceded the meeting of the IRB Supreme Directory where, according to Lynch, Pearse, Clarke and MacDiarmada discussed the 'principal matters' in a generalised manner in order to preserve the secrecy of Military Council deliberations.[30]

> Secret instructions which Pearse had ready in January [1916] were issued subsequently to Commandants of Volunteer Brigade[s] in the South and West (who were IRB men) outlined the territory over which each was to hold [i.e. command] the coming 'manoeuvres'. That of the Cork Brigade was along the north-western part of the County – in Contact with the Kerry men from Tralee and district; the latter to be linked up with those of North Kerry and Limerick; the connection to extend thence through Clare and Galway, to Athlone and the line of the Shannon. Thus, these provincial brigades would be in occupation of pre-selected positions on Easter Sunday, prior to which date the Commandants were to receive further specific instructions secretly from Pearse. From the German shipload of arms and ammunition expected to arrive at Tralee Bay, the scanty military equipment of the Kerry Volunteers on the spot was to be augmented: trains and other transport were to be commandeered to ensure distribution throughout the country.[31]

By January 1916, every Volunteer sector had a specific role to play. Volunteer Headquarters selected Dungannon for the Summer Training Camp which commenced on 10

July 1915 to facilitate 'Ulster Companies' geographically and geopolitically. Pearse had issued the notification for this regional mobilisation dry run on 25 June 1915.[32]

Collating and assessing the clandestine reports used to generate regional contingencies imposed major responsibility on Pearse who, as Director of Military Operations for the Volunteers, comprised the human bridge between the IRB and the much larger front group. Linking 'manoeuvres' to full-blown revolt fell within his administrative remit, as it was he who had the authority to issue the necessary 'General Order'. IRB/Volunteer commanders understood that, having mobilised on predetermined sites at the behest of Headquarters, they would receive 'further specific instructions secretly from Pearse'.[33]

The momentous decision to declare the Irish Republic imbued all Military Council business with urgency and intensified internal security. James Connolly's militancy was re-evaluated as a risk factor. The IRB almost certainly knew that Connolly had taken measures in late 1915 to streamline the ICA following the ill-tempered departure of Sean O'Casey. According to William O'Brien, 'Connolly interviewed each member of the Army individually and stated that he did not desire any man to remain in it who was not prepared to respond to the call to arms which might come any day.'[34] The revised listing of 339 names included recent recruits as well as those who had been with the ICA since its inception.

Connolly's disappearance for three days in January 1916 created deep unease among his inner circle and led to unsubstantiated rumours that he had been abducted or secretly arrested. On Wednesday, 19 January 1916, at 1 p.m., Pearse, Plunkett and MacDiarmada arrived unexpectedly by taxi to surprise Connolly, shortly after he left Liberty Hall for lunch. The next day, he failed to appear in Liberty Hall, and it was ascertained that he had not returned to his lodgings in the Markievicz residence.

As friends assembled to discuss the matter, a telegram, misaddressed to 'Jim Larkin', who was living in the USA, arrived from 'Wardell' in Lucan, Co. Dublin. 'Wardell' promised to 'meet' the fictitious recipient the following afternoon. Presumed to be a coded message from Connolly, its timely arrival defused an ICA contingency plan of commencing armed actions if one of its leaders were arrested. Although untested in the final analysis, this was precisely the type of unilateral agency that perturbed the IRB, who feared a premature outbreak would nullify years of revolutionary foundation.

The IRB Supreme Council met on 23 January 1916 at the Town Hall, Clontarf, where McGinn, a discreet Omagh republican, worked as caretaker. Clarke, Pearse, McCullough, Lynch, MacDiarmada, McCartan, Joe Gleeson and Pat McCormack attended. Leinster delegate Sean Tobin was absent. At previous sessions, Easter had been mooted as a suitable time to mount the insurrection, but the threat of aggressive pre-emption had loomed. A consensus formed that they would resist a raid in arms: 'Everyone produced his revolver to show that he was ready for such an event, except P. H. Pearse who rather shamefacedly admitted that he had forgotten his revolver that morning.'[35] With some dissent, it was agreed that the Rising would commence if the Volunteer leadership were arrested, if conscription were imposed or in the event of an early 'termination of the war'.[36]

The Council then discussed news that Mallin and Markievicz 'had a pact with James Connolly that if any of the leaders were arrested they would start the Insurrection'.[37] Clarke's view was that any violent move by the ICA must fail due to the modest size of the organisation and that it would incur massive and indiscriminate reaction. He did not reveal that Connolly, still officially missing, had just been co-opted to the Military Committee.[38]

McCullough, who was then newly installed as Supreme Council Chair, recalled that MacDiarmada arrived late and, after explaining this lapse as arising from 'Connolly's disappearance', told them that he had persuaded Mallin and Markievicz to 'hold their hands' for a few days.[39] He sought permission from the IRB to threaten non-cooperation of the Irish Volunteers, which, once agreed, was purportedly relayed to Liberty Hall. McCullough later admitted to being 'credulous' and understood that this represented the depth of MacDiarmada's involvement in the affair.[40]

Connolly's reappearance in Leinster Avenue on Sunday morning was equally mysterious. He nonchalantly declined to be drawn into conversation about his recent whereabouts when questioned by William O'Brien and Helena Moloney.[41] On reading the aggressive tone in an article written by Connolly in the *Workers' Republic* of 29 January 1916, Pearse was worried by the transparency of intent conveyed. He told Ryan, 'I am greatly afraid Connolly has said too much this week.'[42] Ryan was apprised by Pearse that 'Connolly now was acting with him' and understood that Pearse was concerned that this liaison would be noticed by Dublin Castle. With a sensitive IRB secret thus broached, Pearse confided, 'it was very difficult to convince Connolly that he should work with them, and that when he eventually agreed he was very disappointed.'[43]

An extended negotiation with Connolly had indeed taken place. A relation of Joseph Plunkett confirmed that Plunkett's visible exhaustion in early 1916 was attributable to 'two days and nights almost continuously discussing the situation with James Connolly before Connolly was finally persuaded to agree to act with him'.[44] Pearse admitted having been 'very worried about Connolly' and troubled by 'holding people in that I really agreed with'.[45]

Although Connolly did not disclose IRB induction or high rank to O'Brien, he did impart that when the moment of truth arrived he would be positioned in the General Post

Office (GPO).[46] An ill-informed Hobson, who admitted being 'kept in ignorance' of such matters despite nominally heading the IRB in Dublin, wondered whether Connolly had 'succeeded in capturing' his 'captors' and 'committing them to a definite insurrection in 1916'.[47] More importantly, Hobson further believed that Clarke and MacDiarmada were 'the principal movers', 'joined by Pearse, MacDonagh and Plunkett'.[48]

Members of the General Council of the Volunteers believed in the early months of the year that 'action could not be long delayed'.[49] Pearse requested that Diarmuid Lynch investigate the 'relative merits' of using Ventry Harbour and other 'advantageous spots in that region for the landing of a cargo of arms and their expeditious distribution therefrom'.[50] Lynch reconnoitred possible weapons-landing sites and confirmed that Fenit Pier, in Co. Kerry, was the best destination of the planned German arms ship.[51]

Austin Stack, Paddy Cahill, Ned Leen and Alf Cotton were deeply involved in the plans to receive and move the German supplies.[52] It was not immaterial that when the Volunteer split hit North Kerry in October 1914, 'only about 20 men sided with Redmond'. The IRB was relatively well organised under Stack in Tralee, Listowel and Castleisland.[53] Pearse advised Stack and Fr Joe Breen, Chaplain of the Volunteers, that the IRB had determined to rise at Easter and that the Tralee district men would be responsible for moving imported weapons across north Munster. Stack's adjutant, Paddy Cahill, was evidently not informed of this until late March, although preliminary arrangements were made in the interim.[54]

An invitation to speak in Doe Castle, Cresslough, Co. Donegal, was issued to Pearse in February 1916 but did not come to pass, owing to the pace of events. Daniel 'Dan' Kelly, who had been an IRB centre in Glasgow and Derry before his transfer to Cashelnagore Railway Station, reorientated his republican activities on Donegal and enlisted the support of the well-regarded McNultys to encourage Pearse to visit. He had represented one of the family in court for illegally using Irish on his cart.

While the Doe Castle address did not go ahead, Pearse and Herbert Moore Pim ventured to Derry in March 1916, an area under Kelly's IRB remit. Kelly postponed a major arms delivery in order to deny RIC reinforcements the opportunity of compromising both republican initiatives. Pearse and Pim would have been legally vulnerable if rifles had been recovered in the possession of the men they were visiting.[55]

On Wednesday, 9 March 1916, the 'Great Volunteer Rally' held in the Athenaeum, Enniscorthy, Co. Wexford, was hailed by locals as 'one of the most impressive national gatherings witnessed in living memory'.[56] Lieutenant Seamus Cullen headed the Volunteer guard detail, which turned out in uniform with bayonet-fixed rifles to emphasise the martial tone of the occasion.

The stirring 'Oro, Sé Do Bheatha 'Bhaile' by Dublin tenor Gerard Crofts was so moving as to warrant three encores from the overcapacity audience of 900. Many would have appreciated that Pearse had reworked and augmented a traditional song regarding military assistance to Irish insurgents. Other talented performers delivered 'The Men of '98', 'God Rest You Robert Emmet' and an Irish-language version of Thomas Moore's 'Speak Not His Name'. The Fenian anthem 'God Save Ireland' was well chosen in view of the 'Manchester Martyrs' theme of the event. This rounded off the entertainment, after which Pearse approached the stage to a 'tremendous burst of acclamation'.[57]

Flanked by two armed Volunteers and seated at a table draped in the Tricolour, the flag associated with the IRB, Pearse commenced in Irish: 'Budh maith liom Riobaird Emmet a mhoadh as Gaedhilg, agus is truagh liom nach bhfuill Gaelhilg again go éir.'[58] Switching to English, he continued:

> We who come together to honour Robert Emmet's memory stand for one of the ancient, indestructible things of the world. Nationality is more ancient than any empire and will outlast all the empires ... whenever in Irish history we seem to forget that fact, some strong man arises and rallies us or some good man redeems us by sacrifice. Tonight we speak of one who made for us the ultimate sacrifice. In Emmet's

day, and once again, the Irish nation had been sold as far as man could sell a nation, but sacrifice like Emmet's saves us … The generation now growing old has led Ireland for thirty years and in all that time has produced no man to say or do a splendid thing … The reason I think is that they have made nationality a material thing – a thing bound up with temporal and material interests. They have thought and talked and preached of freedom as a thing to be haggled over and negotiated … not as a glorious thing to be Achieved. They have failed to see in the nation the image and likeness of God … I believe in one Irish Nation and that free![59]

Once 'thunders of applause' had subsided, Pearse nominated republican separatists Wolfe Tone, Thomas Davis, Fintan Lalor and John Mitchel as the four 'great minds' and 'Apostles of Irish Nationhood'. Emmet was one of the 'martyrs', whose 'Christ-like death' and unilateral actions had 'redeemed Ireland' in 1803, following the military defeat of the United Irishmen in 1798 and imposition of the Act of Union in 1800.

Having invited the audience to stand with him in quasi-religious reverence, the closing segment of Emmet's 'Speech from the Dock' was recited: 'When my country takes her rightful place among the nations of the earth, then, and not till then, let my epitaph be written.' Drawing his own oration to a close, Pearse solicited adherence to the uncompromising ideals of Emmet, stating, 'God may even grant us, though so unworthy, to achieve the wonderful thing for which so many worthier strove in vain.'[60]

Few could have failed to grasp that Pearse identified himself totally with the mission of Emmet and that the inertia that had stalled the republican agenda since the 1867 Rising and dynamite campaign of 1882 was about to be dispelled. Bob Brennan recalled, 'from the tone of his speech it was clear to everyone that the Rising was only a few weeks off. After the lecture he made arrangements to convey the date by code messages to the officers in the various districts.'[61]

At St Enda's, adult members of what had morphed into a republican commune were engaged in 'feverish activity' preparing for revolt. Science master Peter Slattery supervised the filling of 500 cannisters despite having been wounded while manufacturing explosives in the science laboratory. Frank de Burca was deeply involved and on one occasion in the spring of 1916 was delegated by Pearse to collect bomb casings from the Clarke home in Fairview. They were handed over by Kathleen Clarke, whom de Burca personally revered as 'the daughter of the famous Fenian John Daly'.[62] He recalled:

> For some months previous to Easter Monday 1916 … every evening we spent in the 'University Room' making hand-grenades, filling cartridges with shot and fashioning batons

for use against looters ... we managed to procure as much equipment as possible. Each Volunteer had to provide himself with a bandolier, haversack and knapsack. I had a lovely long Lee-Enfield rifle which I had got from the hands of P. H. Pearse himself some months before ... We kept our rifles at the head of our beds.[63]

From late 1915, 'engineering' classes led by Peadar Slattery and Pat Breen met at Volunteers headquarters. Seamus Daly, an IRB man and member of the 2nd Battalion, recalled:

Lessons on the use of explosives and demolitions, field works and field cookery. We also got lectures on house construction which was designed to teach us the art of breaking in from house to house, also the construction of barricades and the proper materials to use ... We carried on with these lectures right up to Easter Week ... Pearse used [to] visit the class occasionally to enquire into our progress. ... [He] told us that soon we might have to be putting our knowledge into effect. He told us to report back to our companies and to ask the Company Captains for six men each. We would teach these men and use them as military engineers when the fight came.[64]

Selected IRB men, who had hitherto enjoyed modest roles in the Volunteers, were advanced to positions of authority as the date for the Rising approached. Bob Brennan was visited in mid-March 1916 by Captain Seamus O'Sullivan, who conveyed Pearse's verbal order that he had been appointed Brigade Quartermaster with the rank of captain. Promotion from private to captain was an exponential increase in responsibility. The advancement stemmed from his prominence in the Wexford IRB.[65]

Certain Volunteer officers were cultivated by the IRB at the last minute, including John MacDonagh, brother of Thomas MacDonagh and lieutenant in the 3rd Battalion (Dublin). He took the oath in order to courier a message from Pearse to Tipperary. Ceannt carried out the initiation on 18 April 1916.[66] Similarly, Fintan Murphy joined the Mitchel Circle of the IRB once sworn in by Pearse.[67]

A meeting at the Mansion House protested the deportation of Liam Mellows and Ernest Blythe and inspired a raucous procession of hundreds unimpeded by the DMP and RIC, who found themselves outnumbered. Mary Louisa Hamilton Norway, wife of Arthur Hamilton Norway, Secretary of the GPO since September 1912, was living in the Royal Hibernian Hotel on Dawson Street (where French officers of General Jean Humbert's expeditionary force to assist the United Irishmen had been accommodated following capture in September 1798). She claimed 'they marched down Grafton Street singing "Die Wacht am Rhein" and revolutionary songs; a slight disturbance with the police took place and some shots were fired.'[68]

The annual St Enda's fête was very different in ambiance and format in 1916 than in previous years, when staff and students had usually performed a play in Irish and English in front of schoolboys, musicians, past pupils and invited guests. For that of 21 March 1916, the engagement of the Headmaster 'and most of the staff ... in more serious work' necessitated the simplifying of performances.[69] Séamus Ó Braonáin arrived in the middle of proceedings, having spent the previous night defending the Volunteer Hall in Tullamore from a police raid. De Burca noted that 'the first shot in the Insurrection had been fired' and that St Enda's 'resounded with our cheers when P. H. Pearse announced the tidings to us'.[70]

Pearse made another important speech behind closed doors. Des Ryan remembered, '[Pearse] knew [it] was his last farewell to the "2nd achievement" of his life. The "3rd achievement" was on the horizon.'[71] Elsewhere, Ryan recorded:

Sgoil Éanna, [Pearse] declared, had gone on for eight years. He hoped it would continue for eighty, but so far as he was concerned its work was done. He had founded Sgoil Éanna to make Irish boys efficient soldiers in the battles spiritual and temporal of their country. In the Irish Volunteers that day were many such soldiers. It had taken the blood of the Son of God to redeem the world. It would take the blood of the sons of Ireland to redeem Ireland.[72]

Bulmer Hobson arranged an all-day meeting of the head-quarters military staff at the residence of James MacNeill, Eoin MacNeill's brother, in Woodtown Park, Rathfarnham, where the Chief of Staff produced a manuscript outlining the formal position on an uprising. According to Hobson, 'Pearse and McDermott at this meeting specifically disavowed any intention to land the Volunteers in an insurrection, and reproached the rest of us for our suspicious nature.'[73] Admitting secret preparations on the part of the IRB Military Council would have courted expulsion.

Pearse later met Hobson at a Dublin restaurant and disclosed, when rising to leave, 'I cannot answer your arguments, but I feel that we must have an insurrection.'[74] Connolly, whom Hobson held in equal disdain, also rendezvoused for a meal and reputedly claimed that 'Ireland was a powder magazine and that what was necessary was for someone to apply the match.'[75] When Pearse learned that Hobson had requested details of 'training and activities' in the Cavan sector from Seamus O'Sullivan, he said to O'Sullivan, 'Now, listen, the less Hobson knows, the better. Send no reports to him, but report directly to me at St Enda's any time you come to town.'[76] Pearse subsequently called O'Sullivan to Dublin and assigned him a 'special job' in Wexford where, in the event of an emergency, he was to assume command.[77]

Briefings of regional Volunteer leaders were held discreetly in Dublin. Frank Henderson of the 2nd Battalion, who evidently did not join the IRB until 1918, was present at one, held on a Saturday night, two to three weeks before the Rising at Volunteer Headquarters – alongside 'every officer of the Dublin Brigade'.[78] Some attended in uniform, and most carried revolvers or automatics. Ceannt and MacDonagh were discussing their personal preparations for mobilisation.

> There was a short pause, Pearse came in, and, after a dramatic silence of a few moments while he stood with his head down, he raised his head quickly and said, 'Is every man here prepared to meet his God?' He said it not loudly but with the force of tremendous seriousness. After that, Pearse proceeded to tell us that any man who was not in earnest, now was his time to get out.[79]

This was evidently the session attended by Cathal McDowell, deputised by McCullough and Burns to represent the Belfast sector on behalf of the IRB and Volunteers:

> Pearse addressed the delegates at the meeting. He reviewed the state of the country and the preparations the Volunteers were making to combat the state of affairs then existent. He suggested that armed camps be set up for Easter, and his words conveyed the impression that something serious was afoot. There was no definite statement made as to what

his plans were … *He stated that somebody might make an effort to call off this mobilisation for armed camps during the Easter holidays, and that no notice was to be taken of such cancellation, except it came direct from himself …* There was a large crowd of delegates at the meeting from all over the country.[80]

McDowell reported on the gathering to the Volunteer Executive in Belfast, but, if McCullough and Burns were informed of the stricture on the cancellation of manoeuvres, this was not related to McCartan.[81]

At a fund-raiser in the Keating Branch Hall in Parnell Square, Pearse made an appearance, armed and in full uniform. Michael Walker, of the 2nd Battalion, remembered that Pearse said

'Volunteers might be called into action at any moment' and appealed for the support of the people with funds, suggesting that the women might even contribute their jewellery. He also appealed to any man who was not prepared to face this issue by reason or any other responsibilities to withdraw from the movement, hand in any arms which they might have and nothing the worse would be thought of them. This brought it home to me very clearly the dangers and realities of the position of matters.[82]

As a clandestine member of the IRB Military Council, Pearse knew that orderly mobilisation required the utmost secrecy if it were not to be pre-empted, as had occurred in Dublin on 23 May 1798, when last-minute leakage of the plans enabled the government to turn out the garrison ahead of the United Irishmen. Young Ireland in 1848 stood no chance of mounting its planned armed protest as intelligence ensured martial law was proclaimed prior to the dissemination of orders to rise. In March 1867, the inherent military capacity of what became the RIC was equal to the main if uncoordinated showing in the Dublin suburbs of local Fenians.

Pearse, Connolly and Clarke were steeped in such history and successfully restricted the greatest secret of their generation to a small cohort of intimates in Ireland, the USA and Germany. 'General Orders' dated 3 April 1916 were sent to every town in Ireland and suggested routine intentions by referencing the uneventful precedent of 1915 and the requirement for reports due on a date beyond the one on which they had already chosen to rise:

1. Following the lines of last year, every unit of the Irish Volunteers will hold manoeuvres during the Easter Holidays. The object of the manoeuvres is to test mobilisation with equipment.

2. In Brigade Districts the manoeuvres will be carried out under the orders of the Brigade Commandants. In the case of the Dublin Brigade, the Manoeuvres will, as last year, be carried out under the direction of the Headquarters General Staff.

3. Each Brigade, Battalion or Company Commander as the case may be, will on or before 1st May next, send to the Director of Organisation a detailed report of the Manoeuvres carried out by his unit.[83]

Volunteers made transparent preparations to muster. Vinny Byrne, one of the youngest at the age of fifteen, was informed on Holy Tuesday, 18 April 1916, that E Company, 2nd Battalion, would meet at Father Mathew Park on Easter Sunday at 11 a.m. He expected to join Company Commander Thomas Weafer and Battalion Vice Officer Commanding Tom Hunter for 'an ordinary parade'.[84] Little of note struck Byrne in the run-up to Easter other than a series of lectures by Connolly on the subject of 'street fighting'. Company officer Mick McDonnell went on to form Byrne and others into the cutting edge of the Dublin Brigade IRA 'Squad' during the War of Independence.[85]

In March and April 1916, Eamon Bulfin recalled being 'engaged [by Pearse] … sending secret orders to O/Cs of the Units in the country. I did not see the contents.'[86]

Cotton and Stack had been briefed by Pearse in St Enda's

in a manner that prioritised the role of Kerry in the insurrection being planned. Cotton, like Hobson, was ignorant of the extent to which Pearse as Director of Military Operations had fostered guerrilla warfare operations throughout the country to reinforce the *coup d'état* in the national capital:

> Pearse made us definitely promise that we would tell no one the information he had given us. I think he wanted to be sure I would give no hint to Hobson, with whom he knew I was friendly. Hobson was opposed to the plans for a Rising, which Pearse entertained. He wanted a fight conducted on guerrilla tactics, and he was largely responsible for that trend in training, which was evident from the articles by O'Connell and O'Duffy appearing in the *Irish Volunteer*. Hobson has told me that he and Pearse had had hot arguments about the matter. On one occasion Pearse had admitted that he could not deny the soundness of Hobson's arguments, but stated: 'we must have a sacrifice'. Hobson's main argument was that gambling everything on one throw was not good tactics, and that the adoption of guerrilla fighting would enable us to make a more sustained effort with better prospects of success.[87]

Pearse, as Director of Military Organisation, set the Easter Rising in train on 8 April 1916 with the publication of 'General Orders' in the *Irish Volunteer*.

On 15 April, Tom Byrne, a Carrickmacross man raised in Dublin, was summoned from an all-night Volunteer social gathering in 41 Parnell Square and instructed to meet Pearse in Rathfarnham. The fact that this pointed invitation reached him after 4 a.m. was indicative of its urgency. Ostensibly a low-ranking Volunteer in B Company, 1st Battalion, Byrne had seen action with MacBride's Irish Brigade in South Africa and had lived in the USA. He was received in New York by Devoy and inducted into Clan na Gael, then transferred into the IRB in Dublin. On being apprised that 'the Volunteer movement had practically started', he attended the foundation event at the Rotunda in November 1913 and participated in its most clandestine operations, not least the Howth and Kilcoole arms landings in 1914.[88] Trusted and effective, it was not immaterial that Byrne was an experienced mineworker familiar with explosives.[89] Byrne was a near-daily visitor to Clarke's shop in Parnell Street in 1915.[90] In early 1916, Clarke deputed him to reconnoitre Harcourt Street Station with Connolly, a location they were to seize 'in the event of trouble'.[91]

Peadar Bracken, Midlands area commander, who had been in hiding since the shootout with the RIC in Tullamore on 21 March, was contacted around the same time by Liam Staines, who had a 'dispatch from Pearse' urging him to await further instructions.[92]

Over the following weeks, plans were amended by the Military Council. Pearse instructed Byrne to assume control of the Kildare Volunteers from the less qualified Ted O'Kelly, whom he retained as second-in-command:

> Pearse gave me no definite word that the Rising was to take place soon. I was not to travel by train to Kildare but to cycle down as I might be spotted by the police at the station. I had a few hours' sleep in St Enda's before leaving for Co. Kildare.[93]

It was no coincidence that Domhnall Ua Buachalla, an intimate of Pearse and fellow militant, accommodated Byrne in Maynooth the following night. Byrne and O'Kelly quickly contacted leading adherents in Prosperous, Newbridge and Rathangan, at which time they discovered that most still lacked weapons. By 20 April, Byrne knew that an insurrection was imminent:

> I received instructions in a dispatch from Pearse that the rebellion was to start on Easter Sunday at 4 PM. I was to mobilise all the Companies in Kildare and they were to march in full kit to Bodenstown churchyard. At 4 PM I was to address them and tell them that the fight was on, that those who wished to fight could follow me, and that those who did not wish to fight could go home. I visited all the Companies and sent word around. There was promise of a big response.[94]

On 8 April in Dunboyne, Co. Meath, Volunteer officer and IRB inductee Sean Boylan received instructions to go to St Enda's. Meeting the man who had commissioned him into the Volunteers made a deep impression:

> Pearse said 'This is Donal O'Hannigan whom I have appointed Officer Commanding Meath, Louth, South Down, South Armagh and Monaghan area.' He told me I would come under O'Hannigan's command. Pearse told me that a German ship would land arms in the country. He instructed me that when I got orders for mobilisation I was to mobilise my men and send out scouts and get in touch with [O']Hannigan … [who] left Pearse before I did and I did not see or hear from [O']Hannigan again until after the Rebellion had started, although I expected to do so.[95]

A source in Dunboyne Castle, home to the Morrogh-Ryan family, which had links by marriage to Major Bertie Kenny of the War Office, learned of a written recommendation that all officers in the Irish Volunteers be arrested under the Defence of the Realm Act. John Moore, valet in the castle and Boylan's trusted 'agent', gained sight of the resolution, which was composed by Lord Frederick Fitzgerald, Charles Hamilton, 'Captain Fowler', 'Mrs Maher' and other 'loyalists'.[96] A concerned Boylan visited Pearse without invitation on 15 April: 'Pearse thought the information very important and subsequent events proved it to be so. It would seem that the document read by Alderman Tom Kelly at the meeting of Dublin Corporation on the 19th April was based on those recommendations.'[97] Kelly had been a founder member of Sinn Féin and first leader of the republican labour tendency on the Corporation.[98]

Winning over a vacillating MacNeill and other members of the Volunteer Executive to unilateral armed action posed a challenge for the Military Council. Recourse was made to forging a document purporting to come from Dublin Castle regarding the imminent suppression of the Irish Volunteers. The 'gist' of the order was described as 'Arrest of leaders, isolation of certain Volunteer centres and seizure of Volunteer drill halls.'[99]

According to Hobson (who insisted that the role he played in circulating the *ruse de guerre* 'all over the country' just days ahead of the Rising was an unwitting one), MacNeill accepted the authenticity of the chimera without disclosing its provenance.[100] Hobson's personal investigations in 1917 concluded that Joseph Plunkett presented the document to Rory O'Connor, who passed it on to P. J. Little, from whom it was acquired by MacNeill. A compliant Colm Ó Lochlainn apparently printed it at Plunkett's request. In Hobson's eyes, Plunkett, 'a member of our [Volunteer Executive] Committee, who was actively associated with Pearse' had taken 'apparently, elaborate precautions to plant the document on MacNeill'.[101] The studied omission of the agency of Clarke, Devoy and Lynch in relation to contemporaneous stratagems of the Military Council was rare reticence from the acerbic Hobson. He cited Plunkett's 'very advanced stage of TB' as a point of mitigation, although this had no bearing on events.[102]

Des Ryan, guardian of Pearse's reputation, discovered that in the aftermath of the Rising that IPP leader John Dillon had consulted Margaret Pearse to ask 'if she had any evidence that the Dublin Castle Order was genuine'.[103] Much to his surprise, she replied in the affirmative. She said that 'there was a man in Dublin Castle who knew about it'.[104] It was claimed that 'scraps' of intelligence had been acquired from DMP offices, one of which specified that the Catholic Archbishop of Dublin was to be 'isolated'. Men identified as working on the forgery project included Ó Lochlainn, O'Connor, Jack Plunkett, George Plunkett and, following consultation in his Mountjoy Square Nursing Home, Joseph Plunkett, who mischievously recommended that the residence of the Archbishop of Armagh be added.[105]

Ryan evidently did not know that Pearse had received intelligence on the same topic from Boylan, which, if not a separate stream of information pointing to an imminent swoop, was nonetheless unnerving. With the sword of Damocles hovering over his head, Pearse projected a calm visage. Ryan ascertained:

Pearse would never commit himself on the matter although he showed it to Liam Mellows, saying, 'Look what they are going to do' or words to that effect. So Miss Margaret Pearse told us at the time. Some of us were very sceptical of it. Peter Slattery asked Willie Pearse jocosely, 'Whoever forged that?'[106]

Once word spread of a pending crackdown, people and arms dumps were moved to an unprecedented extent.[107]

Lacking convincing evidence to substantiate his suspicions, on Palm Sunday, 16 April 1916, Hobson addressed a fund-raising concert organised by Cumann na mBan in 41 Parnell Square. The programmed one-act play produced by *Irish Review* regular Jack Morrow was axed to enable Hobson to speak, claiming that 'this was not Ireland's opportunity and that a more favourable time would come later'.[108] Using what he regarded as careful language, Hobson 'warned them of the extreme danger of being drawn into precipitate action, which could only have the effect of bringing the movement to an end'.[109] It is possible that this intervention, based on pure intuition, had bearing on the response of those present when contradictory orders flashed across the thirty-two counties the following weekend.

Denis McCullough, who was present, was stunned by Hobson's speech: 'I had just left Tom Clarke, who told me the Rising was fixed for the following Sunday and here was the

Secretary of the Irish Volunteers advocating publicly a policy of delay. I feared that divided councils would be fatal to any attempt at an armed Rising.'[110] MacDiarmada was incensed and promised to 'damned soon deal with that fellow'.[111]

Charles Donnelly, seeking to be excused from Larkfield duty the following week, innocently learned the secret of the Military Council from Pearse:

> He said: 'I am going to tell you something that you are not to repeat inside or outside this Hall.' He then told me that the Rising had been planned to take place on Easter Sunday and finished by saying: 'I leave it to yourself whether you come with us'. When I said I would withdraw my request he smiled, shook hands with me and said: 'I thought you would.' This was so unusual that the other Volunteers standing around and out of hearing asked me why he did it. I replied that I had told him a funny story … with the repeated warnings to guard our arms and the air of tension, I already had a feeling that something was in the air.[112]

On 17 April, Pearse addressed E Company, 4th Battalion, advising on rations, equipment and orders pertaining to the Easter Sunday manoeuvres. Members of that company, including IRB man Michael Cremen, were acting as Pearse's bodyguard and were detailed to 'escort' him from the tramway terminus to the Hermitage.[113]

On Spy Wednesday, 19 April 1916, Eamonn Corbett collected Liam Mellows from St Enda's and drove him to Galway in a motorbike and sidecar combination. Mellows had staged a daring escape from Reading Gaol in April 1916, and had been lying low in the college, disguised as a priest.[114] Within the walls of the Hermitage estate he was hailed as 'the life and soul of the party', staying dressed as a priest at all times. Mellows being sent to Connaught ensured that segments of the Galway Volunteers saw action when fighting broke out. By Holy Thursday, virtually all the munitions manufactured and stockpiled in the college over the previous weeks had been dispatched around the city.[115]

Limerick City Officer Commanding (OC) Michael Colivet was apprised by Sean Fitzgibbon on 18 April that 'arms were to be landed in Kerry within a week', and, excepting weapons required for local use, they were to be transported to Abbeyfeale, then sent by rail to Galway. When Colivet questioned the change in previously transmitted orders, Fitzgibbon advised him to confer with Pearse, which he did on 19 April. Pearse explicitly 'instructed him to cancel all other plans … [and] that action was to be started at 7 PM on Sunday'.[116] According to Colivet's close associate, Lieutenant James Gubbins,

Colivet found him surprisingly reticent as to the amount of help expected from abroad. Closely questioned, he would

159

neither confirm nor deny that an expeditionary force was to be expected. The ultimate impression left on Colivet's mind was that men were coming but that Pearse was precluded by some agreement from saying so. He was told he might expect to meet an old friend and took this to refer to [Robert] Monteith. He returned to Limerick and gave an account of his visit to [George] Clancy, [Jim] Ledden and [John] Grant who were in his confidence. He recast his plans in accordance with his new instructions.[117]

Liam Manahan, an East Limerick Volunteer and IRB leader, call in to Dawson Street HQ to confer with Hobson and O'Connell in the late morning, on his way home from business in London. He was 'amazed at their complacency', which seemed all the more incongruous when he encountered an 'excited' MacDonagh and divined that matters were moving forward.[118]

MacDonagh urged Manahan to return immediately to Limerick where important orders awaited his review, but then changed his mind and said, 'As you are here now, you better come and see Pearse.'[119] They went to MacDiarmada's 'office' on the quays, where the arrival of J. J. O'Connell stifled free conversation. It was clear that Pearse could not be accessed at this time, and Manahan departed on the 6.30 p.m. train for Limerick.[120]

Dr de Burca, Ulster IRB delegate and father of St Enda's

resident Frank, cycled from Carrickmacross, Co. Monaghan, to Dublin (a distance of sixty miles) to be briefed by Pearse. He generally visited the city once or twice a week, reporting 'mainly to Pearse but sometimes to Tom Clarke'.[121] He and McCullough met Pearse and Connolly in the Keating Branch offices to receive preliminary instructions on a national uprising. Pearse told them that the Belfast men were to move into East Tyrone and proceed to Connaught, having rendezvoused with a Monaghan contingent under de Burca.[122] McCullough reportedly wept on receiving his orders, which pertained primarily to Antrim and Tyrone.

Pearse and Ceannt visited the 'Kimmage Garrison' at Larkfield, where men they intended to deploy were assembled. McGallogly recalled Pearse's lecture on urban fighting, which, he explained, might be necessary 'if the British acted before we were mobilised'.[123]

That day witnessed the publication of the forged Dublin Castle document, which, Des Ryan recalled, sent 'the temperature up'.[124] The *Irish Independent* inadvertently gave credence to such reports by stating that 'a very unsatisfactory state of affairs prevails in Ireland. The Sinn Féin movement is growing to such an alarming extent that the Government may find it necessary to take drastic action at once.'[125] This 'document of a grave character' reached Cork on 19 April. Liam de Róiste was in 'some doubt' as to its veracity, but he reasoned that 'the effect of the publication of this document may have good results on the public mind in the strengthening of public opinion in favour of the Volunteers'.[126] De Róiste inferred that the Easter manoeuvres 'tend to become serious' in the new context.[127] Monsignor Michael Curran, Secretary to Archbishop Walsh of Dublin, had received advance notice of the forged document's existence as early as 8 April from Dr Seamus O'Kelly, friend of another occasional private confidant, Eoin MacNeill.[128] The palace in Drumcondra had suspected for some time that 'Pearse … was determined to force a rising at any cost, whether in the case of disarmament or otherwise.'[129]

Orders from Pearse warned Peadar Bracken in Westmeath that the 'Rising would take place at 7 PM on Easter Sunday' when he was to 'carry out my instructions' in the Athlone Brigade district.[130] Liam Staines carried similar if not identical messages from Pearse to the Moate area Volunteers, including one to McCormack of Drumraney.[131] A female relative of Michael O'Hanrahan handed Enniscorthy IRB man Seamus Doyle a coded message from Pearse on the same day: 'Brown and Nolans tell me that they will have the books you require on the 23rd July next. Remember 3 months earlier.' The subject had been agreed as a trigger for action in March when Pearse lectured on Emmet whereas the date was that of the Rising of 1803.[132] Having been inducted into the IRB, John MacDonagh, brother of Thomas, departed Dublin for Cashel, Tipperary, on 20 April. The message from

Pearse to Eamon O'Dwyer read: 'The grass seeds on order will be delivered on Sunday, the 23rd, at 7 PM.' O'Dwyer eventually received the note on a farm three miles from Tipperary town.[133] On the train journey back to Dublin, MacDonagh was surprised to encounter other secret messengers, including Marie Perolz and Gearóid O'Sullivan.[134]

Chapter 5

• • • • •

Countdown to the Rising

Patrick and Willie Pearse made arrangements through Des Ryan to stay with the O'Kelly family at 27 Upper Rutland (modern Parnell) Street on the night of 20 April. Michael and Matthew O'Kelly had graduated from St Enda's into the F Company of the 1st Battalion Irish Volunteers, while elder brother Seán T. was a close associate of the Pearses and a leading IRB member. Margaret O'Kelly recalled Seán T. informing their mother that the guests

would probably require meals at irregular times. They turned up on Holy Thursday in the late evening … on bicycles wearing raincoats to cover their full military uniform. They were sticking out in bumps because of all the equipment they were carrying … Pádraig Pearse looked wonderful. Michael drew my attention afterwards downstairs to their yellow tabs and explained to me the significance of the ornaments on their epaulettes. They had no meal that night. They told Michael who was in civilian clothes to hold himself in readiness to run messages for them. Michael felt honoured to be asked, as he was rather afraid of Pearse who was his master at school … I remember him afterwards coming in breathless, probably from Liberty Hall … After they had disposed of their gear to their satisfaction the Pearses left on their bicycles and did not come back that night.[1]

In the dying hours of 20 April, Bulmer Hobson was disturbed in his city office by J. J. O'Connell and Eimar O'Duffy, who delivered the stunning news that a Rising had been planned for Easter Sunday. The trio went directly to MacNeill in Rathfarnham, roused him from his slumber and warned of what was taking place. All four travelled the short distance to St Enda's, where, at 2 a.m. on 21 April, Pearse was awakened.

Preserving hierarchy in the midst of confusion, O'Duffy was required to remain outside when the senior executive members confronted their rival: 'Pearse then admitted that an insurrection was to take place, and told us that nothing we could do could prevent it.'[2]

Fintan Murphy and other IRB residents of St Enda's had just finished work manufacturing munitions around 3.30 a.m. on Friday when Patrick and Willie Pearse arrived into their room. They charged Eamon Bulfin, Conor McGinley and Murphy with delivering dispatches to Clarke, MacDiarmada, MacDonagh and Ceannt. During the hours of darkness the youths cycled across the city, locating men absent from their usual haunts.

MacDonagh could not be found, and, lacking direction, the trio called in to 2 Dawson Street shortly before 10 a.m. to await Hobson's arrival.[3] Hobson appeared and inquired as to the nature of the communications they were carrying. Denied sight of the secret documents, he was distinctly unhelpful. John MacDonagh called in shortly after midday and agreed to bring the Pearses' dispatch to MacDiarmada.[4]

Having retired to Woodtown Park shortly after his visit to St Enda's, MacNeill ordered O'Connell to proceed to Cork to prevent the Volunteers from mobilising while Hobson was charged in writing with doing the same in Dublin city. Pearse had evidently apprised MacDiarmada and MacDonagh of his early morning confrontation as both arrived at MacNeill's house some hours later to reinforce the argument that the Rising was 'inevitable'. Much to Hobson's annoyance, MacNeill revoked his command in Dublin and instructed him to await his arrival in headquarters. The Chief of Staff did not appear.

Identified by former associates as a wild card, Hobson was lured to Martin Conlon's home in Phibsborough, where on arrival he was taken prisoner and brought to a Leinster Executive IRB meeting.[5] Ryan learned that Hobson was braced by 'some friends of his who produced revolvers and arrested him … [He] was not really surprised.'[6] MacDiarmada had evidently made good his intemperate vow to McCullough to neutralise Hobson.

Pearse, however, was initially blamed by The O'Rahilly, who was misinformed of his role. The following day, Geraldine Plunkett was told by her brother Joseph that O'Rahilly

> went up to St Enda's. Pearse opened the door and O'Rahilly drew his gun on him, and abused him. Pearse said nothing at all and O'Rahilly went away. Later in the day, Thomas MacDonagh and Sean McDermott got hold of him, and told him the whole situation, for the first time. He had not been told before about Hobson, that he had been opening letters, was fully aware of the plans, and was taking steps to see that they would not be carried out ... When he found out that he had been carrying unauthorised orders [to Kerry], he was very unhappy and completely agreed with the Military Council.[7]

Sean 'Johnny' Sinnott, Commandant of the Wexford Battalion, received the anticipated cryptic message from Pearse on Good Friday, 21 April 1916. When Bob Brennan viewed the reference to ordering 'school desks', he knew, from prior arrangement, that this 'conveyed the news that the mobilisation for the Rising was fixed for Sunday 23rd at 6 p.m.'[8] In Dunboyne, Co. Meath, Volunteer officer and IRB Centre Sean Boylan was contacted by 'written instructions from

Pearse to the effect that the Rising would start at 6 PM on Easter Sunday'.[9] Two men delivered the order and required that it be verbally acknowledged.[10]

Seamus O'Sullivan, who had been reassigned from Cavan to Wexford under Pearse's instruction, had been called to St Enda's on Holy Thursday but, due to transport problems, did not arrive until midday on Good Friday. He learned that Ned Daly was expecting him in the city and was left 'under the impression that something serious was about to happen'.[11] A chance meeting with J. J. O'Connell on the Rathfarnham Road indicated that his friend was due to be sent to Wexford.[12]

On what was a hectic day, Patrick and Willie Pearse called to Mount Argus, Harold's Cross, to visit Passionist Order associate Fr Eugene Nevin. A conspicuous supporter of the Volunteers, Fr Nevin was absent on business and 'never saw them after'. He noticed a marked increase in Volunteers attending church that weekend and 'crowded round the Confessionals'.[13]

Michael O'Hanrahan, one of the key men responsible for distributing weaponry, arrived to a house beside Fr Mathew Park at around 7 p.m. to visit IRB man and Volunteer Leo Henderson. On seeing his old acquaintance, Leo's brother Frank risked a direct question: 'Well, Micheál, are we going out on Sunday and not coming back again?' He answered, 'Yes, we are going out, and not coming back.'[14]

The SS *Libau* had sailed from Germany under Captain Karl Spindler, changing its name along the way to the *Aud*, a Norwegian freighter. Its cargo of 20,000 rifles, machine guns and 1 million rounds of ammunition might have changed the course of Irish history.[15] It reached Tralee Bay, as planned, on 20 April, meeting the timeline the IRB Military Council had originally requested through the German Consulate in New York, as managed by Devoy.

When the date was adjusted by the IRB to 21 April, word was sent via New York with Mimi Plunkett (Joseph's sister), but did not reach Berlin until after Spindler had sailed. The *Aud* apparently did not possess a high-powered radio transmitter and remained unaware of the mysterious lack of friendly shore contact.[16] The IRB, however, took pains to arrange the seizure of a transmitter from the Wireless College in Cahirciveen. According to Geraldine Dillon (née Plunkett): 'the purpose of the wireless … was really to get the news of the Rising transmitted to the world, especially to America. They knew that their own transmitter was not powerful enough, so they decided to send Con [Keating] to capture the wireless.'[17] This elaborate contingency failed when three Volunteers drove off the unfamiliar Ballykissane Pier, Killorglin, in the dark and plunged to their deaths in the river Laune. Given this sacrifice, no Dublin directed stratagem could then have averted a disastrous denouement to the importation at a critical phase.[18]

Four messages sent by McGarrity in Philadelphia reached McCartan in rural Tyrone, and all couriers dutifully relayed their import to Dublin. Clarke was apprised of contact codes, signals and the Fenit Pier objective and reassured the doubting McCartan by return communication that 'everything was alright'. This optimism was misplaced. British cryptanalysts had broken the German Navy code, and HMS *Bluebell* was lurking on station, ready to stalk the *Aud*. Interception at sea prompted Spindler to scuttle the ship off Daunt Rock, Co. Cork.[19]

Casement, meanwhile, dejected and unwell, had been virtually cast ashore on Kerry's Banna Strand by the German U-boat *U-19* in the early hours of 21 April. There was no reception committee, as local republicans had no inkling of his return. Two companions departed in a forlorn bid to make contact with comrades in the town. A disorientated Casement was arrested by the RIC who found him sheltering in 'McKenna's Fort' and, when taken to Tralee, made an unguarded request to phone MacNeill. He was quickly identified, despite having shaved his signature beard.[20]

News of the loss of the *Aud* reached Limerick city on the morning of Saturday, 22 April, and also of the arrest of a 'prominent prisoner' in Kerry and the detention of Austin Stack. Although several Volunteer/IRB officers understood that an insurrection had been planned for the following day, setbacks in the neighbouring county created confusion which the dispatch of multiple couriers to Tralee and Dublin did not immediately clarify.

James Gubbins eventually conferred with a still 'debonair' MacDiarmada in a private house, who imparted 'confidently … that the Rising would take place, that the lost German ship was only one of many such expeditions'.[21] The agreed code signal, almost certainly worded by Pearse, was telegraphed to Limerick. Recipients knew that the phrase 'the books have arrived' meant 'the rebellion is on'.

Yet the situation was far from settled.[22] Kerryman Fionán Lynch, close friend of MacDiarmada and member of his IRB Circle, recalled:

About 5 AM on Easter Saturday morning there was a terrific rat-a-tat-tat at our door in [44] Mountjoy St[reet] and we all drew our guns in expectation of a raid. The man at the door, however, was Sean Connolly [of the ICA] … and he brought a dispatch to Sean McDermott with regard to Casement's arrest. On Sean's orders Gearóid [O'Sullivan] and myself at once foraged a taxi and drove out to St Enda's with orders to inform Pearse that he should come at once in the taxi with us to Liberty Hall. We reached St Enda's about 6 AM and, when Pearse had dressed, we brought him to Liberty Hall where conferences went on throughout the day.[23]

MacNeill believed that a major armed showing was doomed. He did not, however, immediately cancel manoeuvres scheduled for the following afternoon. Such arrangements, he knew beyond doubt, covered an uprising by the national organisation of which he was nominally Chief of Staff.[24] Liam Ó Bríain ascertained that:

Pearse and McDermott visited MacNeill early on Saturday morning. And for the first time the patriot scholar learned of the *Aud* debacle. This altered MacNeill's views. Protesting that he had been unfairly dealt with, he now feared the British would come down on us with all their might. Therefore, we might as well stand together and meet the coming storm as best we could. The others said, 'Thank God.' At least there was to be unity of action. As the day wore on MacNeill changed his mind.[25]

News of developments began to permeate. Seán T. O'Kelly confided in Min Ryan that he had learned from Arthur Griffith that 'the Volunteers were going to rise the next morning' but had no idea what was likely to occur.[26] She recalled, 'Sean T. was very upset about the whole situation as he was very much in the dark about things and he feared that the Rising might end in a holocaust.' Although not on the Military Council, O'Kelly was hardwired to its personnel and within hours was called upon to assist in circumventing the newly dogged MacNeill. The Chief of Staff's associates, meanwhile, called to a meeting at the Rathgar Road home of Dr Seamus O'Kelly.[27]

At 4 p.m. Pearse received Liam Tannam, Captain of E Company, 3rd Battalion, in the Hermitage. Eamon de Valera had sent Tannam to collect a number of small parcels, which, he believed, contained 'armlets' to distinguish non-uniformed Volunteers from ordinary citizens. Tannam recalled 'the air was electric' as many Volunteer officers surmised the moment of truth was at hand. On being apprised that his company was to muster the following day in Beresford Place and augment the headquarters contingent, he ventured to engage Pearse in an unguarded discussion that confirmed his intuition.

Pearse assented that if fighting broke out, E Company, recruited from men living between Leeson Street and Goatstown, would have a better chance of entering the north inner city in small groups. Pearse then asked Tannam, 'Suppose we have to fight, where do you think would the British hold?' to which Tannam replied, 'the line of the canal'.[28] When Tannam returned to battalion headquarters at 144 Great Brunswick Street, De Valera was amazed by what his subordinate had ascertained.

Connaught IRB leader Alec McCabe, upon learning about the arrest of Casement, shook off his RIC tail and hastened from Sligo to Dublin to see Clarke. They met in a house at the corner of Hardwicke Street. Inside, McCabe found the Military Council. MacDiarmada told him that MacNeill had sent orders on the night of 22 April to stop the Rising, 'but that they had decided to go ahead ... The Staff were standing by ... He said that if forced out of the city [by the British] they would retreat towards the west. He said, "Mobilise as many as you can, destroy communications and await our arrival".'[29]

When Pearse and Connolly left the emergency meeting for further consultations in Liberty Hall, they invited McCabe to walk them over:

As we went towards Liberty Hall there was a discussion between Pearse and Connolly on the coming events. This covered such subjects as mobilisation; the terrible odds they would be up against and how, when the Rising started in the city, they would be out of touch with areas in the country. I ascertained from their discussion that Pearse was for taking to the country, while Connolly was for fighting in the city from house to house. Eventually Connolly agreed that they might be able to retreat into the country from the city. Pearse told me to do my best and said that as they retreated they would be gathering strength by being joined by the country centres of the IRB and some of the Volunteers.[30]

Belfast Volunteers had received orders to mobilise in Coalisland, East Tyrone. Preparations were made to transfer their rifles by taxi on 20 April whereas the 114 men expected were scheduled to arrive in contingents under Cathal McDowell, Archie Heron and Peter Burns/Sean Kelly. A further element was due from Scotland but did not materialise by the evening of 22 April. McDowell led an advance group of thirty, primarily men who were free to travel at midday by virtue of being either unemployed or excused work. Their absence would not be noted by the RIC. Heron and the second group of up to twenty-five departed Belfast by 6 p.m. for Coalisland. The third batch did not entrain on Sunday morning as events had overtaken their mission. McDowell's well-armed men were unimpeded by two RIC men who followed them to their barn billet five kilometres from the town.[31] Those staying in Coalisland's Drill Hall included Nora Connolly O'Brien and five other Cumann na mBan women trained in first aid. Their train had departed Belfast with the Young Ireland Pipers, Volunteers to a man, playing 'The Soldier's Song'.[32]

When poised the following afternoon to strike in the manner agreed, the Meathmen were ordered to desist when Benson, another IRB intermediary, arrived from the capital to aver that Tobin had ordered a halt. It proved difficult to ensure that Meath Volunteers who rallied with Garret Byrne on the Tara Hill site of a large engagement in May

1798 went home. Authorisation to cancel the Easter Sunday mobilisations came primarily from MacNeill, albeit following a period of agonised reflection and hesitancy.[33]

Sean Fitzgibbon and Colm Ó Lochlainn travelled to Kerry in relation to the aborted German arms landing, namely to commission a radio, and quickly reassessed at first hand the unfavourable short-term prospects of advancing the republican agenda.[34] They arrived into Dublin on Easter Saturday morning but failed to locate Hobson. Accompanied by The O'Rahilly, they went to Woodtown Park, where they briefed MacNeill, who then drove them all to St Enda's. According to Ó Lochlainn:

> After some conversation with Pearse in the hall of St Enda's, MacNeill and Pearse came out to the steps of the house and it was there I heard Pearse say to MacNeill, 'we have used you and your name and influence for what it was worth. You can issue what orders you like now, our men won't obey you.' MacNeill said he would do as his conscience and his common sense bade him and if Pearse had any more to say he could meet him at 9 p.m. that evening at Dr Seamus O'Ceallaigh's house at 53 Rathgar Road.[35]

With new resolve, MacNeill became proactive in cancelling the manoeuvres.[36] Dr Jim Ryan, brother of Min, was ordered to deliver MacNeill's handwritten orders to Cork, where he had just handed over a set notifying mobilisation. Identical documents were issued to Min Ryan for Wexford, to Liam O'Brien for Tyrrellspass and Tullamore (Offaly), to The O'Rahilly for Limerick and to Fr Paul Walsh for Galway. MacNeill confirmed the cancellation with a notice released to the press on the evening of 22 April. The most cogent and widely disseminated was published in the *Sunday Independent* the following morning.[37]

This fateful step was debated that night at length in the Rathgar home of Dr O'Kelly, where men of action like Brugha, Fitzgibbon and possibly also Thomas MacDonagh assembled. MacNeill did not convince all those present, and Brugha evidently placated the wavering Seán T. O'Kelly after protracted discussion.[38]

As yet oblivious to the extent of the MacNeillite reaction, Patrick and Willie Pearse spent the night once again in the O'Kelly family home in 27 Upper Rutland Street.[39] Patrick Pearse wrote to his friend on St Enda's stationery: 'A cara, could you put my brother and myself up tonight? It is important that we should be in town. If you cannot, can you get some friend to do it? Please let me know by bearer.'[40] The brothers accessed their second-storey drawing-room billet 'very late' on Saturday night in a state of perturbation.[41]

Margaret O'Kelly answered the door of the family home on the morning of Sunday, 23 April, to find her agitated brother Seán T. seeking admission, an unusual situation determined by his having loaned his keys to the Pearses.

Pádraig descended the stairs towards the hall and Sean ran up halfway to meet him. Pearse must have been shaving because he had a towel in his hand – it was a nice linen one that my mother had specially bought for these important and distinguished guests ... He seemed excited – the only time I ever saw him like that, for he was always so calm and dignified. I heard him distinctly shout in a loud voice, 'Damned cowardice!' He may have said more. Sean said 'Sh!' and rushed up towards him and brought him back into the drawing room where they remained some time ... [I was] rather intrigued at Pearse's strong language ... When I came back from Mass all three had left [for services in Gardiner Street].[42]

Liam Forde, an emissary from Limerick city, spent the night in MacDiarmada's lodgings and was appalled by his host's reaction to the *Sunday Independent*. He became 'frantic' before he 'rent the coat of his pajamas to shreds'. During the short walk to Liberty Hall, his peace of mind returned, and he remarked, 'they should rise, if only with pikes and bayonets; even though defeated their blood would regenerate the nation'.[43]

Eoin MacNeill and Sean Fitzgibbon went to 8 a.m. Mass at Rathfarnham Church to meet and enlist the aid of

John J. Keegan of E Company, 4th Battalion. They had first approached Eamon Bulfin, who, once he surmised the undisclosed mission involved 'calling off the manoeuvres', immediately refused. They evidently also failed to convince Frank Connolly.[44] MacNeill finally succeeded with Keegan, who consented to deliver a written statement to Pearse, Clarke, MacDonagh or Plunkett 'somewhere in the city'.[45]

Pearse was reputably frequenting 44 Mountjoy Square, and Plunkett nearby No. 27.[46] It was clear that Plunkett had just departed the lodgings, taking his luggage. Pearse was not known at No. 44, and Keegan was the second misdirected caller received by a puzzled landlady.[47] Kathleen Clarke gave Keegan a 'very poor showing' when he called enquiring as to the whereabouts of her husband. This, he mused, was understandable for anyone 'diagnosed as a policeman'. The IRB hub of 41 Parnell Square, 'generally crowded out on Sunday mornings with clubs', was eerily deserted. There was 'no one to be seen, not even the caretaker'.[48]

Pearse was located by fellow E Company member Michael Cremen who had stayed in the north inner city to carry out a special mission prior to learning of the published order. Friendly Volunteers directed him to the Jesuit church on Gardiner Street, where Willie and Patrick Pearse were present: 'I asked P. H. Pearse was the MacNeill order a bogus one or a British ruse. He said no, but that I would have further orders later on.'[49] Nothing materialised in the blur of events, and the restless Cremen rejoined many of the company later that night as they camped in the Pine Forest above Rathfarnham.[50]

Nora Connolly returned from Dungannon at around 6 a.m. on Easter Sunday and went straight to Liberty Hall, where she briefed her 'very upset' father on the situation in the north of Ireland. It transpired that he had been misinformed about the encouraging strength of the early turnout in mid-Ulster. He explained that he had argued bitterly with MacNeill the previous night when the loss of the German weaponry was in focus.

Six members of Cumann na mBan were sent under armed escort to key Volunteer leaders to apprise them of the genuine situation in the North and to summon them to Liberty Hall.[51] When Nora Connolly returned, she saw her father in ICA uniform for the first time and found him 'in much better form. He felt that something might be done.'[52] Mac-Diarmada, Clarke, MacDonagh, Ceannt and Plunkett arrived separately after dawn, followed by Pearse, the last to join the breakfast gathering hosted by Connolly on the day earmarked to declare the Irish Republic.

A visiting Cumann na mBan woman returned with a copy of the *Sunday Independent*, which 'amazed' Connolly. Nora Connolly recalled his consternation: 'He did not know it was going to be put in the papers. My father asked Pearse. He just said: "Do you know anything of this?" And Pearse said: "I know nothing of this".'[53] Any other answer in such a febrile environment would have scuppered the Rising.

At 10 a.m., the Military Council assembled in Room 7, where they had habitually convened: 'There was great activity in the Hall. The great front door was closed, and an armed guard along the stairs and along the corridor.'[54] Although requested to remain available, the unimpeachable Nora was denied entry to the meeting room when she wished to confer with her father.

MacNeill's proxy, Keegan, arrived at Liberty Hall, having been directed there by Seán T. O'Kelly. On learning the negative purpose of the visit, O'Kelly gripped Keegan earnestly: 'it must go on.'[55] The unwelcome emissary proceeded to a suspiciously thronged Liberty Hall with difficulty as he was once again marked as a Castle spy. He hailed Countess Markievicz on the landing who told him testily that while she knew 'nothing about' Pearse (who was actually upstairs), she was 'in a quandary to know what to do next'.[56] Connolly had denied her access to the leadership meeting, as she did not hold the qualifying seniority.

Keegan's friend Sean Connolly of the ICA hailed him from a higher floor and facilitated the serving of MacNeill's written statement:

> He opened the door of the Council Chamber and I went
> in and there sure enough was Comd Pearse coming towards

the door. I saluted him and handed him my dispatch. Before he read it, he asked me 'did I want any answer to it' to which I replied 'I don't think it requires any answer, it is, as far as I know, the commands of the Chief of Staff'. He then read the dispatch and said, 'tell him it shall be so'. I got one hurried glance around that Council Chamber and at the further end of room from me I saw MacDonagh, Clarke, McDermott and Plunkett with a few others whose backs were towards me.[57]

Keegan returned swiftly to Woodtown Park, where MacNeill 'anxiously' awaited news. On being apprised of Pearse's verbal acquiescence, 'he expressed "thanks to God for that"'.[58] The attitude of Pearse was more significant than other Military Council members as he, like MacNeill, possessed national-level authority in the Volunteers; he was not simply an IRB revolutionary. A countermanding order endorsed by Pearse would have settled the question.

As matters stood, when Michael Staines delivered news of the cancellation to 3rd Battalion headquarters, he came close to detention at gunpoint by Eamon de Valera and Seán Heuston.[59] Mick Hayes was sent to St Enda's 'to enquire from Pearse what was happening', but Eamon Bulfin and the others remained in the dark: 'We did not know actually where Mr Pearse was at the time.' They themselves had unsuccessfully sought access to Liberty Hall at around 1 p.m.[60]

Irish Volunteers loyal to MacNeill underestimated the authority vested in the free-standing ICA contingent by the IRB clique of which Pearse was the prime interlocutor. Pro-IRB elements in Volunteer Headquarters and the unanimous Military Council deliberated all morning before secretly rescheduling the Rising. Standing down those already poised to revolt preserved the surprise factor in a sophisticated conspiracy and deceived Special Branch, RIC and Military Intelligence observers.

Dublin Castle discerned from Casement's demeanour in Tralee and MacNeill's actions that the immediate threat of insurrection had been reduced if not totally negated.[61] Pearse played his part in this subterfuge by issuing dispatches from Liberty Hall at around 1 p.m. on Sunday confirming the import of MacNeill's direction. Additional 'couriers', however, were enjoined to attend an evening meeting at 18 North Frederick Street. According to the Henderson inquiry, 'by them went forth the final order for the Rising on Easter Monday'.[62]

At around 4 p.m., as the Military Council meeting began to dissolve, Liam Forde watched as Pearse reemerged: 'placing his arm affectionately around Forde's shoulder, he told him everything was off for the present, but "hold yourself in readiness for further orders"'.[63] In a seemingly extravagant act, Pearse arranged a car to bring Forde straight to Cashel with a sealed message for Pierce McCann.[64]

An armed ICA detachment gathered outside Liberty Hall while expectant onlookers loitered. The ICA moved off as if on a routine exercise to distract the DMP from the dispersing Military Council. They had determined to proceed with the Rising at 12 p.m. on Easter Monday and imparted this to various trusted ICA members.[65] Pearse, MacDiarmada and probably other Military Council members drafted revised instructions in the North Frederick Street office that were 'sent out … to the country Volunteer leaders to carry out their orders on Easter Monday'.[66]

In North Kerry, republicans were in disarray in the face of the combined losses of Ballykissane Pier, McKenna's Fort and Daunt Rock. The pre-emptive arrest of Austin Stack and Con Collins removed popular men of considerable joint IRB and Volunteer authority at a critical juncture. On Easter Sunday, a reduced cadre under Paddy Cahill assembled in Tralee. They were surprised when Robert Monteith, who had been landed on the Friday by Captain Raimund Weisbach's *U-19*, arrived into their midst and threw some light on the bizarre reverses. Willie Mullins, meanwhile, was tasked with briefing HQ and 'took the word of the arrest direct to the Military Council in Dublin, direct to Pádraic Pearse and James Connolly'.[67]

A stand-off occurred in East Tyrone when Cathal McDowell challenged the order to demobilise when confronted in his billet by Denis McCullough, Herbert Moore

Pim, Pat McCartan and Fianna Éireann commander Seamus Dempsey, who had driven from Belfast 'early on Sunday morning'.[68] McDowell reminded McCullough that Pearse had instructed commandants to ignore cancellation orders that did not emanate from his hand. When the senior IRB man remonstrated and emphasised his authority, McDowell averred that only Peter Burns, 'the officer in charge during military operations', could impose his will.[69] McDowell was told that Burns was temporarily intoxicated, but this proved an exaggeration if not fabrication. McCartan learned of Pearse's fail-safe and concurred that MacNeill's instructions could be honourably disobeyed.

On the drive back to Coalisland, Dempsey 'expressed his determination to fight'.[70] Arranging a meeting of all Antrim Volunteer officers in Tyrone proved impossible, and McDowell's search for Archie Heron ensured he was absent when a consensus accepted MacNeill's position. While clearing his billet, McDowell encountered Nora Connolly, who divulged that 'her father and Pearse were not in agreement with those orders and were determined to go out and fight. She did not inform me when they intended to start'.[71] With great reluctance, McDowell acceded to Burns' orders to lead the Belfast group to Cookstown to catch the Belfast train.[72] Their followers only then realised they were being sent home.[73]

Min Ryan arrived by rail in Wexford town with instructions for J. J. O'Connell to remain stood down. At around

2 p.m., Ryan was driven to Enniscorthy where she passed the same orders to Fr Patrick Murphy.[74] Yet Sean Sinnott, a leading Volunteer officer in the town, received a 'dispatch' from Pearse at 8 p.m. stating that mobilisation was merely postponed overnight. Units were ordered to turn out on the evening of 24 April by which time Dublin would have struck the first blow. Wexfordians, nonetheless, had already decided to participate despite the withdrawal of Kilkenny contingents arising from GHQ disarray.[75]

The Athlone Brigade ceased mobilisation preparations when Liam O'Brien handed OC Peadar Bracken a copy of the 'countermanding order' in Tullamore. Recently briefed by Pearse, Bracken lost no time travelling to Dublin with Seamus Brennan to 'ascertain what the situation was'.[76] In his absence, his brother Paddy Bracken and Seamus Malone attacked the town's railway bridge with explosives that failed to detonate.[77]

Derry City OC Seamus Cavanagh mobilised a small urban force on Easter Sunday and waited until 5.30 a.m. on Monday before Denis McCullough sent word from Belfast to desist. Joe O'Doherty was thirty minutes too late to ensure Derry Volunteers interacted with comrades in Strabane and Omagh in West Tyrone.[78]

In Carrickmacross, Dr de Burca was assailed by MacNeil-lites when spurring Monaghan men to revolt as per the orders of Pearse.[79]

Kildare OC Tom Byrne, appointed by Pearse just two weeks before, first received news of the countermanding order from the *Sunday Independent*. As he ventured to Naas to obtain further details, motorbike courier Dick Stokes came 'tearing through the town' and halted suddenly beside him on the street. Stokes produced a succinct dispatch signed by Pearse: 'Postponed until twelve o'clock tomorrow.' Renewed promises of compliance were received from various company commanders.

Byrne had been tasked by the IRB with blowing up Sallins railway bridge among others using sixty sticks of gelignite, which had been procured in Phibsborough on 23 April. Ordered to cycle back to Kildare to avoid surveillance, it fell to 'Miss Sheehan' to move the explosives to Newbridge by train, where courteous soldiers assisted her in getting the heavy baggage into town.[80]

Frank de Burca and other members of E Company, 4th Battalion, had been dismayed, when leaving Mass on Sunday morning, to learn of MacNeill's orders and the seeming finality with which they had been issued. They and others linked to St Enda's inner circle know more than most what this signified. It was appreciated that 'Commandant Pearse … had addressed our company the previous week and had hinted as much as was safe, to coming events. He impressed upon each and everyone present in the drill hall to go to

Confession and to make his peace with God before going out on "the manoeuvres".'[81]

Word arrived to await 'further instructions', and de Burca was present in St Enda's when 'the brothers Pearse called back to see their mother and sister late this evening'.[82] Des Ryan was shocked by Patrick's appearance: 'I never saw Pearse so silent and disturbed. He simply would not speak to anyone.'[83] The pair 'went off quietly' and recovered something of their spirit.[84]

In the course of the night, Dr Kathleen Lynn, who was linked to the ICA, drove Eamon Bulfin and the remaining improvised explosives from St Enda's to Liberty Hall. A refocused Pearse entrusted Ryan with carrying a message to Connolly. The ICA leader 'just nodded, said it would be all right as he would meet Pearse later'.[85]

A communications breakdown between Pat McCartan in Carrickmore, Co. Tyrone, and Dan Kelly in Cashelnagore/Creeslough, Co. Donegal, ensured that twenty-six men mobilised as planned on Easter Sunday to cut telegraph wires. Pursued by the RIC, Kelly's men 'ordered' them 'back into their barracks' and told them to remain there.[86] Seamus McNulty was part of the group and conducted inspections of rail and road bridges they intended to drop. Their militancy probably stemmed from their joint IRB membership. McNulty had liaised with Devoy in late 1915 and carried

US dispatches to Ireland for Clarke. Kelly was in contact with Pearse and had hosted MacDiarmada, MacBride and Joe McGarrity when meeting the Glasgow IRB. Strangely, 'no definite orders' arrived from McCartan on 23–4 April 1916.[87]

On 24 April, Michael Staines was summoned to North Frederick Street for a 2 a.m. meeting with Pearse and MacDiarmada:

> Pearse said: 'We are going into action at 12 o'clock today and, as the representative of the Dublin Brigade we want your consent.' I said to him 'Have you done everything possible with MacNeill?' He replied: 'Yes … we can't do more' … He said, 'We are all going to be arrested anyhow, and on behalf of this generation we will have to make a gesture.'[88]

A debate had indeed taken place in Dublin Castle regarding arrests under the Defence of the Realm Act and selective internment, with suggested dates of 24 or 25 April. If the Lord Lieutenant, Lord Wimborne, had prevailed with an immediate crackdown, an even more expansive form of the Military Council conspiracy may well have come to pass.[89]

Mrs O'Kelly did her best to show hospitality to the esteemed Pearse brothers when they slipped into her house for a few hours' sleep in the very early hours of Easter Monday. On leaving for mass, Mrs O'Kelly had left instructions with her daughter that the men be served a huge cooked break-fast, which included a tureen of bacon and eggs and another of mutton chops: 'She said they must be very hungry and God knows when they will get a meal again. She must have known more than I did.'[90]

While the woman of the house contemplated the consoling mysteries of faith and resurrection, the aspiring revolutionaries, rooted in the world of imminent violence, loitered nervously and politely until invited into the dining room. They devoured all the cooked food as well as an entire loaf of bread. Their admiring host was not unmindful of the pathos of what this conveyed and retained the tablecloth as a cherished relic, as well as a set of wire-cutters left upstairs.[91] She recalled:

> After breakfast they went upstairs again and apparently started to collect all their equipment. They arrived down fully dressed ... Their uniforms were covered by the gabardine raincoats without belts and they had the same lumpy appearance. They asked for mother to thank her for her hospitality. I explained that she was still at Mass. I should imagine it was then about 10 o'clock ... They took their bicycles which were in the hall, wheeled them down the four steps. They mounted the bicycles and turned to wave to me. I can see them still. They rode down along Upper Rutland Street in the direction of Liberty Hall.[92]

While going down Gloucester Street, the brothers cycled past their acquaintance, Fr Aloysius of the Capuchin Friary on Church Street, without noticing him. He discerned their intense preoccupation and astutely concluded, 'there was something in the air.'[93]

Patrick Pearse had 'scribbled' several 'special messages', which were distributed from St Enda's and required Eamon Bulfin, Joe Sweeney and Des Ryan to mobilise their company in Rathfarnham. Ryan believed these were issued around 10 a.m., which provided two hours' notice to reach Liberty Hall. Another batch issued by Pearse on Monday morning urged Volunteer leaders to disregard MacNeill's cancellation.[94]

Nora Connolly, having rested overnight in the Leinster Road home of Markievicz, reported to Liberty Hall by 8 a.m., where she learned of her rural mission from her father:

He said Pearse was sending a message to the people in the North; and we were to take it. He told us that the fighting would start in Dublin at noon ... There was a verbal message for McCullough and a written message for Dr McCartan ... We were only there a short time when Pearse arrived; and he too told us that he wanted us to take this message ... When Pearse arrived, Daddy told him to write out the message for us; and he went off to another room to write it. When he came back, he had a poster in his hand; and he opened it, and said: 'This is the Proclamation of the Republic. This will be posted up, when we go into action. I want you all to read it, and memorise it as much as you can. When you reached these people, tell them you have read this; then tell every Volunteer you meet that we will be fighting from twelve o'clock on; and, even though they have not received their orders, to hold themselves in readiness; and they will receive orders.'[95]

The Cumann na mBan couriers destined for the southern counties of Ulster departed in time to catch the 10 a.m. train from Amiens Street Station. A jocose Thomas MacDonagh quipped, 'there you go tripping, while we are going out in two hours to risk our lives'.[96] The ambiance in Liberty Hall was otherwise serious if not subdued: 'Pearse ... was all business. He showed us the Proclamation in order that we could learn the important parts of it and repeat it as our password to those whom we must try to persuade to come out.'[97] As they left, a preoccupied Pearse said, 'Goodbye girls, God bless you; don't desert the boys.'[98]

By early afternoon they reached East Tyrone where the local OC was 'in a blazing fury' at the haste with which the second Belfast contingent Pearse and Connolly incorrectly believed to be in situ had been recalled. It was assumed that the two groups of dismissed Belfastmen would return and, if impeded by the RIC on main routes, would be conveyed across Lough Neagh by 'Fenian fishermen'.[99]

Eilish 'Lizzie' Allen was sent to McCullough to inform him 'that Pearse had said to mobilise, the fight was going on – we had seen the Proclamation, to tell them to hold themselves in readiness for mobilisation'.[100] A male emissary reached McCartan on the night of 24 April, bearing a long overdue standard note from Pearse: 'We start at noon today. Carry out your orders.'[101]

Nora Connolly 'sent Aghna [Ina Connolly] to the home of Dr Pat McCartan, near Carrickmore in Tyrone. McCartan and Denis McCullough were the principal IRB men in the North … They both felt that with the loss of the arms ship there was no hope of a successful fight.'[102] This was not fully grasped until 27 April when a Tyrone Volunteer captain drove her to McCartan's home for a bitter reunion. In the critical hours and days, she waited in the remote homestead of an ex-Fenian, but no further orders arrived from Dublin and the East Tyrone men quietly dispersed.[103]

Receipt of multiple contradictory messages induced two Limerick City brigades to cancel mobilisations. Commandant Michael Colivet, a recent IRB acolyte under local centre George Clancy, hedged his bets by leading 130 Volunteers out of the city to Killonan for an Easter Sunday 'bivouac'.[104] By 2 p.m. on 24 April, Nora Daly arrived into Killonan with orders from the capital: 'The Dublin Brigade goes into action at noon today (Monday). Carry out your orders. P. H. Pearse.' After debate, the battalion staff reached a 'unanimous decision' that 'Pearse's dispatch could not be acted upon' as it appeared to be predicated on unreliable information on the situation in Munster. Returning to the Fianna Hall in Limerick, they entered a city with 2,000 alert soldiers, two artillery batteries and the RIC, yet 'no attempt' was made to arrest their officers. Colivet and his associates were exonerated by an IRA inquiry headed by Cathal Brugha on 10 March 1918.[105]

Similarly, Liam de Róiste and various Cork City and County Volunteer companies left Sheares Hall for Macroom before being recalled due to late arrival of the cancellation.[106] A message from Pearse reached Mary MacSwiney, Cumann na mBan member and sister of prominent Cork City IRB man Terence, on Easter Monday from the hands of a 'Miss [Brigid] Foley'.[107]

Terence MacSwiney spent most Holy Week nights sleeping in Sheares Hall, as did Tomás Mac Curtain.[108] Mac Curtain and MacSwiney arrived back in Sheares Hall late in the evening having endeavoured to curtail premature violence. They were unsure how to interpret the phrase 'we start here at noon today' and, especially, the unorthodox endorsement that read 'PHP' instead of 'P. H. Pearse'. Pearse used the abbreviation sparingly. A further message from Pearse was delivered by a 'Miss [Una] Brennan' by which time it had been ascertained that Dublin had risen.[109]

Volunteer Sam 'Sonny' P. O'Reilly was a seventeen-year-old machinist in Broadstone Station with Midland Great Western Railway in August 1913 when 'the working men of Dublin … locked out of their jobs … [were] brutally clubbed and killed on the streets by the DMP and the RIC, English agents of Dublin Castle'.[110] His father, J. K. O'Reilly, was a republican who toured America during the Boer War raising funds for the Irish Brigade. He penned the popular nationalist anthem 'Wrap the Green Flag Around Us Boys' and participated in the 1916 Rising with five sons: Sam, Desmond, Kevin, Thomas and Donald. Sam O'Reilly was acquainted with Connolly, and, on 25 November 1913, joined Daly's 1st Battalion on its inception.[111] The O'Reillys were already intimates of MacDiarmada, a frequent visitor to their North Circular Road house and a man known as having 'toured all Ireland on a bicycle for the IRB'. John MacBride, Arthur Griffith and Harry Boland regularly convened on Sunday mornings with MacDiarmada in the O'Reilly home.[112]

Sam O'Reilly departed 15 Claremont Avenue home at 8 a.m. on 24 April to assist the mobilisation of the 1st Battalion in the Gaelic League Hall on 5 Blackhall Street.[113] They had been instructed to assemble with firearms and rations for three days. By 11 a.m., approximately 175 men were present when the shades were drawn, doors locked and lights illuminated. Commandant Ned Daly said, 'Men, our training

period has come to a close. When we leave this room, we go
to fight for freedom of Ireland. If any man does not wish to
join in the fight, he may remain in the hall after we leave.'[114]
Nearly all proceeded to parade in Blackhall Place where
Daly imparted further details of the plan at 11.45 a.m.:

> Men of the 1st Battalion, I want you to listen for a few
> minutes and no applause must follow my remarks. Today
> at noon an Irish Republic will be declared and the flag of
> the Republic will be hoisted. The Irish Republican Army
> communications – and our other elements in the city –
> may be precarious situations. In less than an hour we may
> be in action.[115]

Daly's stress on the IRA designation signalled to those
conversant with revolutionary terminology that they were
being identified as the IRB at war. This mirrored the con-
current interpretation of Óglaigh na hÉireann by Diarmuid
Lynch. Shedding the Redmondite 'advanced nationalist' husk
in 1914, albeit an unforeseen transition, facilitated the revelation of this republican core.[116]

At around 10 a.m., Desmond FitzGerald called to The
O'Rahilly at 40 Herbert Park to apprise him that 'the
Rising is on'.[117] Faced with the prospect of missing the
action, O'Rahilly succumbed to the temptation to participate. O'Rahilly's nephew, Dick Humphreys, joined them

in GHQ, where he was reunited with Pearse, a man whose work in St Enda's he had chronicled alongside his own teenage experiences.[118]

Other former students turned out with alacrity. Frank de Burca was awakened by Eamon Bulfin in time to rally at the local church at 10 a.m.: 'we donned our equipment and made our way in twos and threes to Rathfarnham Church. Mrs and Miss Pearse bade a fond farewell to each ... we mustered thirty-seven strong when we got the order to march.'[119]

Before they could board the No. 17 tram for O'Connell Street, en route to Liberty Hall, the tenacious MacNeill appeared and remonstrated with the republican officers present, warning that they 'were being led into a trap'.[120] His assistant, Sean Lester, advanced arguments 'to which they paid no attention'.[121] Undeterred, the men left on the tram. Charles Donnelly headed a 'cyclist party' of twelve Volunteers who followed, with an unarmed Michael Cremen in the lead, checking the route ahead for military patrols.[122]

They glimpsed the occupation of Jacob's Biscuit Factory from the tram, and, by the time they reached the George's Street–Dame Street intersection, 'a burst of rifle fire' was audible from their left. Turning right into Dame Street and halting outside the Bank of Ireland on College Green, the late-running Volunteers were suddenly stranded when their nervous driver abandoned his seat. They marched in fours down the quays before crossing Butt Bridge to reach Liberty

Hall. Arriving shortly after the headquarters body had moved off, they dashed 'at the double' into Lower Abbey Street and across O'Connell Street into the Prince's Street side of the GPO. The area was 'thronged with sightseers, some dumbfounded at the sight while others raised a cheer'.[123]

By 10.30 a.m., Athlone Brigade OC Peadar Bracken located Pearse in Liberty Hall. He had spent the night with George Plunkett's garrison in Larkfield. The sixty men who followed Plunkett from Harold's Cross to the city centre by tram were lectured by Pearse on 'street fighting and barricades'.[124] London-born Joe Good, a comrade of Bracken's, recalled being 'honoured with an address by Patrick Pearse' in Kimmage who then imparted the news that they comprised 'a Company of Headquarters Battalion'.[125] Bracken sought revised orders for the Offaly sector which he intended 'to call out … for the Rising' despite reversals already sustained. Suspecting the high level of damage caused by MacNeill's emissaries, a pragmatic assessment by Pearse dictated that Bracken could not achieve much in the Midlands sector. Personal and political qualities that had occasioned his promotion were not to be squandered. He recalled:

> Pearse said he wanted me here and sent me over to James Connolly, who handed me my commission as Captain, with instructions to take over half of the Kimmage Garrison, and typed orders to occupy Kelly's gunpowder shop and Hopkins

and Hopkins, commanding O'Connell Bridge area. I arrived at my allotted posts about 11.50 a.m. with my half company. Seamus Robinson was my second in command.[126]

The corps tasked with seizing the GPO moved out of Liberty Hall and massed just prior to midday in Beresford Place. This was a mixed group of Volunteers, including those who rallied from Scotland and England as the Kimmage garrison, alongside the ICA. A cab was available to move heavy war *materiel*, and O'Rahilly's car shifted munitions formerly under his control. Quietly and efficiently, a uniformed Post Office employee descended manholes, which had been mapped by Diarmuid Lynch, to destroy telegraphic wiring. Well-planned sabotage occurred all over Dublin, accumulating into a phenomenon of urban warfare never before seen in Western Europe.[127]

At 11.50 a.m., Connolly ordered the Beresford Place column, numbering some 150 men and women, to proceed towards O'Connell Street. As they passed Lower Abbey Street, onlookers commented on the seamless cooperation of the Volunteers and ICA.[128] Pearse and Plunkett marched alongside Connolly, Willie Pearse and Sean McGarry, while Michael Collins, W. J. Brennan-Whitmore and other HQ personnel closely followed.[129] Once positioned opposite the main entrance of the GPO, the vanguard was ordered by Connolly to 'charge' inside.

Stunned military and DMP were taken prisoner before they could resist, while most of the staff and all of the public were told to leave.[130] Michael Staines confronted seven soldiers on an upper level, who displayed courage bordering on foolishness when they attempted to challenge with unloaded rifles the Volunteers ascending the stairway. The slight wounding of their Scottish sergeant presaged their honourable surrender.[131] Captured Connaught Rangers offered to fight with the rebels but when firmly rebuffed – as much for their own long-term welfare as any other consideration – reluctantly agreed to run the field kitchen.[132]

Around a dozen men simultaneously entered the GPO from the Henry Street door, and a chosen party, primarily men of Pearse's late-arriving Rathfarnham unit, rushed to the rooftop. The republican Tricolour was mounted on the Henry Street corner of the complex in its most significant context since its adoption by Young Ireland in 1848. A second flag, comprising a green field bearing the legend 'Irish Republic', was placed on the Prince's Street corner.[133]

Following discussion with Connolly, Pearse instructed Collins and Brennan-Whitmore to supervise the barricading of the building.[134] Brennan-Whitmore was elated: 'The GPO was quickly, quietly and even bloodlessly seized. The general staff headquarters of the Irish Republican Army and the seat of the provisional government of the Irish Republic was established.'[135] Having secured possession of the spacious granite building, work parties hastily readied it for defence by breaking out glass and boarding up windows and doors with leather-bound books.

Cremen spoke briefly with Pearse who gave him permission to retrieve some stashed weaponry. Leaving the building, he glimpsed Pearse and Connolly standing on O'Connell Street to watch the raising of the Tricolour over the GPO: 'As Connolly shook hands with Pearse, I heard him say, "Thank God, Pearse, we have lived to see this day!"'[136]

Chapter 6

• • • • •

President and Commander-in-Chief

Patrick Pearse appeared under the GPO Grand Portico, on Sackville (O'Connell) Street, at around 12.45 p.m., and read aloud the proclamation, 'Poblacht na hÉireann, Provisional Government of the Irish Republic to the Irish People', to a gathering of confused, curious and supportive city-dwellers. Brennan-Whitmore observed the scene:

> The front door was opened and Pearse and Connolly, with a small escort, passed outside. Pearse read out the Proclamation and then had it posted up publicly. The crowd kept its distance respectfully enough until the little party had passed back into the building when a rush was made to read the notice. Those in the rear called on those in front to read it aloud. Many sentences were loudly cheered and at the end there was a great ovation.[1]

Reflecting on the events, Lynch recalled:

President Pearse, surrounded by an armed guard, emerged into O'Connell Street and read the Proclamation of Independence. The few cheers that greeted this epochal announcement furnished an index of the denationalised state of Ireland after an era of Parliamentarianism … Time elapsed before the Irish people recognised the fact that the Insurrection of Easter Week effected a necessary revivication of the national soul of Ireland … With the posting of the Proclamation of the Irish Republic as a Sovereign Independent State, the seven signatories thereto became its Provisional Government. Five of them were in the GPO now the Republican GHQ: Pádraic Pearse – President of the Provisional Government and Commander-in-Chief of the IRA, James Connolly – Commandant-General of the Dublin District, Commandant Joseph Plunkett, Tom Clarke and Seán MacDiarmada.[2]

Labourite William O'Brien theorised that Eoin MacNeill's complicity might have generated a proclamation bearing his name. Tom Clarke could then have been listed or regarded as 'president', pairing the Chief of Staff of the Volunteers with the de-facto leader of the IRB. However, without MacNeill's participation, 'the best known man next to Mac-Neill was Pearse', who had the additional appeal of being a national figure as well as Volunteer Director of Military Organisation. Clarke was not nominated as president, and his widow's contention to the contrary probably stemmed from her privileged knowledge that he was accorded the honour of lead signatory.[3]

Pearse tasked Charles Donnelly with distributing the Proclamation 'through the city'. He was assisted by an eighteen-year-old newsboy, who took the initiative of selling his bundle. On being gifted the money to assist his impoverished family, and reminded that the document was to be handed out freely, the youth 'collected the balance of the Proclamations' and departed. Donnelly did not record the reaction of Pearse or Connolly to the news of unexpected capitalist endeavour, although the stated explanation that the cash had been collected with a view to buying food for the garrison mollified the commanders. He was clearly sincere and on the following day was permitted to join the defenders of the GPO.[4]

The Proclamation referenced the illegitimate British suppression of Irish independence with the assertion that the 'long usurpation of that right by a foreign people and government has not extinguished the right'.[5] Pearse had stressed this point in New York in March 1914 when he referred to Ireland's 'old tradition of nationhood', a phrase that appeared in the Proclamation's first sentence.[6]

The IRB, the Irish Volunteers and the ICA demonstrated their acceptance of the historic joint appeal to 'Irishmen and Irishwomen', perhaps the first sincere invocation of its kind in the world, giving female activists a role in the uprising. Women took on the dangerous role of dispatch runners and in so doing exploited traditional expectations of their innocuousness. They also carried out vital support work by nursing, foraging and cooking to support the fighting personnel.[7]

All four battalion sectors contained a headquarters in a prominent building and improvised nearby strong points to defend irregular perimeters. Rail line, control equipment and rolling stock were sabotaged in the north city in and around Broadstone, Phibsborough, Harcourt Street and Amiens Street Station. The south-side line was damaged near the port of Dun Laoghaire. Overhead telegraph wires and subterranean cables accessed by manholes were cut. Several key bridges were barricaded and efforts made to trench roads useful to military traffic. Many setbacks were encountered: a detail ordered to crater the road between Stanhope Street Convent and Richmond Hospital were 'unused to picks' and relented after an hour's fruitless labour.[8]

Monsignor Michael Curran cycled to the GPO to question Pearse, whom he 'knew well', on behalf of Archbishop W. J. Walsh. He found his acquaintance 'flushed but calm and authoritative'. Curran stated, 'if there was anything that could be done, I would do it … but I see now that nothing can be done. "No," he said, "we are going to see it out".'[9] Declining an offer to convey messages, Pearse asked for assistance in arranging confession in the Pro-Cathedral.[10]

The commanders of the hesitant DMP and RIC decided that their forces were incapable of countering what appeared to be a coup and withdrew to their numerous city stations and barracks as military forces were summoned.

Many contemporaries were gripped by the drama of the situation. Having served breakfast to Patrick and Willie Pearse that morning, Margaret O'Kelly was setting up a Cumann na mBan first-aid station above J. J. Walsh's shop at 26 Blessington Street when she discerned a commotion:

> We heard the prancing of horses' hoofs on the cobblestones of the streets. We rushed to the windows and we saw a troop of Lancers with pennants flying and carrying carbines galloping down Blessington Street into Frederick Street. We could not see them past the turn of the street but we still heard them galloping. Presently we heard gunfire, but we did not see them return.[11]

Min Ryan commented that 'the first thing that made us realise there was a war on was a dead horse, lying on its back with its feet up'.[12]

Messages received by 2 p.m. from the various zones occupied by the Volunteers 'showed the general situation to be fairly satisfactory'.[13] Rebel dispositions inside the GPO evinced careful reconnaissance, tasking and implementation. No time was lost in setting up a first-aid section, armoury and larder. Supplies were brought in from local stores, including the Imperial Hotel, Clerys and the Metropole Hotel. A 'special telephonic connection' was rigged to enable Connolly to converse with men posted on the roof.[14]

Liberty Hall, a staging area for late mobilising men, was evacuated and a cache of munitions conveyed to the GPO after 3.30 p.m. in fifteen vehicles appropriated for the purpose. Those who retrieved precious resources from Liberty Hall obeyed stern injunctions to resist engaging British forces as they marched, oblivious to danger, along the north-side Liffey quays.[15]

Initially, Pearse was 'well pleased with the way everything was going'.[16] When casualties began to mount, he sent Joseph Murray to summon a doctor, a mission that ended in failure when he found both selected medics were absent.[17]

On leaving the GPO, telegraph-messenger Jack Rowan returned home to the vicinity of Beggars Bush Barracks, where, around 3 p.m., he watched as Volunteers manning a barricade erected on the railway bridge spanning Bath Avenue to South Lotts Road opened fire on a marching contingent of 'Home Defence'/'George Royals' men. Despite being preceded by a dispatch rider and having prudently loitered on Shelbourne Road, the veteran retired soldiers were ordered to use the primary route of Haddington

Road. This entailed moving into the line of sight of IRA positions, an act of imperial bravado halted by death and injury. Their commander wisely reconsidered and re-routed his men via the sheltered access of Shelbourne Lane. An inebriated Royal Dublin Fusilier was killed shortly afterwards having goaded a Volunteer into making a difficult shot from the bridge vantage. Those bottled up in Beggars Bush Barracks subsequently played a minor role in the suppression of the Rising.[18]

Rumours of gunplay, looting, secondary uprisings, forced entry of houses and commandeering of property perturbed the pro-government population. Sir Arthur Irwin, a Roscommon-born judge who had worked in colonial Burma, wrote from Ailesbury Road to inform his daughter that 'the Sinn Féiners had risen & were shooting in Dublin'. A close relative had been 'missed by an inch' by persons unknown, but Irwin may have been consoled by the fact that the message had been relayed by telephone at 4.20 p.m. This signified that the rebels were not in total control of the capital.[19] City loyalists learned that a detachment of Volunteers exited the GPO and turned into Crown Alley with a view to seizing the Telephone Exchange in Temple Bar Square when accosted by an elderly woman who told them it was 'crammed with military'. The high-value building was, in fact, unprotected, and failure to seize or destroy its specialist equipment prior to the arrival of its military guard assisted Dublin Castle's counterattack.[20]

The root cause of this apparent oversight was that the sixty-strong City Hall ICA party headed by Sean Connolly became embroiled in the bloody fracas at the Dame Street entrance of Dublin Castle. Connolly shot DMP man James O'Brien and was mortally wounded in City Hall shortly afterwards. An element of his small force retreated into the Daily Express/Evening Mail building on the Parliament Street and Cork Hill corner facing the Castle without fulfilling secondary orders of wrecking local telecommunications.[21] Michael Staines believed that the Rathfarnham Company were earmarked to aid this effort but had not reached the city in time.

Reports that Dublin Castle remained in enemy hands led to 'consternation' in the GPO as Pearse, according to Staines, intended making it his main base. This may have been a pre-countermanding-order contingency as it was an unrealistic and undesignated objective on Easter Monday. Manpower available to the Military Council was insufficient to defend even a small portion of the sprawling Dublin Castle complex.[22]

At 5 p.m., members of the Central Branch of Cumann na mBan, who had gathered in Wellington Street at midday only to be temporarily dispersed, 'were called in' by GHQ Staff for reassignment, as were 'members of Inghinidhe na h-Éireann, of Liverpool Cumann na mBan, of The [Irish] Citizen Army and of Clann na Gaedheal'.[23] The common denominator of the militants hailing from Ireland, Scotland

and England was their willingness to pay the ultimate price to achieve the Irish Republic.

Over the course of the evening, further ad-hoc reinforcements were summoned or received into the GPO. More mature Volunteers, who had originally been regarded as a reserve, were called upon to assist. The Hibernian Rifles, under Captain J. J. Scollan, were roused from 28 North Frederick Street 'where they had awaited the call'.[24] The contingent included J. J. Walsh, a former AOH-IAA leader in Cork, who had unsuccessfully attempted to rally with Oscar Traynor's Fairview Volunteers.[25]

In the late afternoon, Jeremiah Joseph O'Leary, one of the Kimmage Garrison Volunteers, was disconcerted by 'big crowds' breaking into shops on Earl Street and Abbey Street, carrying off their contents. Thomas Leahy, a 2nd Battalion Volunteer and ICA member, witnessed looters being 'warned by P. H. Pearse that they would be fired on as they were bringing disgrace on the country and the Irish people'.[26] O'Leary reported to the GPO, where he found Pearse and Connolly sitting on stools, having sandwiches and tea during a lull:

> Connolly was rather abrupt and probably resentful of my butting in, but Pearse said that there was a shortage of men, that he had none available to take up police duties, and he asked me to try and organise a Volunteer Force to take up the task. He indicated a box of wooden batons which lay

in a corner of the main hall and said I might arm the men with these.[27]

A short address by O'Leary at the base of one of the pillars supporting the portico produced a small number of willing persons. They collected batons and headed outside, where the restive crowd dynamics militated against efficacy. Finding that they were unequal to the task of keeping people on the move, the mission was abandoned within hours.

At around 6 p.m., Min Ryan was surprised to be able to walk from Dorset Street into Sackville Street: 'people were standing around in groups every place, watching for developments. There was not much excitement.' Ryan was intrigued by the Tricolour flying over the GPO as she had 'never seen' it 'flying like that before'. Moving towards the HQ, she caught sight of Connolly 'in full uniform'.[28]

The exhausting work of barricading buildings continued through the hours of darkness, and various roads were blocked to prevent vehicular access. Furniture, bicycles, barrels and giant paper rolls from the Irish Times were pressed into service as defensive shields. Noblett's, the confectionary firm at 34 Sackville Street, was occupied by Volunteers, who smashed holes in the walls to enable concealed movement towards the Imperial Hotel. Reis & Company Chambers at the Sackville Street and Lower Abbey Street corner were also taken over by a contingent that subsequently detached men to enter the well-constructed Hibernian Bank.[29]

As the evening drew on, word of the actions in the city centre reached cadres of men and women who were either primed to act or who gleaned that participation was still possible. Meanwhile, British troops based in the Curragh arrived by train into Amiens Street Station and the North Wall, while others were mobilised in England and Wales.

Outside the city, the MacNeillites succeeded in keeping the vast majority of the Irish Volunteers safely at home. Tom Byrne and Ted O'Kelly found that their men had not turned out at Bodenstown for the midday appointment. Discouraged, there seemed little point in blasting the Sallins train line, and gelignite procured for the purpose was stashed in rabbit holes. This reticence, effectively disobeying orders from Pearse and jettisoning scant resources, could not be readily justified.

In Maynooth, however, it was discovered that the irrepressible Domhnall Ua Buachalla had gathered sixteen men and was determined to rouse others working in Ireland's main Catholic seminary.[30] He had received word from Pearse on Sunday to 'await further orders'.[31] Watching RIC men, who left their barracks without firearms, dared not interfere, and a momentary threat of violence by O'Kelly was defused. Grateful RIC men later credited Ua Buachalla. Cheered by seminarians, the armed contingent received a blessing from

Monsignor Hogan, President of Maynooth College, before proceeding to Clonsilla Bridge to rendezvous with Sean Boylan's Dunboyne Volunteers. The Meathmen did not appear, owing, it transpired, to Benson's negative orders, prompting the Kildare group to proceed through Finglas into Glasnevin Cemetery where they spent the night.[32]

Jimmy McElligott, unable to reach his unit in Jacob's Factory, instead joined the Rathfarnham men in the GPO during the evening. He confirmed that his brother, just arrived from Tralee, had found 'all was quiet down South. Dublin was alone in the fight!'[33] Contrary to earlier reports, Kerry was not 'in a blaze', and, much closer to home, U-boats had not been 'operating in Dublin Bay'.[34]

In the late evening, Claire Gregan appeared at HQ and spoke to several of the leaders. She was conversing with a captured British officer when Pearse approached. On being asked directly 'What is going to happen?', Pearse replied that 'he did not know'. The detained Briton was more forthright and, without deliberate malice, stated that the British military would 'shell them out' of the building.[35]

During the night, Dr Charles J. MacAuley called into the GPO to treat wounded rebels and confer with his kinsman Eoin MacNeill. On finding MacNeill was not present, Dr MacAuley sought his regular patient Joseph Plunkett, to whom he was directed by 'a prominent looking Volunteer … Pearse'. Plunkett informed him that the dagger in the pocket of his green shirt had belonged to Lord Edward FitzGerald, military strategist of the United Irishmen in May 1798.[36]

Following the suppression of the Rising, Dr MacAuley was directed to Mackey's seed shop in Sackville Street by his colleague Dr Seamus O'Kelly. He received a glass vial containing a slip of paper with a pencil-written message: 'All orders given by the Chief of Staff (John MacNeill) must be countersigned by me. Signed P. H. Pearse.' This note was interpreted by MacNeill's lawyers as a magnanimous bid by Pearse to absolve the nominal head of the Volunteers from complicity in the Rising.[37]

After spending the night in Glasnevin Cemetery, the Maynooth Volunteers under Domhnall Ua Buachalla pressed on to the GPO, arriving at around 7 a.m. on 25 April. Tom Byrne, who had detached from the men in Glasnevin and gone to the GPO, re-encountered the column as they neared HQ. Although still weary from Monday's trek, the perceived urgency of reinforcing the City Hall outpost on Dame Street induced Connolly to send them as reinforcements.[38] Patrick Colgan recalled, 'General Pearse spoke to us … He told us how glad he was to have us with them in the fight; that our action in marching from Kildare, even if we did no more in the Rebellion, would gain us a place in history.'[39] They were joined by eighteen of Scollan's Hibernian Rifles with whom they crossed the Ha'penny Bridge and soon entered the Exchange Hotel on Parliament Street.[40]

City Hall had been retaken by the British, and the plan was suggested to break into the hotel from an adjacent house owned by Sir Patrick Shorthall. From the roof of the building, the mixed force of Volunteers and Hibernians plied soldiers bravely storming the Daily Express office: 'Donal Buckley, shot a few of them.'[41] Hibernian Edward Walsh received a mortal wound to the stomach before Joseph Murray, whom Pearse had dispatched to search for arms, recalled the men to the GPO.[42]

Positions occupied by B Company, 1st Battalion, in Cabra became untenable as British reinforcements poured into the area and used artillery to blast Volunteer barricades at point-blank range. Sam O'Reilly was among those isolated from Daly's main redoubt in the Four Courts. They fell back through the north inner city on the 25 April and met Pearse and Connolly at the GPO. One of the leaders 'knew him well' and ordered him to lead ten men to reinforce the barricade sealing the north end of O'Connell Street. This was an important posting as its possession prevented the British encroaching to the point that they could use field guns to pour devastating direct fire on the HQ.[43]

Obtaining accurate information of the various outposts dotted around Dublin was impossible, and incorrect, obsolete or unfounded stories complicated the duty of command vested in Pearse and Connolly. Dire news, however, was received around 9 a.m. when a telegraphic operator attached to the Hibernian Rifles, J. J. Walsh, impersonated a British staff official to contact Cork, Limerick, Thurles and other regional centres in the south and west, and they learned for a fact that most rural Volunteer units had adhered to Mac-Neill's directives. Lynch mused, 'Disappointing it was truly; but not of much consequence now ... It was hoped and believed that the men of the provinces would follow Dublin's lead as soon as the news reached them.'[44]

In Waterford city, Irish Volunteers 'were standing ready to move at a moment's notice' when 'word came ... that our services were not required at present'.[45] Within three hours of hearing the unwelcome prognosis, a hastily produced *Irish War News* presenting an upbeat overview was distributed from the GPO:

The Irish Republic was proclaimed in Dublin on Easter Monday, 24th April, at noon. There has been heavy and continuous fighting for nearly twenty-four hours. The populace of Dublin are plainly with the Republic and the Officers and men are everywhere cheered as they march through the Streets. The whole centre of the City is in the hands of the Republic, whose flag flies from the GPO. Commandant-General P. H. Pearse is Commander in Chief of the Army of the Republic and is President of the Provisional Government. Commandant-General James Connolly is commanding the Dublin districts. Communication

with the country is largely out, but reports to hand show
that the country is rising and bodies of men from Kildare
and Fingall have already reported in Dublin.[46]

Issuing a release in this format, signed by Pearse, attested
to the significance of explaining the effort to locals. It also
served the purpose of establishing the legitimacy of a cause
intended to secure recognition of the Irish Republic.

Two electricians were tasked with rigging a 'wireless
apparatus' in Reis's, the former home of the defunct Irish
School of Wireless Telegraphy. By 5.30 a.m., the device was
in 'working order', and communiqués penned by Connolly
were broadcast, including the wording of the Proclamation
and reports on the campaign to effect the realisation of the
Republic it announced.[47] Rory Henderson wrote that news
of the declaration of the Republic was 'continuously tapped
for hours … One of the receivers of the message was a ship
at sea and it was through this medium that the first news of
the Rising reached America and the European Continent.'[48]

On Tuesday, 2 April, Diarmuid Lynch recalled, at

about 12.45 PM … a bodyguard for Pádraic Pearse was
ordered out. This comprised a squad under Capt George
Plunkett and about an equal number under me. We accompanied Pearse to the centre of O'Connell Street opposite the main entrance to the GPO where, standing on an

improvised elevation, he read the Manifesto to the Citizens of Dublin.[49]

This manifesto was 'The Provisional Government to the Citizens of Dublin' in which Pearse once again emulated the United Irishmen of 1803. Robert Emmet's comrade, Philip Long, had issued an address to the 'Citizens of Dublin', which clearly dictated the title chosen by Pearse.[50] Emmet's concept of Ireland taking its place 'among the nations' was also repeated verbatim, words which were cited not only in the Proclamation of 23 July 1803 and the 'Speech from the Dock' on 19 September 1803, but also in the text of 1916's Easter Monday Proclamation. Pearse informed the 'Citizens of Dublin' that:

Ireland's honour has already been redeemed; it remains to vindicate her wisdom and her self-control. All citizens of Dublin who believe in the right of their Country to be free will give their allegiance and their loyal help to the Irish Republic. There is work for everyone; for the men in the fighting line, and for the women in the provision of food and first aid … Such looting as has already occurred has been done by the hangers on of the British Army. Ireland must keep her new honour unsmirched. We have lived to see an Irish Republic proclaimed. May we live to establish it firmly, and may our children and our children's children enjoy the happiness and prosperity which freedom will bring.[51]

Men of the Fingal Company bolstered the Kelly's Corner outpost at the junction of Lower Sackville Street and Bachelor's Walk and, having advanced via a 'boring extension' to Abbey Street, gained the necessary line of sight to counter British sniper fire from TCD. By 2 p.m., Volunteers at Annesley Bridge harassed British military engineers as they attempted to repair sabotaged rail tracks and operating systems. Soldiers approaching Leinster Avenue were repulsed with loss of men and prisoners.

The City Hall and Westmoreland Street positions had been evacuated by Volunteers, who lacked the strength and equipment to defend buildings located so close to strong military positions. Soldiers barracked in Athlone, Belfast and Templemore arrived into Dublin, as did 1,000 men from the Curragh. Artillerymen from Athlone brought four eighteen-pounder cannon with them. By early evening, it was necessary to pull back from Fairview and Annesley Bridge to avoid being overwhelmed by British infantry massing in the north city suburbs.

On nearing the GPO, where they hoped to receive further orders, some Volunteers 'rushed' from Sackville Place and were momentarily mistaken for hostiles – light casualties ensued.[52] Future IRA Chief of Staff Sean Russell organised the rearguard of the column and escorted British prisoners whose presence had earlier confused the military on Clonliffe Road, Drumcondra.[53]

Former Fairview Commandant Charles Saurin was obliged to obtain first aid for a minor head wound sustained during the relocation to O'Connell Street and was disappointed to find that he had missed an address from Pearse. Oscar Traynor related 'the gist' of the short inspirational speech to Saurin who understood that 'Dublin by rising had redeemed its honour, lost when Emmet failed in 1803 through lack of the capital's support.'[54] The new arrivals were sent to take over nearby large buildings, not least the Metropole Hotel, which Traynor commanded by 9.30 p.m. His forty-strong Metropole group later incorporated the Mansfield building in their thinly manned defensive zone. Thirty men under Frank Henderson entered Henry Street to the rear of the GPO, and a similar if not larger body diverted to the Imperial Hotel under Frank Thornton when unable to reach City Hall.[55]

Mary Humphreys ventured into the GPO from the south suburbs on Monday and Tuesday to distribute 'prayer leaflets and medals of Our Lady' for men of religious inclinations. Her maternal instincts were sensitised by the presence of her nineteen-year-old son Dick, whose safety could not be guaranteed under deteriorating circumstances. Pearse did not wish to see his former student come to harm but, to minimise injury to youthful pride, stressed the obligations of family integrity over national duty. Speaking in Irish, Pearse took Humphreys aside and urged, 'you had better go home. If anything happens [to] your uncle [The O'Rahilly], there will be no man there.'[56] Humphreys reluctantly complied, only to come under fire from Volunteers holding Boland's Mill who did not recognise him as an ally in the dark. He 'returned to the fight' fresh from Mass in Haddington Road the following day.[57]

Expectations of a heavy night attack on the GPO from forces advancing from the Phoenix Park were unfulfilled, although British machine guns emplaced in the watchtower of Tara Street Fire Brigade Station, the roof of the Rotunda Hospital and TCD added to the problems of those hemmed within shrinking rebel lines. Other centres of British strength included the Custom House, Amiens Street Station, Butt Bridge and the Rotunda Gardens.[58]

Barricades were constructed in Henry Place and at both ends of Moore Street while the laborious task of 'boring' between key buildings continued.[59] Min Ryan, who had joked darkly on arrival into the GPO whether she would be shot for assisting MacNeill in preventing the Rising, gamely confronted Clarke on his projection of an Irish republic. She then observed the energised Pearse:

The headquarters people were not doing any fighting in the GPO. They were watching things. Pearse spent most of his time in the front part of the Post Office … There was a counter where you could get stamps. All these young fellows – the Plunketts, Mick Collins and crowds of others, including the members of the Larkfield Camp, were manning the windows. The Headquarters Staff sat there talking quietly.[60]

Overnight, slow and methodological progress was made breaking through buildings leading to the GPO, a promising rate facilitated by the requisitioning of much needed tools from a shop on Henry Lane and the assistance of professional construction workers who were also Volunteers. Having opened a passage into the landmark Coliseum Picture Theatre on Sackville Street, efforts were made to breach contiguous buildings extending towards Arnotts.

Much involved, Frank Henderson was called to meet Pearse 'during the night': 'Pearse ordered me to take a party of men and erect barricades in Henry Place and Moore Lane, in order to hold up any attempt by the British to advance by the back lane from Parnell Street and Moore Street. We completed this work in the darkness of the night in deserted streets, and reported back when it was finished.'[61]

British firepower increased in effect on the morning of 26 April as machine-gun positions with commanding views of the Sackville Street environs laid down 'a fierce barrage'.[62] Sackville, Marlborough, D'Olier and Abbey Streets became extremely dangerous for anyone venturing into the open.[63]

Few men, if any, saw the gunning down of the father of Eimar O'Duffy, who had been 'running from Moore Street into Henry Street' to avoid being shot when he was felled by British automatic weapons: 'He died in the middle of the road.'[64] Converging enemy forces were evidently not firing at defined targets, even though the city centre had not been evacuated of civilians, and both the civic-orientated DMP and counter-insurgent RIC had seemingly melted away. A proclamation ordered a 7.30 p.m. to 5.30 a.m. curfew in the city and county of Dublin. With the city already under martial law since the previous day, a second edict extended the measure to the entire country for a month.[65]

The striking 'Plough and Stars' flag of the ICA was hoisted on the Imperial Hotel at around 7 a.m., a defiant act given the ruination visited by British firepower on Liberty Hall and the association of the landmark Sackville Street premises with the persecution of Jim Larkin during the 'Lockout'.[66] This had the desired effect of drawing British machine-gun fire towards the large water tank in the roof, where, as with the Tricolour on De Valera's 3rd Battalion HQ in Boland's Mill, munitions and attention were misdirected.

The republican green flag hanging from an upper window of the South Dublin Union was visible from the Royal Hospital Kilmainham and irritated General Sir John Maxwell to the extent that he offered two guineas bounty for its seizure. None of his subordinates accepted the probably suicidal challenge.[67] Another major British endeavour, the shelling of Liberty Hall, was pointless from a military perspective as the ICA and Volunteers had departed with their stores in broad daylight on Monday. Nonetheless, the *Helga* powered up the Liffey and, unable to navigate beyond the loop line rail bridge connecting Amiens and Tara Street Stations, blasted the evacuated premises from the Common Street area. Crewmen on the *Helga* were obliged to take cover when Peadar Bracken's men fired on them from Kelly's and Hopkins & Hopkins on the corner of Eden Quay and Sackville Street.[68]

Min Ryan's Cumann na mBan cluster spoke to MacDiarmada on Wednesday morning. He directed them to take detained prisoners' messages, as Pearse insisted they should be forwarded. Three private letters were composed by captured British officers and were approved for delivery by the republican women, who walked as far as Drumcondra to deliver them by hand, despite having not slept.[69]

Soldiers from Beggars Bush Barracks, meanwhile, shot and killed a driver working for Horan's Grocery on Grand Canal Street at around 10 a.m. The victim had been permitted by Volunteers occupying the shop to attend to his horses and died 'riddled with bullets' when running across South Lotts Road.[70]

Some of the heaviest fighting of the Rising occurred in the vicinity of Mount Street Bridge at 12.30 p.m., when the 7th and 8th Battalions of the Nottingham Regiment 'Sherwood

Foresters' approached from Northumberland Road. The area was within De Valera's 3rd Battalion zone. Once leading elements of the first 800 of 2,000 British soldiers drew alongside 25 Northumberland Road, approximately thirteen Volunteers, headed by Lieutenant Michael 'Mick' Malone, opened fire from the house, as well as from Clanwilliam House and the Parochial Hall. This had a devastating effect on a column forced to march from Dun Laoghaire due to rail sabotage.[71] After fierce resistance, a Volunteer recalled, 'there was a great pile of dead and dying on the Bridge'.[72] James Rowan, a resident of Bath Avenue, 'saw the British military retreating down Haddington Road after they had been fired on from a house in Northumberland Road. They were scattered in all directions and very badly disorganised.'[73]

Repeated counterattacks were made into the evening. A large building known as the Distillery drew much misdirected fire owing to its flying a Tricolour and its use by three or four Volunteer snipers. Malone and three other men perished in an action that killed four British officers and wounded an additional fourteen. An estimated minimum 216 men from 'other ranks' were killed or wounded in Dublin according to official accounts in the Royal Hospital.[74]

A nine-pounder cannon firing from the corner of D'Olier and College Streets blasted the 'Kelly's Corner' (aka 'Fort') position of the Volunteers to the extent that HQ ordered a retreat into the Metropole Hotel. Connolly had recourse to a pulled line for exchanging messages with the Imperial Hotel but ventured in person towards the dangerous interface to assess the situation at first hand. His diligence resulted in an arm injury as he returned towards the GPO at 4 p.m.

Rebel wounded and Cumann na mBan 'nurses' were pulled back shortly afterwards into the Sackville Street redoubt from the untenable Hibernian Bank and Hoytes Oil Works. The Henry Street approach to the GPO, however, became increasingly consolidated with common walls between houses being breached to the point that the Coliseum could be reached unobserved. British fire from the Capel Street intersection remained tolerable under the circumstances.[75]

Leslie Price stood with Clarke, Staines, MacDiarmada, Willie Pearse, Gearóid O'Sullivan and Joseph Plunkett as Patrick Pearse 'read an address' in the 'front portion of the Post Office'.[76] It was patently obvious that the British were inexorably tightening their grip and that casualties were mounting, while ammunition, food and medical supplies were running perilously low. Price was retasked by Staines with keeping communications open with Daly's men in North King Street and made hazardous ammunition deliveries to Fr Mathew Hall after midnight.[77]

Pearse was credited with making 'frequent visits' to the GPO's relatively low and exposed parapet, where his brother also made morale-boosting inspections.[78] Posted to a window overlooking Henry Place, cool-headed Liverpool Volunteer

Patrick Caldwell found that 'except for occasional shots which seemed to enter this room we were not otherwise under any fire'.[79] A request to use explosives from stores held by Staines to fell Nelson's Pillar was rejected by Pearse after earlier debate in his absence, owing to the danger posed by its likely path of collapse.[80]

Hard decisions had to be made on a continual basis informed by what was visible or what could be ascertained from dispatch runners. At around 5.30 p.m., a man in civilian clothes, 'true of many of the IRA' in 1916, according to Lynch, reached the Dublin Bread Company restaurant, claiming that Pearse had ordered its evacuation. The twelve or so present obeyed, despite concerns as to the veracity of the instructions. Generally, such tactical orders were the prerogative of Connolly. They departed in two groups, one of which was obliged to take cover when moving through Marlborough Street. A possible pro-British ruse was quickly perceived as an error given that fifteen men were immediately selected to reoccupy the Dublin Bread Company and Reis's so as to impede anticipated enemy advances over O'Connell Bridge and through Middle Abbey Street.

Around five men died moving between Earl Street and Marlborough Street. The remainder pressed onwards to their destinations via Lower Abbey Street. Nine of the initial fifteen survived the overnight posting during which time the Dublin Bread Company and Hopkins' corner were shelled and bracketed by automatic weapons. Both premises were burning when the upper floors of Reis's collapsed forcing hasty abandonment. One man was wounded running the gauntlet back to headquarters.[81]

A well-known DMP detective, who casually inquired 'how long' the Volunteers believed they 'could hold out', approached the barricade manned by Donnelly and others. The Rathfarnham man contacted Pearse, seeking advice as to whether the interloper should be shot. Permission was denied. Incredibly, a patrol in which Donnelly participated that night accosted the same detective near Parnell Street while he was wearing military uniform and carrying a box with civilian clothes. Although clearly guilty of spying, the two 'soldiers' were held as ordinary prisoners in the GPO. The man whose life was spared by Pearse was reunited with 'G men' colleagues within days and assisted in identifying rebel prisoners massed in the Rotunda Gardens.[82]

Open movement was dangerous, and it was noted in the GPO that the frequent and indiscriminate use of machine guns posed a major threat to civilians seeking the protection of large buildings around Sackville Street as well as those venturing for 'less worthy' purposes.[83] The heat wafting across Sackville Street from the burning upper stories of Clerys discomfited Volunteers posted on the GPO roof, and the Rathfarnham men were relieved and brought to the ground level for much needed sleep.[84] They saw that the leaders, 'Pearse,

Connolly, Plunkett, McDermott and Tom Clarke … slept in turns' on mattresses laid on the floor behind the central counter.[85]

Des Ryan noted that although 'his real work was done', Pearse 'was busy enough' and, contrary to the untrue story circulated by Winifred Carney, did not sequester himself in an office to write. Ryan asserted with dutiful hyperbole that Pearse 'was the most central figure in that dangerous front room'.[86] During a quiet moment, Pearse was sitting on a barrel watching the flames from Tyler's Corner when he engaged Ryan in an unguarded conversation:

He suddenly turned to me with the question: 'It was the right thing to do, wasn't it?' 'Yes', I replied in astonishment. He looked at me again more keenly. 'If we fail, it means the end of everything, Volunteers and all'[.] 'Yes', I answered. He looked back at that fantastic and leaping blaze. He spoke again: 'When we are all wiped out, people will blame us for everything. But for this, the war would have ended and nothing would have been done. After a few years, they will see the meaning of what we tried to do'. He rose and we walked a few paces ahead. 'Dublin's name will be glorious forever', he said with deep passion and enthusiasm. 'Men will speak of her as one of the splendid cities, as they speak now of Paris! Dublin!'[87]

In MacNeill's rural retreat near Ballyboden, a number of Volunteer leaders opposed to the Military Council listened to the echoing noise of the bombardment with dread. MacNeill, who had been staying with a local Augustinian community to avoid arrest, 'looked very badly … but he did not talk much' according to Claire Gregan. Her fiancé Bulmer Hobson, liberated by his IRB captors in north Dublin, was part of the close-knit group. He too 'was very much upset and depressed'.[88]

On Thursday morning, Min Ryan's Cumann na mBan unit once again, amid hazard, reported to the GPO from their Moore Street access point. MacDiarmada greeted them and imparted important news: 'Commandant-General (Pearse) would like to send out a few messages.'[89] They were displeased to hear they were leaving HQ so soon. Their task entailed contacting Mrs Pearse 'on the south side' and delivering 'another message to the people in the country, asking them to support him'.[90] Ryan did not differentiate between the relative importance of the very different missives, but it was obvious that the Irish Volunteer/IRB document was a priority.

The couriers chanced the Ha'penny Bridge crossing at a time when the Sherwood Foresters, aggrieved from heavy casualties in Northumberland Road, lined both quays of the Liffey.[91] Walking along Dame Street, Ryan's curiosity was piqued by a passing armoured car: 'I was seized with a feeling that this was something diabolical and devastating.'[92] Whereas

Mrs Pearse was contacted by the courier from the GPO, it proved impossible to move beyond the outer city limits and 'get out of town. The place began to be surrounded.'[93] The rural Volunteers may never have received the final message of the Director of Military Operations.

Having taken part in two days of heavy skirmishing with enemy infantry and artillerymen, Sam O'Reilly was aggrieved when ordered back from a Sackville Street barricade to the GPO. Pearse 'mollified' him by placing his hand on his shoulder and declaring, 'O'Reilly, when the uprising started on Monday we hoped and prayed that we could establish a Republic for twenty-four hours. And here we are, seventy-three hours afterwards, and we have accomplished more than we had hoped for on Easter Monday morning.'[94] Londoner Joe Good observed in relation to that day that their 'headmasterly leader, P. H. Pearse … was very approachable' in the main hall: 'The Volunteer privates took every opportunity to have a word with him, like schoolchildren with a favourite teacher.'[95] Connolly, in the eyes of the socialist Good, 'held the men together'.[96]

Desmond FitzGerald recalled discussions in the GPO between Pearse and Plunkett on the future of Ireland in the event of a German victory in the Great War. Although allegedly anticipating tolerance of Irish aspirations, given the shared anti-British mentality and token level of wartime alliance, they mused that Berlin would probably seek to establish 'an independent Ireland with a German prince as king'.[97] The trio mused that 'the ruler ... would have to become completely Irish' in order to promote local allies useful for neutralising British revisionism while containing those with 'loyalist' sympathies.[98]

London anticipated that the reinforcements dispatched to Ireland ensured military victory, and on 27 April General Sir John Maxwell was given 'plenary power to proclaim martial law over the whole of the country'.[99] Quashing Volunteer outposts and overwhelming their redoubts was a mere matter of time and logistics, underwritten by political will and the Treasury. Yet equally resolute and patriotic insurgents, fighting for self-determination in their native country, held the Royal College of Surgeons, the Four Courts, Jacob's Factory, the South Dublin Union, Boland's Mill and, more tenuously, the torrid precincts of the GPO.

All could be inundated but probably not without human cost that would have temporarily raised Ireland to the level of a side theatre in the Great War. President Woodrow Wilson's efforts to secure Congressional support in the USA for an unprecedented European military intervention might be jeopardised.

Sir Alfred Bucknill, Deputy Judge Advocate to the British Forces in Ireland from 1916 to 1919 was central to obviating this nightmare scenario.[100] Bucknill was personally briefed by Prime Minister H. H. Asquith to ensure that General Maxwell fulfilled his duties with probity and legality and was given 'a pretty free hand to deal with the insurgents'.[101] The British authorities in Ireland were concerned that the summary execution of Francis Sheehy-Skeffington in Portobello Barracks would lead to embarrassing questions being raised in the House of Commons by his liberal acquaintances. Maxwell, according to Downing Street, had been suspiciously evasive when pressed to reveal the true nature of the Captain Bowen-Colthurst affair and unacceptably slow to admit 'a *mistake* had been made' (emphasis added). Two prominent middle class pro-enlistment Home Rulers, a famous pacifist and, allegedly, member of Dublin Trades Council, had been killed in cold blood. Bucknill determined on arrival that the lack of explicit provision within the Defence of the Realm Act for trying and executing armed insurgents negated its utility. It was insufficiently draconian. Maxwell, contrary to his declared intention to proceed under the terms of the special legislation cherished by Dublin Castle, reverted to the traditional capital offence statute of 'aiding the enemy'.[102] The Establishment, as Irish revolutionaries appreciated from historical precedent, would exact their pound of flesh. The precise formulation used in courts martial read 'Did an act, to wit, did take part in an armed rebellion, and in the waging of war against His Majesty the King, such act being of such a nature as to be calculated to be prejudicial to the Defence of the Realm, and being done with the intention and for the purpose of assisting the enemy.'[103]

Fr Murphy was in Enniscorthy's Athenaeum on 26 April 1916 when all but two Volunteer officers of the battalion agreed to rise the next day in response to Connolly's order transmitted to Commandant Paul Galligan. A map in the possession of Galligan 'had all the places occupied by the IRA marked'.[104] Parts of north Wexford were, therefore, belatedly seized, despite the withdrawal of Kilkenny from the equation. Although strongly emplaced, the Volunteers saw little fighting due to the caution of the state forces.[105] Delaying train movement of British reinforcements from Rosslare port was more critical than either Pearse or Connolly would have divulged in writing.

Lynch's assessment of the situation on the morning of 27 April was vivid and pragmatic:

> Overwhelming and modernly equipped enemy cordons had been tightened around the GPO and its adjacent outposts. Their fire increased on all sides. The Republican forces whose only armament (apart from hand grenades) consisted of rifles and shot guns, while unable to push them back kept them at bay … [Connolly and Saurin] were on the [Middle Abbey Street] sidewalk planning their next moves, [when] one of the buildings in the immediate vicinity showed a large gaping hole where a shell had just penetrated. The building of the barricade was hampered by snipers from some distant point, but the work was progressing well when

the shelling intensified, soon the terrific crash of explosion nearby made impossible its completion.[106]

The Metropole/Mansfield defences just inspected by Connolly repelled British infantry closing in from Marlborough and Abbey Streets. Rifle barrels became so hot from prolonged usage that they were rendered inoperable until oil obtained from sardine tins provided a means to cool them down.

Matters in the GPO were deteriorating, with evidence of mounting pressure on the rear approaches to HQ. Access from Mary Street and Denmark Street could not be adequately defended with the scant resources on hand, and a group of fifteen men sent to O'Neill's on the corner of Liffey Street were powerless to prevent a reconnaissance by an armoured car. Other city garrisons could no longer be regularly contacted, and, by the afternoon of 27 April, the heroic work of Cumann na mBan and Na Fianna Éireann in carrying messages was drastically curtailed. In yet another risky short-range foray, Connolly received a serious leg wound near Williams Lane, rendering him 'virtually hors de combat'.[107] On the same day, Des Ryan noted that Patrick and Willie Pearse had 'a narrow escape when they inspected the O'Connell St positions'.[108]

Volunteers of the 3rd Battalion under Daly and Paddy Holahan were engaged:

Firing was continuous. The British forces had started that morning to move up North King Street. They came from the Capel Street end … Our party in Moore's Dairy [near North Brunswick Street corner] engaged a party of the enemy who were attempting to come through Monks Bakery … Rumours began to reach us about how the fighting was progressing. One of the rumours was that the Germans had landed and were advancing along the Naas Road … We were joined by the men of the Mendicity Institute garrison.[109]

The threat posed by flames obliged the abandonment of Tyler's, Noblett's and the Imperial Hotel during the late evening. The hotel's first-floor ceiling was on fire when the men withdrew. The GPO remained on alert as a British attack was anticipated. Small numbers of those evacuated reached HQ, as did part of the unit in the Coliseum Picture Theatre. Lynch saw 'a raging furnace' as separate fires spread and joined: 'molten plate glass flowed to the sidewalk'.[110]

The GPO garrison surmised from the pressure on their outposts, proliferating casualties and intensity of enemy fire that their days were numbered. It fell to Pearse to address the issue in a realistic manner designed to offer reassurance at a time when surrender had not been discussed. Most of the men not covering key defence points were summoned to the main hall to listen to a 'communiqué', possibly drafted for publication. Joe Good was too distant to hear all of its content, but he heard that the leadership was 'making arrangements for the final defence of headquarters and [was] determined to hold it while our buildings last'.[111]

All those involved were thanked for their efforts and apprised that they not only deserved to 'win' but 'win it they will, although they may win it in death'.[112] Pearse's voice 'rose near the end', at which time he claimed the deeds of Easter Week justified a seat at the 'peace table' for the Irish Republic when the global war terminated. This placed the endeavour in the context of securing far-reaching political objectives in the immediate future.[113]

Fourteen-year-old Roddy Connolly, the only son of James Connolly, spent most of Easter Week in the GPO. William O'Brien risked his life to pay daily visits until Wednesday when the situation had grown desperate. James Connolly told O'Brien, 'You had better not come again' and requested that he take his son to safety.[114] In the event, two men brought the youth to 43 Belvedere Place.[115] Back at HQ, 'not a soul was now to be seen, only a huge wall of flames towering to the sky and great billows of smoke. The noise of bursting shells and tumbling walls and roofs was indescribable.'[116] Machine guns plied Sackville Street, and a horrified de Burca watched as a civilian was cut down beside Nelson's Pillar.[117]

A contingency plan was raised to move *en masse* to the Four Courts, and George Plunkett sent three men to assist the boring of houses in Henry Street. Clarke wished them well as they proceeded via the 'ghostly' auditorium of the Coliseum Picture Theatre and into the Waxworks. Tunnelling had been halted, and the men decided to rest. De Burca awoke 'in the middle of the night' as Pearse and two others inspected the position.[118]

Sir Alfred Bucknill arrived into the Irish capital hours before dawn on 28 April. He recalled a nocturnal dystopia. Under cover of night the Englishman was conveyed by ship to a city in revolt when empowered with virtual omnipotence regarding the eradication of those deemed punishable for its subversion. Bucknill sailed slowly from the shallow Irish Sea into the tidal black river Liffey, the UK's *Heart of Darkness*, or, as he classified the situation with determinist, exculpatory and delusional precision, 'civil war':

We arrived in the very early hours of the morning and steamed up the North Wall, silent and dark. The Custom House stood out against a background of fire. There were at least four distinct fires burning, and great flames were leaping up in different places as if the whole city north of the Liffey was doomed. Occasionally we heard the crack of a rifle and the knocking of machine gun fire. We arrived at the quay and found a vessel lying alongside with a gun mounted on her bows. The crew of this vessel had left but there was one man on board in charge of the gun and he helped us to tie up alongside … After some delay in getting our luggage ashore, we mounted the cars and drove away to [British Army Headquarters at the] Royal Hospital. It was impossible to go direct as the Four Courts and the Post Office were held by the rebels and there was no other way except to go round by the North Circular Road. We passed Liberty Hall, which had been shelled on the previous day, and then pursued a somewhat exciting course owing to the excessive vigilance of our picquets who challenged us almost every 50 yards … We arrived safely at Royal Hospital about 3 a.m.[119]

In the early hours after dawn on 28 April, orders were given to withdraw Volunteers from the outposts on Liffey and Abbey Streets, although men holding 1A Liffey Street were inadvertently omitted, an oversight ascribed to the overworked and ailing Connolly. Any sense of relief that the night infantry assault had not materialised was tempered by the resumption of a heavy and more accurate artillery bombardment in which direct hits were scored on the GPO.

Unable to quench the flames spreading from the O'Connell Bridge corner of the roof during the late morning brought home the necessity of abandoning the position within a matter of hours.[120] Volunteers from the Metropole/Mansfield positions arrived into the GPO before, following discussion with a determined Pearse, they returned to the crumbling defence line.[121]

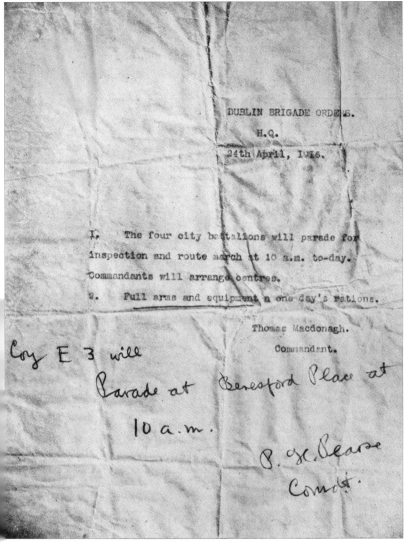

DUBLIN BRIGADE ORDERS.

H.Q.

24th April, 1916.

1.   The four city battalions will parade for
inspection and route march at 10 a.m. to-day.
Commandants will arrange centres.

2.   Full arms and equipment an one day's rations.

Thomas Macdonagh.

Commandant.

Coy E 3 will
Parade at Beresford Place at
10 a.m.

P. H. Pearse
Comdt.

Thomas MacDonagh's mobilisation order
for the Dublin Brigade on Monday, 24 April
1916, co-signed by Patrick Pearse.

POBLACHT NA H EIREANN.

THE PROVISIONAL GOVERNMENT
OF THE
IRISH REPUBLIC
TO THE PEOPLE OF IRELAND.

IRISHMEN AND IRISHWOMEN : In the name of God and of the dead generations from which she receives her old tradition of nationhood, Ireland, through us, summons her children to her flag and strikes for her freedom.

Having organised and trained her manhood through her secret revolutionary organisation, the Irish Republican Brotherhood, and through her open military organisations, the Irish Volunteers and the Irish Citizen Army, having patiently perfected her discipline, having resolutely waited for the right moment to reveal itself, she now seizes that moment, and, supported by her exiled children in America and by gallant allies in Europe, but relying in the first on her own strength, she strikes in full confidence of victory.

We declare the right of the people of Ireland to the ownership of Ireland, and to the unfettered control of Irish destinies, to be sovereign and indefeasible. The long usurpation of that right by a foreign people and government has not extinguished the right, nor can it ever be extinguished except by the destruction of the Irish people. In every generation the Irish people have asserted their right to national freedom and sovereignty: six times during the past three hundred years they have asserted it in arms. Standing on that fundamental right and again asserting it in arms in the face of the world, we hereby proclaim the Irish Republic as a Sovereign Independent State, and we pledge our lives and the lives of our comrades-in-arms to the cause of its freedom, of its welfare, and of its exaltation among the nations.

The Irish Republic is entitled to, and hereby claims, the allegiance of every Irishman and Irishwoman. The Republic guarantees religious and civil liberty, equal rights and equal opportunities to all its citizens, and declares its resolve to pursue the happiness and prosperity of the whole nation and of all its parts, cherishing all the children of the nation equally, and oblivious of the differences carefully fostered by an alien government, which have divided a minority from the majority in the past.

Until our arms have brought the opportune moment for the establishment of a permanent National Government, representative of the whole people of Ireland and elected by the suffrages of all her men and women, the Provisional Government, hereby constituted, will administer the civil and military affairs of the Republic in trust for the people.

We place the cause of the Irish Republic under the protection of the Most High God, Whose blessing we invoke upon our arms, and we pray that no one who serves that cause will dishonour it by cowardice, inhumanity, or rapine. In this supreme hour the Irish nation must, by its valour and discipline and by the readiness of its children to sacrifice themselves for the common good, prove itself worthy of the august destiny to which it is called.

Signed on Behalf of the Provisional Government,

THOMAS J. CLARKE.

SEAN Mac DIARMADA.   THOMAS MacDONAGH.
P. H. PEARSE.   EAMONN CEANNT.
JAMES CONNOLLY.   JOSEPH PLUNKETT.

At around 12.45 p.m. on Monday, 24 April 1916, under the Grand Portico of the GPO on O'Connell Street, Patrick Pearse read the text of the Proclamation of the Provisional Government of the Irish Republic to the confused, curious and supportive city-dwellers.

Four other members of the Provisional Government – (clockwise from top left) James Connolly, Seán MacDiarmada, Joseph Plunkett and Tom Clarke – were in the GPO with Pearse during Easter week.

The Provisional Government

... TO THE ...

CITIZENS OF DUBLIN

The Provisional Government of the Irish Republic salutes the CITIZENS OF DUBLIN on the momentous occasion of the proclamation of a

Sovereign Independent Irish State

now in course of being established by Irishmen in Arms.

The Republican forces hold the lines taken up at Twelve noon on Easter Monday, and nowhere, despite fierce and almost continuous attacks of the British troops, have the lines been broken through. The country is rising in answer to Dublin's call, and the final achievement of Ireland's freedom is now, with God's help, only a matter of days. The valour, self-sacrifice, and discipline of Irish men and women are about to win for our country a glorious place among the nations.

Ireland's honour has already been redeemed; it remains to vindicate her wisdom and her self-control.

All citizens of Dublin who believe in the right of their Country to be free will give their allegiance and their loyal help to the Irish Republic. There is work for everyone: for the men in the fighting line, and for the women in the provision of food and first aid. Every Irishman and Irishwoman worthy of the name will come forward to help their common country in this her supreme hour.

Able-bodied Citizens can help by building barricades in the streets to oppose the advance of the British troops. The British troops have been firing on our women and on our Red Cross. On the other hand, Irish Regiments in the British Army have refused to act against their fellow countrymen.

The Provisional Government hopes that its supporters— which means the vast bulk of the people of Dublin—will preserve order and self-restraint. Such looting as has already occurred has been done by hangers-on of the British Army. Ireland must keep her new honour unsmirched.

We have lived to see an Irish Republic proclaimed. May we live to establish it firmly, and may our children and our children's children enjoy the happiness and prosperity which freedom will bring.

Signed on behalf of the Provisional Government,

P. H. PEARSE,

Commanding in Chief the Forces of the Irish Republic, and President of the Provisional Government.

An appeal to the citizens of Dublin from the Provisional Government in the GPO, signed by Patrick Pearse.

IRISH WAR NEWS

THE IRISH REPUBLIC.

VOL. I. No. I   DUBLIN, TUESDAY, APRIL 25, 1916.   ONE PENNY

"IF THE GERMANS CONQUERED ENGLAND."

In the London "New Statesman" for *April 1st*, an article is published—"If the Germans Conquered England," which has the appearance of a very clever piece of satire written by an Irishman. The writer draws a picture of England under German rule, almost every detail of which exactly fits the case of Ireland at the present day. Some of the sentences are so exquisitely appropriate that it is impossible to believe that the writer had not Ireland in his mind when he wrote them. For instance :—

"England would be constantly irritated by lofty moral utterances of German statesmen. England would assert—quite sincerely, no doubt—England was free, freer indeed than she had been before. Prussian freedom, they would say, was the only real freedom, and therefore England was free. They would point to the flourishing railways and farms and colleges. They would possibly point to the contingent of M.P.'s which was permitted, in spite of its deplorable difficultness, to sit in a permanent minority in the ......

stag. And not only would the Englishman have to listen to a constant flow of speeches of this sort ; he would find a respectable official Press secretly bought over by the Government to say the same kind of things over and over, every day of the week. He would find, too, that his children were coming home from school with new ideas of history. . . . They would ask him, if it was true that until the Germans came England had been an unruly country, constantly engaged in civil war. . . . . The object of every schoolbook would be to make the English child grow up in the notion that the history of his country was a thing to forget, and that the one bright spot in it was the fact that it had been conquered by cultured Germ ny."

"If there was a revolt, German statesmen would in ...

---

4   IRISH WAR NEWS

STOP PRESS !

THE IRISH REPUBLIC

(Irish) "War News" is published to-day because a momentous thing has happened. The Irish Republic has been declared in Dublin, and a Provisional Government has been appointed to administer its affairs. The following have been named as the Provisional Government :—

Thomas J. Clarke.
Sean Mac Diarmada.
P. H. Pearse.
James Connolly.
Thomas Mac Donagh.
Eamonn Ceannt.
Joseph Plunkett.

The Irish Republic was proclaimed by a poster, which was prominently displayed in Dublin.

At 9.30 a.m. this morning the following statement was made by Commandant-General, P. H. Pearse :—

The Irish Republic was proclaimed in Dublin on Easter Monday, 24th April, at 12 noon. Simultaneously with the issue of the proclamation of the Provisional Government the Dublin Division of the Army of the Republic, including the Irish Volunteers, Citizen Army, Hibernian Rifles, and other bodies, occupied dominating points in the city. The G.P.O. was seized at 12 noon, the Castle was attacked at the same moment, and shortly afterwards the Four Courts were occupied. The Irish troops hold the City Hall and dominate the Castle. Attacks were immediately commenced by the British forces and were everywhere repulsed. At the moment of writing this report, (9.30 a.m., Tuesday) the Republican forces hold all their positions and the British forces have nowhere broken through. There has been heavy and continuous fighting for nearly 24 hours, the casualties of the enemy being much more numerous than those on the Republican side. The Republican forces everywhere are fighting with splendid gallantry. The populace of Dublin are plainly with the Republic, and the officers and men are everywhere cheered as they march through the streets. The whole centre of the city is in the hands of the Republic, whose flag flies from the G.P.O.

Commandant-General P. H. Pearse is commanding in chief of the Army of the Republic and

is President of the Provisional Government Commandant General James Connolly is commanding the Dublin districts. Communication with the country is largely cut, but reports to hand show that the country is rising, and bodies of men from Kildare and Fingall have already reported in Dublin.

MORE PIRACY.

The condition of affairs illustrated in the following comment from "The Advocate," a New York Irish Redmondite paper, is not at all unlike piracy on the high seas. In its latest issue to hand "The Advocate" says :—

"Since the British Government began to seize the mails we have been informed by some of our Swedish acquaintances that the little cheques they have sent to the old folks at home have never reached their destination. If this be true, and we have no reason to doubt it, then the British Government stands convicted of the most contemptible kind of petty larceny which the criminal annals of the world can show. Sweden is just now experiencing a depression in all kinds of business owing to being cut off from other neutral nations by Great Britain, and consequently a little help from their exiled brethren is much needed in countless Swedish households. Now, it may be asked what Great Britain hopes to accomplish by preventing the exiled Swedes from helping their suffering kindred at home ? The reason is not far to seek. The Socialist party is very strong in Sweden, and is growing stronger in proportion to the increase in the difficulty of the masses to make ends meet. Now, Great Britain knows that were it not for the opposition of the Socialists Sweden would long since have entered the war on the side of Germany, hence it is to her interest to add by every means at her disposal to the Socialists' power. Therefore in robbing the mails of these little cheques she is robbing deserving people of the means of tiding over the dull season, and expects that, driven by necessity, many will turn to the Socialists in their extremity, and thus Sweden's continued neutrality will be secured. This is the explanation our Swedish acquaintances give of England's thieving conduct in this regard. For the honour of our poor human nature, let us hope the case is not as bad as it is said to be."

The shelled GPO
and O'Connell
Street.

In order to prevent the further slaughter of Dublin
citizens, and in the hope of saving the lives of our
followers now surrounded and hopelessly outnumbered, the
members of the Provisional Government present at Head-
Quarters have agreed to an unconditional surrender, and the
Commandants of the various districts in the City and Country
will order their commands to lay down arms.

P. H. Pearse

29th April 1916
3.45 p. m.

I agree to these conditions for the men only
under my own Command in the Moore
Street District and for the men in
the Stephen's Green Command.

James Connolly

April 29/16

On consultation with Commandant Ceannt
and other officers I have decided to
agree to unconditional surrender also.

Thomas MacDonagh.

Patrick Pearse's notice of surrender, written on 29 April 1916,
and co-signed by James Connolly and Thomas MacDonagh.

Above: Patrick Pearse and Elizabeth O'Farrell (her boots can be seen next to Pearse's) surrender to Brigadier General William Lowe and his son John.

Left: Patrick Pearse in memoriam.

Guided by common sense, Frank de Burca sought Pearse's permission to fall back from the forlorn house-boring operation on Henry Street and resume guarding the GPO. HQ was 'now an inferno', and nervous Volunteers sang to keep their spirits up as water sprayed on the flames lapping the roof dripped down through the thickening smoke into the lower levels.[122]

Pearse, on the basis of a conversation with a Post Office engineer, claimed the floor between them and the Instrument Room on the upper level, which was burning, was fireproofed. Seamus Ua Caomhanaigh disabused him of this notion and assisted The O'Rahilly in supervising the removal of explosives from the path of encroaching flames.[123] Cracks began to weaken the masonry of the outer walls and were noticed around the time that the hitherto-constant water supply began to fail. Threatened by collapsing floors, it was obvious that the base could no longer be maintained.[124]

Connolly believed a declaration was desirable and composed a typescript address, 'To Soldiers' as Commandant-General, Dublin Division:

> We are here hemmed in because the enemy feels that in this building is to be found the heart and inspiration of our great movement. Let us remind you what you have done. For the first time in seven hundred years the flag of a Free Ireland floats triumphantly in Dublin city … We have every

confidence that our allies in Germany and our kinsmen in America are straining every nerve to hasten matters on our behalf … Never had a man or woman a greater cause; never was a cause more grandly served.[125]

The devastating impact of close-range and high-arc cannon fire answered in full the formerly rhetorical question vis-à-vis the depths to which Whitehall would descend to cleave an overwhelmingly unwilling Ireland to a perishing Empire. In retrospect, the prowess of the Imperial General Staff who consigned tens of thousands of Britons, Irish and 'colonials' to pointless deaths in the Somme in July 1916 vindicated negative republican assessments of their professional acumen. Brute force and ruthlessness, once amplified by the projection of unlimited logistical capacity in Dublin, were undeniably tokens of London's resolve.

If, as seems probable, Pearse and Connolly accepted the basic premise of the 'England's difficulty' theory cherished by US sponsors, Britain had retorted when provoked with an escalating regime of state terrorism indicative of a zero-sum game of power reassertion. Connolly, one of the Irish revolutionary leaders who, in *Workers' Republic*, anticipated die-hard resolution of this order, represented himself as being aggrieved by such callousness in his address to the 'Soldiers' on 28 April:

The British Army, whose exploits we are forever having dinned into our ears, which boasts of having stormed the Dardanelles [in Turkey] and the German lines on the Marne [in France], behind their artillery and machine guns [in Dublin] are afraid to advance to the attack or storm a position held by our forces. The slaughter they suffered in the first few days has totally unnerved them and they are not attempting again an infantry attack on our positions.[126]

By midday, an eighteen-pounder cannon was positioned behind the military barricade on Parnell Street, 'facing down Moore Street in the direction of the GPO'. This was the heaviest calibre artillery piece available. Infantry Sergeant Samuel Henry Lomas, who moved from Watford to Dun Laoghaire on 25 April, witnessed the scene: 'Four shells were fired which caused the rebels to quake, as for some considerable time, the rifle fire was silent, with the exception of a few snipers.'[127] Many taken prisoner in the days ahead were wounded and clad in dishevelled uniforms, primarily from holding positions under artillery fire where resolve entailed blood and trauma injuries as well as grime attributable to stone shards, falling plaster and dust agitated by shelling.[128]

Contact with other Volunteer positions had become difficult, and, when Michael Ua Caomhanaigh departed the GPO with a message from Pearse for MacDonagh in Jacob's Factory, his failure to return simply added another mystery to the scenario. It transpired that he was simply trapped in his destination, as 'the British military were everywhere'.[129]

Chapter 7

* * * * *

Court Martial and Execution

Preparations for a general escape were laid from midday on Friday. On Thursday evening, Louise Gavan Duffy had delayed the dismissal of the women at HQ by petitioning her former employer. 'Pearse said we could stay. He said he did not think he had a right to prevent anybody taking part in the Rebellion who wanted to stay.'[1] Pearse addressed the women before they left under a Red Cross flag for Jervis Street and the North Circular Road, claiming,

> when the history of the week would be written, the highest hono[u]r and credit should be given to the women whose bravery, heroism and devotion in the face of danger surpassed that of the women of Limerick in the days of Sarsfield. He then ordered them, except those of the nursing station, to proceed.[2]

Pearse and Plunkett 'call[ed] the various companies to attention before they [were] marched into the yard' around

2 p.m.[3] Thomas Harris was present as 'Pearse was issuing instructions that each man was to take 24 hours' rations with him.'[4] Amid ongoing shelling, the roof of the GPO was cleared and an interior defence position prepared inside the main hall, using coal-filled mailbags as protection.

The front portico, where the Irish Republic had been declared that Monday, was ablaze by 3 p.m., and fire spread into the ground floor. The remaining garrison, reduced by the departure of the Cumann na mBan women yet augmented by the last of the retreating Coliseum outpost, moved into the Sorting Office at the rear of the building.[5]

At 5 p.m., a captured Royal Army Medical Corps officer and city-centre priest, Fr John Flanagan, led the wounded from the GPO via Prince's and Middle Abbey Street to nearby Jervis Street Hospital. An escort of twenty-three men was permitted to accomplish the duty and return to HQ. Connolly refused the opportunity to retire in safety and was attended by two trained nurses and Carney.[6]

By 7 p.m. Friday evening, the GPO was no longer a tenable position. Much of the roof was burning or smouldering: 'myriads of live sparks fell through the open shaft to the immediate vicinity of the Henry Street basement room in which the stocks of gelignite and bombs had been placed for safety'.[7] Fires raged out of control around the building, and British shelling threatened imminent annihilation. Fearing a catastrophic explosion, relays of Volunteers once again relocated the cache into a storeroom adjacent to Prince's Street courtyard.[8] The only option was to pull back through the maze of side streets and alleys towards Moore Street, which ran parallel to Sackville Street and linked Mary Street.

Pearse made what appeared to be an impromptu speech but which probably had been long ruminated upon. Fintan Murphy noticed that Pearse 'looked weary … but not defeated – still the same quiet voice which had inspired us on so many occasions'.[9] O'Reilly, who had been detailed to engage in sniping from the roof of the building, recalled his words: 'Let me, who has led you into this, speak on my own, and my fellow commanders' names. In the name of Ireland present, and to come, speak their praises, and ask those, who come after them to remember them.'[10] This prayer-like invocation was consistent with Pearse's deep-seated sense of historical continuity and faith in the propaganda of the deed.

Lynch remembered Pearse's words:

I desire now, lest I may not have an opportunity later, to pay homage to the gallantry of the soldiers of Irish Freedom who have, during the past four days, been writing with fire and steel the most glorious chapter in the later history of Ireland. Justice can never be done to their heroism, to their discipline, to their gay and unconquerable spirit in the midst of peril and death.[11]

Cheered by this endorsement, the men sang 'The Soldier's Song'. Around thirty selected as a 'advance party' exited into Henry Street at 8.10 p.m., led by The O'Rahilly, and passed through one of the last extant friendly barricades in the area. They were hoping to reach Williams & Woods Soap and Sweet Manufacturers (aka 'the jam factory') at 204–6 Parnell Street.[12] Pearse appointed Seamus O'Sullivan second-in-command of the detachment.

After some discussion, he failed to convince The O'Rahilly to move forward using available cover and stealth.[13] Knowing a British emplacement had a line of sight to the only route available to reach their objective, the men 'charged up Moore Street' towards Henry Place. Their fixed bayonets indicated they expected close-quarters fighting, but this was forlorn. Withering British fire from the corner of Parnell Street pinned them down in the alleyways running off Coles Lane and Moore Street and mortally wounded the fearless O'Rahilly. He was hit near Sampson's Lane, opposite Henry Place, when attempting to advance from temporary cover in a doorway.[14] A letter to his wife written in his own blood on scrap paper was recovered from his uniform, as was the final dispatch issued by Connolly. Francis Macken of the Rathfarnham company also perished.[15]

Meanwhile, after Pearse had spoken, Captain M. J. O'Reilly was instructed to lead a stretcher party carrying Andrew Furlong to Jervis Street Hospital. Patrick Caldwell had been

standing by, ready to move Connolly, when his friend Furlong received a serious knee wound. Caldwell, laden with
equipment, was redirected to assist his immobile comrade.
When moving through four or five 'bored' houses, Willie
Pearse caught up with them and ordered them back to the
GPO. By the time they arrived, the building was about to be
emptied of its occupants.[16]

A British sniper firing from a Henry Street roof was hit-
ting men using the exit chosen by Pearse to evacuate the
HQ. He asked Ua Caomhanaigh to 'try to get him':

> I went into a room beside the Henry St door and took up
> a position at the window. This was on the ground floor; all
> the upper floors were then aflame … I put a few shots near
> where I thought he might be and waited for results. I heard
> no more shots and waited patiently in that room for a very
> long time … Eventually Pearse came in. 'I was nearly for-
> getting you, Seamus' said he. 'They are all gone. We are the
> only ones left now.' I went with him then to the side door
> and found I was one of the last six left in the Post Office –
> Pearse, George Plunkett, myself and three others.[17]

In the absence of a report from O'Rahilly, Pearse pursued the objective by sending Liam Tannam to reconnoitre 'a place to which the garrison could be evacuated'.[18]
Seven Volunteers followed Tannam past the dangerous

Moore Lane opening covered by the British from the Parnell Street barricade and on into Moore Street. Telling the men to enter the 'corner house of Moore Street', Tannam returned to the GPO via the Henry Street angle to the crumbling HQ. He found the Henry Street door 'rather crowded' and shouted at the men to 'come on'.[19] On locating Pearse, he guided the Dubliner to the Henry Place angle to show him interim positions identified for accessing Moore Street. Pearse re-entered the doomed GPO to supervise its final abandonment.[20]

At 8.30 p.m., the last of the garrison mustered to leave for Moore Street as dusk approached. The mobile Metropole/ Mansfield group sustained three casualties crossing Sackville Street to join their comrades. Prisoners were freed, but three serving in Irish regiments elected to stay. Within ten minutes, the building was emptied. Harry Boland apprised the man guarding the munitions that it was time to quit. A most reluctant Clarke joined Plunkett and MacDiarmada at the head of the column in which Connolly was carried by stretcher. Pearse organised the rearguard element.[21]

Caldwell, having obeyed orders from Willie Pearse to carry the injured Furlong back to the GPO, arrived into the midst of the rearguard headed by Patrick Pearse:

When we got back to the Post Office we found that it was for all practicable purposes completely evacuated by the Volunteer garrison. Willie Pearse brought us to an exit door facing Henry Place and Patrick Pearse was standing at this door at the time and he instructed us to make a run for it into Henry Place. The wounded man was taken across first. Patrick Pearse went across soon after and I followed immediately behind him and joined two Volunteers who were behind a barricade in Henry Place ... Commandant John[n]ie [aka Sean] McLoughlin, a Fianna boy, gave us instructions to evacuate the barricade and move up Henry Place towards Moore Street. At this time he was carrying a sword in his hand.[22]

The Volunteers appeared hesitant as they exited the GPO and were undoubtedly wary of stumbling into hidden British strong points. The fate of O'Rahilly's 'advance party' remained unknown. An officer of the Royal Irish Regiment believed that those who waited in a side street beside the Coliseum 'seemed uncertain what to do' until Pearse addressed the group: 'in a few minutes they were cheering and rushed after him in the direction of Moore St'.[23]

The evacuation involved approximately 320 people who 'congregated in houses along Moore Street' around 9 p.m.[24] This was not accomplished without considerable difficulty. Machine-gun fire directed from the roof of the Rotunda Hospital raked the Moore Lane and Henry Place intersection as the Volunteers pelted across in intervals towards No.

10 Moore Street. De Burca of the Rathfarnham Company recalled:

> The street was being swept by machine gun fire from Mary Street direction, we had to make a dash across in ones and twos into Henry Lane. Bulfin made the journey with great speed. My turn was next … I could see the bullets like hailstones hopping on the street and I thought that twould be a miracle to get to the other side scatheless. With head down as if running against heavy rain, I ran as I never ran before or since.[25]

Men preparing to make the crossing were momentarily concerned by the absence of Pearse who had conducted a final check of the building: 'after what seemed an interminable time … Pearse returned, begrimed with soot and dust, his face and eyes swollen with the heat, and passed through to Henry Street.'[26] He followed Ua Caomhanaigh in the last group and 'walked quietly' across Henry Street into Henry Place. This was made possible by the suppression of the formerly troublesome enemy sniper covering the zone. They reached the right-angle bend in Henry Place running to the left towards, but not as far as, Moore Street. Getting to Moore Street entailed passing the Moore Lane T-junction, which, if a narrow gap, was in sight of British positions to the right at the Parnell Street end. Ua Caomhanaigh:

This corner appeared to be under continuous machine gun fire and our people were watching an opportunity to run across the danger spot in ones and twos. When it came to our turn Pearse sent me across in front of him and he came behind me. I had just got across when I heard Pearse stumble and fall. I thought he had been hit and ran back to help him but he was all right. He had struck his foot against a stone and tripped. I think he was the last across.[27]

The immediate objective was in sight: the side door of a house on the Moore Street corner. Impacting rounds blasted whitewash dust plumes from the outer wall of the nearby Mineral Water Stores.[28] Good cover was obtained when a Volunteer wrenched open a doorway, enabling the men to move inside the *Freeman's Journal* printing works.[29]

Avoiding heavy fire from actual British positions to their right from the Parnell Street barricades, small groups hurried into Cogan's Grocery, 10 Moore Street.[30] To avoid having to use the exposed front door, they smashed through the side wall into the alley and pushed a commandeered dray into Moore Lane to provide protection during the last exposed dash to the breach point.[31]

Once this temporary sanctuary was reached, the work of opening access into the adjacent buildings immediately began. This labour brought the concealed rebels wall by wall towards their opponents and the end-of-terrace house,

25 Moore Street. Michael Collins, exuding confidence in the most stressful of circumstances, directed the boarding-up of windows.[32] Laden with supplies, Tom Leahy faltered when entering No. 10 but was quickly pulled to his feet by Vincent Poole and P. H. Pearse.[33] After consultation with Oscar Traynor, who pinpointed the position on a streetmap, Pearse reputedly selected the central Hanlon's fish shop at 20–1 Moore Street as the new 'headquarters'.[34] No. 16 Moore Street, Plunkett's Butchers, was where the decision to surrender was taken, on 29 April, in the first-floor back room.[35]

British positions ringed the mostly abandoned enclave. De Burca saw dead bodies of civilians shot by the soldiers, 'one poor man with a white flag grasped in his hand, lying dead on the door step of his house'.[36] Liverpool Volunteer Seamus Donegan told Ua Caomhanaigh about seeing a young girl being struck in the head by a British round inside her home. John King, another Liverpool participant, lay undiscovered in the darkness with a serious hip wound when comrades inadvertently stumbled over him.[37]

According to Ua Caomhanaigh, 'The 18th Royal Irish, a regiment of Irishmen in the British Army, had shot at everything that moved in the street and at such short range their shooting was deadly.'[38] Casualties sustained during the night included an elderly man who was mortally wounded yet clung grimly and audibly to life for hours. After dawn, a distressed five-year-old girl came out of a shop and repeatedly told her mother that her grandfather was dead.[39]

Boring continued towards the Sackville Lane axis. Pearse decided that an outpost was required, and a small detachment was sent through or over the warehouse at Henry Place in order to secure a position at the Henry Street end of Moore Street. Uncontrolled fires from the blazing GPO rendered this hopeless.[40] After midnight, Charles Donnelly was moving along a laneway when he saw Pearse 'at the last house of this lane with a frontage in Moore St ... after some conversation with him he instructed me to bring the men for food from the stores to the Moore St house.'[41]

Connolly's injuries rendered him incapable of exercising further command. Under an oleograph of the Sacred Heart and a portrait of Emmet, he lay, conscious, on a bed, speaking to those who came and went. A delirious and wounded Dublin Fusilier called in, saying 'Jim Connolly' over and over again, and Joe Good watched as

Pádraig Pearse went to him at least once, and stayed talking with this wounded man for some time. At other times he would move from house to house, talking gently with our own men. He would then return and sit again with Joe Plunkett at the edge of Connolly's bed'.[42]

Ua Caomhanaigh saw Pearse emerge from a meeting of the Executive Council to appoint Fianna Éireann leader Sean McLoughlin Commandant-General in place of Connolly. The young man had acquitted himself well during the GPO evacuation. Leo Henderson was promoted to Captain.[43]

Most of the Military Council, minus Clarke, occupied a single room in 16 Moore Street during the hours of darkness. The situation in Moore Street was less critical than at the GPO, but it was unstable. The IRA was surrounded by vastly superior military forces who kept a respectful distance. The terrace of two-storey redbrick houses did not offer significant defensive advantages given the weight of opposing forces, and food, water and ammunition were in short supply.

Erecting a barricade to provide cover for crossing into Sampson's Lane commenced, but the lack of materials and the 'continuous enemy barrage' halted construction.[44] Consideration was given to a costly bayonet charge on British positions guarding the Moore Street end of Sackville Lane. Closing with enemy barricades under crossfire from waiting automatic weapons and elevated snipers would have been virtually suicidal. Joining the undefeated Four Courts garrison seemed impossible. 'Resolute' men loitered unseen in the double yard at the rear of Hanlon's, 20–1 Moore Street, awaiting orders.[45] At least two British machine guns covered the Parnell Street barricade supported by an artillery piece.[46]

Michael Cremen noticed that a storehouse to the rear of 25 Moore Street had a first-floor bay window capable of providing covering fire, and Willie Pearse and Eamon Bulfin confirmed its utility.[47] According to Cremen, 'As [Patrick] Pearse was a man who spoke little, I fell asleep with the impression that my suggestion was being agreed to. Seeing events in retrospect, it seems that Pearse's mind was then concerned with surrender.'[48]

Matters were not clear-cut. Harry Boland, J. J. Walsh and Peadar Bracken were standing by with the assault party when Diarmuid Lynch arrived to query if Pearse 'was aware that we were about to go into action'.[49] When Walsh replied that 'he thought not', Lynch postponed the charge until darkness, a plan Cremen believed had already been agreed.[50] Bracken, for his part, recalled that a message was sent to the leadership at around 2 p.m. regarding the timing of the attack. This elicited an unexpected reply that none should occur as 'there was a truce'.[51]

The seven men of the Provisional Government had reassessed the situation in pragmatic terms. Clarke wanted to fight on, at least personally, to the death. Pearse, as outlined in a written account for his mother and posterity, 'was in favour of one more desperate sally before opening negotiations'.[52] This proved the minority position, and he yielded to the majority with whom he quickly, on reflection, concurred. Static defence and valorous charges both courted losses in a campaign that could not be carried by force of arms in Dublin alone.[53]

John Twamley arrived to guard the room where Connolly lay and 'saw Pearse kneeling beside and talking to him. Immediately after this I heard we were surrendering.'[54] There was no general consultation with the men and few women remaining. Even Bulfin, so often the link between Pearse and the national republican movement, was initially unaware of the reasoning behind the cancellation of the barricade assault.[55]

Elizabeth O'Farrell, 'fully trusted by Pearse and all the leaders', performed the dangerous role of opening dialogue with the British.[56] Her message read, 'The Commandant-General of the Irish Republican Army wishes to treat with the Commandant-General of the British Forces in Ireland.'[57] Escorted to the door by MacDiarmada at 12.15 p.m., O'Farrell waved an 'improvised flag', which attracted 'a burst of sustained firing'.[58] When the possibly impulsive bullet storm ceased, she bravely stepped into Moore Street and 'very slowly' approached British positions on Parnell Street.[59]

Key issues included arrangements for a ceasefire to enable face-to-face negotiations and the status of such talks. This entailed two precarious trips between opposing strong points. O'Farrell ascertained from Brigadier General William Lowe, who had commandeered Clarke's shop at 75B Parnell Street, that unconditional surrender was demanded. At 1.40 p.m.,

General Lowe specified that 'P. H. Pearse' could and should come to his position.[60] According to Pearse,

> We decided in order to prevent further slaughter of the civil population and in the hope of saving the lives of our followers, to ask the General Commanding the British Forces to discuss terms. He replied that he would receive me only if I surrendered unconditionally, and this I did.[61]

Reposing trust in his enemies, at 3.30 p.m. Pearse accompanied O'Farrell to see Lowe and a small group of staff officers outside 70 Parnell Street at the Moore Lane corner.[62] His presence confirmed that he was indeed inside the 'cordon' yet uninjured as a British 'official intimation' in Dublin stated that day. Connolly was not dead, and Markievicz, as a pressed Pearse insisted, was elsewhere.[63]

Having watched Pearse venture out alone, 'as firm as a rock', Des Ryan went into the 'headquarters room' where the remaining commanders were grouped: 'Plunkett is calm. Tears are in McDermott's eyes. So too with Willie Pearse. Connolly stares in front of him.'[64] Ryan learned from Willie Pearse that Connolly had been 'asked out to negotiate', a role performed by Patrick Pearse, and that the leadership wished 'to save the men from slaughter'.[65] Orders were circulated that there was to be 'no shooting on any account' while arrangements were made to surrender.[66] MacDiarmada toured the terrace, imparting the news to generally despond-ent and semi-mutinous fighters.[67] He ordered Sam O'Reilly to fashion a white flag from a bedsheet which was hung from a window.[68] The restive men ascertained that

> Commandant Pearse in consultation with Commandant Connolly and the other officers had decided that enough had been achieved to save Ireland's honour and 'that it was time to arrest the slaughter of the civilian population by British shells and bullets.' It was about 3 o'clock in the afternoon when the unconditional surrender took place.[69]

Word of the decision was also relayed by Captain Frank Henderson and Joseph Plunkett.[70] O'Reilly recalled:

> The British terms demanded 'unconditional surrender'. And they wanted Pearse and Connolly brought out first. Pearse, his head held high, walked out and Connolly was carried on a stretcher. Word came that we soldiers were to march out. We assembled our troops and McDermott stood up on a box and addressed the men. He said: 'March out with your heads held high, as if in victory. Your actions this week have redeemed the Irish Nation'. I marched out at the head of the troops, down Moore St, on to Henry St and into O'Connell St. Our troops in the march numbered about 300. A British officer ordered us to proceed towards

O'Connell Bridge. On further orders we marched to the Parnell Monument. The British Officer wanted us to lay down our arms. The men wouldn't do so until I gave the order to ground arms.[71]

The Volunteers retained their weapons 'because we didn't know if that white flag would mean anything'.[72]

Caldwell witnessed a potentially serious 'altercation' between MacDiarmada and Captain Lea Wilson after the men had piled their arms outside the Gresham Hotel on Sackville Street. The Irishman responded to an insulting suggestion that the Volunteers had no positions with a curt 'We can see about that.'[73]

Pearse, meanwhile, was taken to the British Army Headquarters in Parkgate Street, Kilmainham, where he 'wrote and signed an order to our men to lay down their arms'.[74] News that the 'wretched "Commandant" of the insurgents' had been in Army Headquarters provided Birrell with rare good news for Asquith.[75] The original text was copied and distributed:

In order to prevent the further slaughter of Dublin citizens, and in the hope of saving the lives of our followers now surrounded and hopelessly outnumbered, the members of the Provisional Government present at Headquarters have agreed to an unconditional surrender, and the

Commandants of the various districts in the City and Country will order their Commands to lay down arms. P. H. Pearse, 29th April 1916, 3.45 p.m.[76]

The pace of events caught many off guard. Deputy Judge Advocate Bucknill met General Byrne in Parkgate after lunch:

Whilst we were there, we heard that probably the whole affair was over, and shortly afterwards Pearse the rebel leader arrived and saw General Maxwell. Pearse surrendered immediately and sent out notices to his followers to do [the] same. I saw this man later on in the day at Arbour Hill [Detention] Barracks where he was removed. I went there with General Byrne. Pearse was dressed in green uniform with yellow staff tabs and he had a hat rather like a Colonial's with one side turned up. He was tall and well set up, with high cheek bones and eyes deep set. I remember that he said he had brought some money with him to pay for his food and he requested that he might have special food, but this request was not then granted.[77]

Pearse was taken to Arbour Hill in the course of the evening, where many of those he had parted with in Moore Street were being concentrated. He informed his mother, 'Willie and all the St Enda's boys are here.'[78] The bulk of those who had been in the GPO and Moore Street were kept overnight in the Rotunda Gardens.

Caldwell watched as Clarke and Plunkett were 'called out and taken over to a special place'. Michael Collins was also picked out of the crowd by Captain Lea Wilson, who reputedly remarked, 'I wouldn't trust that so-and-so.'[79] Ryan believed the officer to be 'either drunk or mad with hysteria' and visibly held in contempt by many of his own subordinates.[80] Lea Wilson was positively identified as the man responsible for harassing Clarke and MacDiarmada after their surrender and was shot dead by the IRA in Gorey in June 1920.[81]

Yet the IRA were undefeated on 29 April 1916, and, with the notable exception of the skillfully evacuated GPO HQ, retained all four battalion command posts in the Four Courts, Boland's Mill, Jacob's Factory and the South Dublin Union. John 'Sean' Shouldice, a lieutenant in F Company, 1st Battalion, moved between strong points and barricades in the sector controlled by his comrades until ordered to fall back on the Four Courts:

> Comt Daly addressed us, and stated that orders had been received from General Pearse that we were to lay down our arms and surrender unconditionally. This was the cause of an outburst amongst the men and some of the officers who replied that they would fight on sooner than surrender …

Daly, however, sympathised with them and stated that personally he would prefer to fight on under these conditions, but the orders from General Pearse were definite and had to be obeyed … The Four Courts was gradually being surrounded by strong military forces and the final surrender occurred about 7 p.m.[82]

Fr Augustine, a member of the Capuchin Friary on Church Street, pursued his vocation during Easter Week, tending to the rebel wounded in Fr Mathew Hall. Serious cases were transferred to Richmond Hospital. Augustine learned of the surrender order from Pearse at around 7 a.m. on 30 April and was concerned that Volunteers would not comply unless shown a hard copy. To this end, he and Fr Aloysius went to Dublin Castle at 8 a.m., where General Lowe confirmed the authenticity of the typed copies in circulation; he was not, however, able to produce a spare.

Lowe volunteered that Connolly was present and arranged a private meeting. Although confirming the veracity of orders he had given, Connolly stressed that his signature pertained solely to men under his direct command in Dublin; it was Pearse who led the national organisation. Sensing confusion in the city and a possible problem demobilising the Volunteers around the Four Courts, Lowe immediately put his chauffeur and car at the disposal of the Capuchins.

We drove at once to Arbour Hill Detention Barracks to see Pearse who, after a short while, was ushered into the room by a soldier who then stood at the end with a loaded rifle. Pearse advanced with noble mien and such soldierly bearing that the word 'Napoleonic' shot at once through my brain. In answer to my question he said that he had signed a document of unconditional surrender stating the reasons why he had done so, but that one of our Fathers had been here a short time previously, and as he assured him no copy of it could be found, he wrote another.[83]

Back in Church Street, the men ascertained that Fr Columbus Murphy had indeed acquired an additional surrender order from Pearse that convinced Paddy Holahan to comply. The Four Courts Volunteer garrison duly stood down. An armistice facilitated discussions between Lowe and MacDonagh outside Jacob's Factory.[84] MacDonagh was concerned that Pearse might have acted under duress and demanded access to him. He certainly liaised with Ceannt before briefing his own officers, at which time he personally 'counselled surrender'.[85]

MacDonagh assembled the men in the basement of Jacob's, where the news was poorly received. Vinny Byrne recalled, 'There was a Franciscan Father in the building at the time, and he was pleading with the men to lay down their arms quietly.'[86]

Three RIC men brought Pearse's document to Enniscorthy under a white flag. Fr Murphy, assisting Bob Brennan at Volunteers headquarters, was among those discomforted by advance word of 'the unconditional surrender of our noble Commandant Pearse'. Neither a special edition of the *Free Press* nor copies of telegrams instructing Volunteers to stand down were taken at face value. Brennan's men demanded a delegation see Pearse in Dublin. Colonel French, a native Wexfordian serving in the British Army, permitted Seamus Doyle and Seán Etchingham to pass through military checkpoints for this purpose. According to Etchingham:

We were brought to Arbour Hill Barracks, attended by quite a number of staff officers. We were escorted into the Main Hall, and the cell door was unlocked and flung open, the officers remaining in the hall. As we entered, Pearse was rising from a mattress in the far end of the cell, upon which he had been lying covered with his great coat. He wore the uniform of the Irish Volunteers, which was complete, except for the Sam Browne belt. The rank-badges were still on the collar of his tunic … He seemed to be physically exhausted, but spiritually exultant … He told us that the Dublin Brigade had done splendidly – five days and five nights of almost continuous fighting – of The O'Rahilly's heroic death in Moore Street, and of the no less heroic death of our country-man, Captain Tom Weafer, at his position in the Hibernian Bank in O'Connell Street. The surrender was ordered, he told us, to save the lives of the people of Dublin, who were being shot by the British in the streets, adding that he saw them being shot himself.[87]

A military orderly went to get stationery and a pen for Pearse to write an explicit surrender order for Wexford. While he was gone, Etchingham said, 'Pearse said in a whisper, "Hide your arms, they'll be needed later," and so we said farewell. The memory of the handclasp and the smile remains with me.'[88] Doyle, whose account mirrored that of his companion, confirmed Pearse's comment on weapons.[89]

On turning to leave, Doyle recalled saying, '"We will soon meet again I suppose." He looked at me but said nothing. Although he seemed very tired his morale seemed to be very high and he gave me the impression he was well satisfied with what had happened.'[90] Doyle related the secret message to Enniscorthy IRB man Sean Whelan. Pat Keegan, nonetheless, wished to take to the mountains with a flying column when a report of the meeting was given in the Athenaeum.[91]

A British 'military touring car' transferred Pearse to Richmond Barracks shortly afterwards, where his court martial took place.

After an enforced gap in publication, the *Irish Times* reappeared on Dublin streets on the morning of Monday, 1 May, with an editorial regarding 'The Insurrection' that named

'P. H. Pearse' as one of the seven 'ringleaders'. The editor opined, 'we do not deny a certain desperate courage to many of the wretched men who today are in their graves of awaiting the sentence of their country's laws'.[92]

A typewritten document signed by Connolly identified MacDonagh, Ceannt, Mallin, Daly and De Valera as commanders. Orders appointing MacBride to assist in Jacob's Factory and others instructing Heuston to capture the Mendicity Institute were vital to securing their convictions, as was a letter from MacDiarmada summoning Volunteers to Liberty Hall on 24 April 1916.[93]

Bucknill received a letter from Maxwell answering Pearse's verbal request that the British accept his admission of full responsibility for the Rising in lieu of executing his men. This was passed unopened to Pearse in Richmond Barracks, 'who seemed quite calm and self-possessed, thanked him for the letter, read it and put it in his pocket without comment'.[94]

William O'Brien and others detained in the Custom House were brought to Richmond Barracks on 1 May, passing a hostile crowd on the way of 'mainly ... separation allowance women'.[95] On the morning of 2 May, he was sent to the gymnasium, where many high-ranking Volunteers were congregated, including MacDonagh, Ceannt, Mac-Bride and O'Hanrahan. O'Brien was informed that Pearse had been there earlier to share breakfast but had then left as 'it was understood that he slept in Arbour Hill'.[96]

Pearse was also sighted in Richmond Barracks by Volunteers awaiting trial, who saluted him 'in a very respectful manner'.[97] When Gerald Doyle, a member of B Company, 4th Battalion, arrived on 2 May, Harry Boland and Jack Shouldice told him that their leader had been 'brought into the end section of the block where Courtmartials were taking place. He had been there for some time'.[98] They awaited his reappearance:

> Pearse came out of the building and faced us on the green. All at once, all prisoners sprang to their feet and stood to attention. He smiled at us, saluted, and marched off under an escort of officers … His very attitude gave courage to everyone of us who were to face our trial, in turn.[99]

Thomas Pugh of B Company, 2nd Battalion, also sighted Pearse in the square: 'cleanly shaved and brushed and looking ten feet high, with a huge guard around him'.[100]

Courts martial were operated by military officers, no legal counsel was provided to defendants, and they were not bound by the same strict rules about evidence as were civil trials. Even so, acquiring and collating the factual details and testimony necessary to convict hundreds of captured rebels on capital charges posed challenges. Bucknill recalled that 'it was obvious from the commencement that there would be great difficulty in getting sufficient legal evidence to pin any particular offence against any particular person'.[101] It was pertinent that the rebels had 'surrendered with arms in their hands' because possession of weaponry constituted circumstantial evidence of engagement in a conspiracy to assist 'the enemy'.[102]

Designated 'Prisoner No. 1', Pearse's court martial was presided over by Major-General Charles Guinand Blackader. Lieutenant Colonel G. German and Lieutenant Colonel W. J. Kent were also on the panel. Various military and DMP witnesses testified to Pearse having exercised command in the GPO, although nobody had witnessed him firing upon let alone killing soldiers.

It was a closing remark in a letter Pearse had written to his mother on 1 May from Arbour Hill Barracks that was seized upon by the court martial as evidence of his 'aiding the enemy'. The phrase in question read, 'I have reason to believe that the German expedition on which I counted actually set sail but was defeated by the British fleet.'[103] The intercepted private letter was produced as evidence, and Bucknill claimed that 'the prosecution would have been in some difficulty without this postscript'.[104]

Pearse clarified: 'I asked and accepted German aid in the shape of arms and an expeditionary force. We neither asked for nor accepted German gold.'[105] This confession was damning, as was the presence of Pearse's name on the Proclamation and Address. On being found guilty and sentenced to 'death by being shot', General Maxwell quickly confirmed the decision, and Pearse was transferred to Kilmainham Prison that evening.[106]

Following his in-camera court martial, Pearse set out his recollections about what had taken place and in particular what he had said to those he accepted would sentence him to death. Having acknowledged being 'Commandant-General Commanding in Chief the forces of the Irish Republic' and 'President of their Provisional Government', he averred that he stood over 'all ... acts and words done or spoken in these capacities'. He had told his captors,

> I fully understand now, as then, that my own life is forfeit to British Law, and I shall die cheerfully if I can think that the British Government as it has already shown itself strong, will now show itself magnanimous enough to accept my single life in forfeiture and to give a general amnesty to the brave men and boys who have fought at my bidding.[107]

Denied access to her son, Mrs Pearse was additionally deprived of the letter. The document was intended to be more than a personal message, containing as it did passages that read as the political testament of an unrepentant revolutionary facing execution:

> We do not expect that they will spare the lives of the leaders. We are ready to die and we shall die cheerfully and

proudly. Personally I do not hope or even desire to live, but I do hope and desire and believe that the lives of all our followers will be saved ... You must not grieve for all this. We have preserved Ireland's honour and our own. Our deeds of last week are the most splendid in Ireland's history. People will say hard things of us now, but we shall be remembered by posterity and blessed by unborn generations.[108]

Following conviction, Pearse and MacDonagh were visited by Fr Aloysius, while Clarke received Fr Columbus.[109] Fr Aloysius was awoken late on Tuesday night with the news that a military car awaited him as 'Prisoner Pearse desired to see me.'[110] Sniper fire obliged the vehicle to approach Kilmainham indirectly.

A car was sent to bring Mrs Pearse to Kilmainham on the eve of the executions, yet, notwithstanding its official purpose, it was halted by military patrols and not permitted to proceed.[111] When the matter was raised in the House of Commons on 15 May, the Under-Secretary of State for War resorted to semantics to insist that Mrs Pearse had not been 'refused' access.[112]

In the meantime, Fr Aloysius 'spent some hours', stretching into the early part of 3 May, speaking separately to Pearse and MacDonagh:

When I met Pearse I said 'I am sure you will be glad to know that I gave Holy Communion to James Connolly this morning.' I can't forget the fervour with which, looking up to heaven, he said 'Thank God, It is the one thing I was anxious about' ... They received the M[ost] B[lessed] Sacrament with intense devotion and spent the time at their disposal in prayer. They were happy – no trace of fear or anxiety. Pearse had written some notes for his mother. He said that he knew I could not take them, nor would he wish me to do so, but would be glad if I could ask the officer in charge to have them conveyed to his mother ... Between 2 and 3 all visitors were ordered to leave. I thought that it would be my right to remain to the end but the officer said I should leave ... when I reached Church Street I offered Mass for them.[113]

Brigadier E. W. Maconchy, OC of the 59th Division, organised the executions, in conjunction with Brigadier G. Young who was in charge of the prison. At 9 p.m. on 2 May, Sergeant Lomas was instructed to assemble forty-eight men and four sergeants at 3 a.m. the next day for 'a special duty'. The men paraded as required and marched from Arbour Hill to Kilmainham Gaol, where they were tasked with forming four twelve-man firing squads. One man in twelve was issued a blank cartridge to permit the private illusion of non-complicity in what was a cold-blooded affair.

Captain H. V. Stanley attended the executions, which proceeded after a short delay arising from a query on the court-martial paperwork.[114] Pearse, MacDonagh and Clarke descended to the Stonebreakers Yard, where they were halted in a passage to be blindfolded. Pieces of paper were pinned to their coats to mark the heart as target. Two areas were used by the firing squads, selected on the basis that they could not be seen from cell windows. Sergeant Lomas noted:

> At 3.45 the first rebel MacDonoghue [Thomas MacDonagh] was marched in blindfolded, and the firing party placed 10 paces distant. Death was instantaneous. The second, P. H. Pierce [sic] whistled as he came out of the cell (after taking a sad farewell of his wife [sic]). The same applied to him. The third, J. H. Clarke [Tom Clarke], an old man, was not quite so fortunate, requiring a bullet from the officer to complete the ghastly business (it was sad to think that these three brave men who met their death so bravely should be fighting for a cause which proved so useless and had been the means of so much bloodshed).[115]

The inaccuracies in Lomas's report may well have stemmed from the extremity of the occasion. In 1954, Bucknill confided in F. H. Boland, the Irish Ambassador in London, that 'officers in charge of the execution squads had to report to him, as legal officer of the Command, for the certification of their deaths. It was one of these officers who told him that Thomas MacDonagh was whistling when he came down from the steps into the execution yard.'[116] This second-hand account was almost certainly correct, the Lomas testimony confusing the first two victims. Pearse, the most famous and senior of the IRA commanders, would have been the first of the sixteen to be executed. Moreover, Pearse was not married, unlike MacDonagh.[117]

In his last letter to his family, Pearse wrote,

> This is the death I should have asked for if God had given me the choice of all deaths, to die a soldier's death for Ireland and for freedom. We have done right. People will say hard things of us now, but later on they will praise us. Do not grieve for all of this but think of it as a sacrifice which God asked of me and of you.[118]

The bodies were taken to Arbour Hill Detention Barracks for burial in a pre-prepared 'large grave'.[119] A pit lined with quicklime had been commissioned by General Maxwell immediately following his arrival from London.[120] While Fr Edward Morrissey, Chaplain of Kilmainham Prison, exercised his prerogative to be present for the executions, he was not permitted to conduct religious ceremonies. Arbour Hill Chaplain, Fr Francis Farrington, was roused from his Aughrim Street home at 3 a.m. and taken to Arbour Hill. He 'read the burial service' over the three bodies at 4 a.m.[121] Farrington detailed, for the clerical record, 'the arrival of the remains, in pools of blood, still warm and limp, eyes bandaged and mouths open. Those who brought them back said, of Pearse in particular, that he died like a soldier and a man.'[122]

No provision was made to deliver the remains to the next of kin. British statute law required that those executed inside prisons must be interred on site (Section 6 of the Capital Punishment Act, 1864). This prevented traditional funeral rites, not least of which burial in consecrated ground, and was presumably intended to add to the deterrence of the death penalty. Yet Maxwell had ordered the removal of the bodies from Kilmainham to Arbour Hill and, in so doing, violated the letter of the law while dismissing any avenue of magnanimity. He destroyed the bodies of those executed, a ritualised medieval desecration, and endeavoured to deny them posthumous veneration: 'the executed rebels are to buried in quicklime, without coffins'.[123] Maxwell confirmed on 25 May, 'Irish sentimentality will turn those graves into martyrs' shrines to which annual processions etc will be made.'[124] Dr Edward O'Dwyer, Bishop of Limerick, castigated this callousness and on 17 July 1917 was widely reported as criticising the denial of Christian burial.[125]

In Kilmainham, Staines recalled, 'On the 3rd May we heard the three volleys and we knew that they were gone ... Next morning we heard four volleys and knew four more were gone.'[126] Secrecy inculcated dread. Gerald Doyle, once reliable information filtered through, was more assured: 'as the day of our trial came and we knew the way in which P. H. Pearse, Thomas MacDonagh and Tom Clarke met their death, we were also keyed up to show our captors that we also would have courage to face our doom.'[127]

A 'stop press' edition of the *Evening Mail* announced the first executions on the morning of 3 May.[128] Later that morning, Fr Aloysius travelled to St Enda's to speak to Mrs Margaret Pearse. He gave his opinion that he did not think that Willie Pearse would be shot: '"No", she said, "I believe they will put him to death too. They were inseparable. Willie would never be happy to live without Pat."'[129] Mrs Pearse was stoic when informed of the execution of her second son and seemed 'a picture of calm sorrow, resignation and hope'.[130] She told Fr Eugene Nevin, a family associate, 'thank God they both died for Ireland. I am sure they are pleased and what pleased them in life they knew pleased me, so I am satisfied.'[131] An associate of ex-IPP leader John Dillon told their sister, Margaret Mary Pearse, that he 'never saw [Dillon] in such a towering rage as the day Pearse was executed and never so downhearted as the day that Willie Pearse was executed'.[132]

Dillon received Fr Aloysius at his home in North Great George's Street on 7 May. He said that despite the damage inflicted on the Home Rule programme, 'he admired their courage and respected their convictions. He had always had esteem for Patrick Pearse … Anything he could do to prevent further executions he certainly would do. He took my car and drove straight to the Castle and got through a tele-gram to John Redmond in Westminster.'[133] Dillon's interces-sions failed to induce the authorities to surrender the bodies of the Pearse brothers for Christian burial.[134] Meanwhile, diplomatic representations from Paris, Washington, DC and further afield steeled Prime Minister Asquith to rein in General Maxwell and to act, with notable exceptions, more leniently towards those sentenced to death and long terms of imprisonment. T. M. Healy KC, who had known Pearse as a barrister and in general life, noted on 18 June 1916, 'This has been one of the most successful rebellions in the world, from the standpoint of its authors. It has revolutionised Irish feeling, and I suppose that was what Pearse aimed at.'[135]

In 1947, Hobson erred in declaring that the Military Coun-cil had 'no plans ... which could seriously be called military' and that conscription was likely to flow from a misfired 'dem-onstration'. He viewed the Rising as 'locking a body of men up in two or three buildings to stay there until they were shot or burned out'.[136] It was MacNeill's associates who reduced 1916 to the overwhelmingly urban zones where it took place contrary to plans laid by the Military Committee. This is sig-nificant as Hobson, more than anyone, promoted the false-hood that the Rising was underpinned by a cult of 'Blood Sacrifice', which his skeletal pastiche image of Pearse seem-ingly lent credence. In January 1948, Hobson reflected:

He was a sentimental egotist, full of curious Old Testament theories about being the scapegoat for the people, and he became convinced of the necessity for a periodic blood sacrifice to keep the National spirit alive. There was a certain strain of abnormality in all this. He did not contribute greatly to the hard grinding work of building up the movement, but as soon as we had succeeded in getting a small organisation and a handful of arms he seized the opportunity to bring about the blood sacrifice.[137]

This assessment discounted the importance of Pearse as an IRB authority and mentee of the powerful Clarke. His administrative, public-relations and fund-raising efforts as Director of Organisation were unquestioned, even if his seniority in the IRB derived from co-option.[138] It is true that his public rhetoric, in common with contemporary reformists, revolutionaries, generals, prime ministers, dissidents and poets across the Western world, drew promiscuously upon biblical allusions. Stressing virtues of duty, selflessness and courage in a greater cause, within the numbing context of industrialised warfare, was par for the course from Dublin to Sydney.

If Pearse was prepared and possibly wished to die securing a democratic Irish republic, he was by no means a morbid Celtic jihadist. He and other IRB–Volunteer leaders held that the Rising was inherently justifiable owing to its progressive objectives. Irish sovereignty would be either achieved or advanced.

The political agenda for which Pearse gave his life and which warranted him a place in Irish history was soon vindicated. When, in the course of 1917, the IRA regrouped organisationally, the republican message of Sinn Féin grew in appeal to the electorate. Obliged to extend the franchise to most men and women in December 1918, the explicit manifesto of an independent, sovereign, Irish republic was massively endorsed by the first truly democratic elections in the United Kingdom of Great Britain and Ireland. This mandated the Irish War of Independence in January 1919 when the unrecognised First Dáil incorporated the text of the 1916 Proclamation into its democratic programme. Pearse and his comrades had indeed succeeded in breathing new life into an ancient nation.

Bibliography

Primary (Select)

American Irish History Society (New York), Cohalan Papers

Bureau of Military History, Irish Military Archives, Witness Statements

National Archives of Ireland, Chief Secretary's Office Papers

National Library of Ireland, MS 17,306

Pearse Museum, Office of Public Works, MSS

University of Limerick Special Collections, Glucksman Library, Geary Papers,

Daly Papers

Private collections

O'Reilly Papers, Private Collection (Holt Moore)

Statement of James (Jim) Clarke, Private Collection (Pierse/Buckley).

Printed primary (newspapers and periodicals)

An Barr Buadh

An Claidheamh Soluis

An Macaom

An tÓglach

Connaught Tribune

Daily Herald

Enniscorthy Echo

Freeman's Journal

Gaelic American

Hibernian

Irish Freedom

Irish Independent

Irish Republican News

Irish Times

Irish Volunteer

Irish War News

Irish Worker

Kildare Observer

Leinster Leader

Limerick Chronicle

Limerick Leader

Limerick Post

Ná Bac Leis

Nationality

New York Journal-American

Northern Patriot

United Irishman

Saoirse

Shan Van Vocht

Sinn Féin

Sunday Independent

Western People

Wolfe Tone Annual

Workers' Republic

Printed primary (other)

Ashe Fitzgerald, Mairéad (ed.), *A Terrible Beauty: Poetry of 1916* (Dublin: The O'Brien Press, 2015).

Brennan-Whitmore, Charles, *Dublin Burning: The Easter Rising from behind the Barricades*, new edition (Dublin: Gill & Macmillan, 2013).

Dublin's Fighting Story, 1916–21: Told by the Men who Made It, with an introduction by Diarmuid Ferriter (Cork: Mercier Press, 2009). First published 1950.

Good, Joe, *Inside the GPO 1916: A First-Hand Account* (Dublin: The O'Brien Press, 2015).

Jeffrey, Keith (ed.), *The Sinn Féin Rebellion as They Saw It* (Dublin: Irish Academic Press, 1999).

Limerick's Fighting Story, 1916–21: Told by the Men who Made It, with an introduction by Ruán O'Donnell (Cork: Mercier, 2009).

MacBride, Seán, *That Day's Struggle: A Memoir, 1904–1951*, ed. Catriona Lawlor (Dublin: Curragh Press, 2005).

MacEoin, Uinseann, *Survivors: The Story of Ireland's Struggle as Told through Some of Her Outstanding Living People Recalling Events from the Days of Davitt, through James Connolly, Brugha, Collins, Liam Mellows and Rory O'Connor to the Present Time*, 2nd edn (Dublin: Argenta, 1987).

Martin, F. X. (ed.), *The Howth Gunrunning and the Kilcoole Gunrunning*, new edition (Dublin: Irish Academic Press, 2014). First published 1964.

—— (ed.), *The Irish Volunteers, 1913–1915: Recollections and Documents*, new edition (Dublin: Irish Academic Press, 2013). First published 1963.

Mullin, James, *The Story of a Toiler's Life*, new edition (Dublin: University College Dublin Press, 2000). First published 1921.

O'Buachalla, Seamus (ed.), *The Letters of P. H. Pearse* (Dublin: Colin Smythe, 1980).

—— *Pádraig Mac Piarais agus Éire Lena Linn* (Dublin: Mercier, 1979).

O Gaora, Colm, *On the Run: The Story of an Irish Freedom Fighter*, new edition (Cork: Mercier, 2011).

O'Rahilly, Michael (The O'Rahilly), *The Secret History of the Irish Volunteers* (Dublin: Irish Publicity League, 1915).

Pearse, Mary Brigid (ed.), *The Home-Life of Pádraig Pearse, as Told by Himself, His Family, and Friends* (Dublin: Browne & Nolan, 1934).

Pearse, Patrick, *The Story of a Success: Being a Record of St Enda's College, September 1908 to Easter 1916*, ed. Desmond Ryan (Dublin and London: Maunsel & Company Ltd., 1917).

—— *Plays, Stories, Poems* (Dublin, 1980).

Pearse, Patrick, Thomas MacDonagh, Arthur Griffith, James Connolly, Brian O'Higgins, *Diarmuid Ó Donnabháin Rosa, 1831–1915: Souvenir of Public Funeral to Glasnevin Cemetery, Dublin, August 1st, 1915 with second edition* (Dublin: O'Donovan Rossa Funeral Committee, 1915).

Plunkett, Geraldine, 'Foreword', *The Poems of Joseph Mary Plunkett* (Dublin, n.d.).

Stephens, James, *The Insurrection in Dublin* (Gerrards Cross: Colin Smythe, 1978). First published 1916.

Secondary

Augusteijn, Joost, *Patrick Pearse: The Making of a Revolutionary* (London: Palgrave Macmillan, 2010).

Barton, Brian, *From Behind a Closed Door: Secret Court Martial Records of the 1916 Easter Rising* (Belfast: Blackstaff, 2002).

Collins, Lorcan, *James Connolly* (Dublin: The O'Brien Press, 2012).

Combri Group, HQ16: The Citizen's Plan for Dublin, Part 1 (Dublin, 2012). Available online at www.gaelicadventure.org/pdfs/h16.pdf (accessed 3 November 2015).

Comerford, R. V., *Charles J. Kickham: A Study in Irish Nationalism and Literature* (Dublin: Wolfhound, 1979).

Connell, Joseph E. A., Jnr., *Dublin Rising 1916* (Dublin: Wordwell, 2015).

Cronin, Jim, *Millstreet's Green and Gold* (Cork, 1984).

Crowley, Brian, *Patrick Pearse: A Life in Pictures* (Cork: Mercier, 2013).

de Burca, Seamus, *The Soldier's Song: The Story of Peadar O Cearnaigh* (Dublin: P. J. Burke, 1957).

Edwards, Ruth Dudley, *Patrick Pearse: The Triumph of Failure* (Dublin: Irish Academic Press, 2006). First published 1979.

Ellis, John, *The Social History of the Machinegun* (Baltimore, Md.: Johns Hopkins University Press, 1986).

Greaves, C. Desmond, *Liam Mellows and the Irish Revolution* (London: Lawrence & Wishart, 1971).

Hammond, Joseph W., 'Town Major Henry Charles Sirr', *Dublin Historical Record*, 4 (1) (1941): 14–75.

Jordan, Anthony J., *Seán MacBride* (Dublin: Blackwater Press, 1993).

Kenna, Shane, *Thomas MacDonagh* (Dublin: The O'Brien Press, 2014).

Kenna, Shane, *Conspirators: A Photographic History of Ireland's Revolutionary Underground* (Cork: Mercier Press, 2015).

16 LIVES: PATRICK PEARSE

Le Roux, Louis N., *Patrick H. Pearse* (Dublin: The Talbot Press, 1932).

Lee, J. J., 'Pearse, Patrick Henry', in James McGuire and James Quinn (eds.), *Dictionary of Irish Biography from the Earliest Times to the Year 2002* (Cambridge: Cambridge University Press, 2009–).

Litton, Helen, *Edward Daly* (Dublin: The O'Brien Press, 2013).

Litton, Helen, *Thomas Clarke* (Dublin: The O'Brien Press, 2014).

Macardle, Dorothy, *The Irish Republic* (London: Victor Gollancz, 1937).

Malone, Tom, *Alias Sean Forde: The Story of Commandant Tomás Malone, Vice OC East Limerick Flying Column, Irish Republican Army* (Dublin: Danesfort Publications, 2000).

Martin, F. X. (ed.), *Leaders and Men of the Easter Rising: Dublin 1916* (London: Methuen, 1967).

Ní Ghairbhí, Róisín, *Willie Pearse* (Dublin: The O'Brien Press, 2015).

Ó Broin, Leon, *Dublin Castle and the 1916 Rising* (Dublin: Helicon, 1966).

O'Donnell, Ruán, *Robert Emmet and the Rising of 1803* (Dublin: Irish Academic Press, 2003).

Ó Súilleabháin, Adhamhnán, *Domhnall Ua Buachalla: Rebellious Nationalist, Reluctant Governor* (Dublin: Irish Academic Press, 2015).

O'Sullivan, Donal J., *District Inspector John A. Kearney: The RIC Man who Befriended Sir Roger Casement* (Victoria, BC: Trafford, 2005).

Pearse, Patrick, *Collected Plays/Drámaí an Phiarsaigh*, ed. Róisín Ní Ghairbhí and Eugene McNulty (Dublin: Irish Academic Press, 2013).

Ryan, Desmond, *A Man Called Pearse* (Dublin and London: Maunsel & Company Ltd., 1919).

—— *The Rising: The Complete Story of Easter Week* (Dublin: Golden Eagle Books, 1957).

Thornley, David, 'Patrick Pearse: The Evolution of a Republican', in F. X. Martin (ed.), *Leaders and Men of the Easter Rising: Dublin 1916* (London: Methuen, 1967), pp. 151–63.

Townshend, Charles, *Easter 1916: The Irish Rebellion* (London: Allen Lane, 2005).

Walsh, Brendan, *Boy Republic: Patrick Pearse and Radical Education* (Dublin: History Press Ireland, 2013).

Zelenetz, Alan, 'Education and the Gael: Pádraig Pearse's Scoil Éanna', *Proceedings of the Harvard Celtic Colloquium*, 18/19 (1998/9): 445–56.

Notes

Chapter 1

1. Róisín Ní Ghairbhí, *Willie Pearse* (Dublin: The O'Brien Press, 2015), pp. 21–3; Brian Crowley, *Patrick Pearse: A Life in Pictures* (Cork: Mercier, 2013), Chapter 1; and P. H. Pearse, 'Fragment of Autobiography', MS, Pearse Museum. For general family background see Louis N. Le Roux, *Patrick H. Pearse* (Dublin: The Talbot Press, 1932); Ruth Dudley Edwards, *Patrick Pearse: The Triumph of Failure* (Dublin: Irish Academic Press, 2006), first published 1979; and Joost Augusteijn, *Patrick Pearse: The Making of a Revolutionary* (London: Palgrave Macmillan, 2010).

2. *Irish Freedom*, December 1913.

3. *Irish Freedom*, January 1914.

4. Desmond Ryan, *A Man Called Pearse* (Dublin and London: Maunsel & Company Ltd., 1919), pp. 27–9; and Ní Ghairbhí, *Willie Pearse*, p. 28.

5. P. H. Pearse, 2 May 1916, NLI, MS 17,306, pp. 1–2. For a variant, see Brian Barton, *From Behind a Closed Door: Secret Court Martial Records of the 1916 Easter Rising* (Belfast: Blackstaff, 2002), p. 117.

6. Ní Ghairbhí, *Willie Pearse*, pp. 31–2.

7. Ní Ghairbhí, *Willie Pearse*, p. 37.

8. Pearse, 'Autobiography', MS, Pearse Museum. See also Brian Crowley, '"His Father's Son": James and Patrick Pearse', *Folk Life, Journal of Ethnological Studies*, 43 (2004–5).

9. Crowley, *Patrick Pearse*, pp. 22–3.

10. *Irish Freedom*, December 1913.

11. See J. J. Lee, 'Pearse, Patrick Henry', in James McGuire and James Quinn (eds.), *Dictionary of Irish Biography from the Earliest Times to the Year 2002* (Cambridge: Cambridge University Press, 2009–).

12. *Irish Times*, 10 September 1900.

13. Ní Ghairbhí, *Willie Pearse*, pp. 50–1.

14. *Census of Ireland, 1901*, Form B 363.

15. Ní Ghairbhí, *Willie Pearse*, p. 64.

16. See *Irish Times*, 24 December 1907, for report of Willie Pearse's prize-winning sculpture. Ní Ghairbhí, *Willie Pearse*, p. 64.

17. David Thornley, 'Patrick Pearse: The Evolution of a Republican', in F. X. Martin (ed.), *Leaders and Men of the Easter Rising: Dublin 1916* (London: Methuen, 1967), pp. 151–63,

at p. 155. Cited in Alan Zelenetz, 'Education and the Gael: Pádraig Pearse's Scoil Éanna', *Proceedings of the Harvard Celtic Colloquium*, 18/19 (1998/9): 445–56.

18. Edward O'Neill and Patrick H. Pearse, Circular, c. November 1896, in Seamus O'Buachalla (ed.), *The Letters of P. H. Pearse* (Dublin: Colin Smythe, 1980), p. 485.

19. Patrick Pearse to Eoin MacNeill, 20 December 1897, in O'Buachalla, *Letters of P. H. Pearse*, p. 3.

20. *Irish Times*, 27 June 2015.

21. Ryan, *A Man Called Pearse*, p. 30.

22. James Mullin, *The Story of a Toiler's Life*, new edition (Dublin: University College Dublin Press, 2000), p. 202.

23. Ua Caomhanaigh, BMH, WS 889, pp. 1–13. See also *Connaught Tribune*, 5 April 1902.

24. Ua Caomhanaigh, BMH, WS 889, pp. 1–13.

25. Sean T. O'Kelly, BMH, WS 1765, p. 4.

26. O'Buachalla, *Letters of P. H. Pearse*, p. 3.

27. *Weekly Irish Times*, 31 January 1903.

28. *Irish Times*, 17 March 1904.

29. Zelenetz, 'Education and the Gael', p. 449.

30. O'Kelly, BMH, WS 1765, pp. 70–3.

31. Crowley, *Patrick Pearse*, p. 39.

32. Colm O Gaora, *On the Run: The Story of an Irish Freedom Fighter*, new edition (Cork: Mercier, 2011), p. 54.

33. O'Kelly, BMH, WS 1765, pp. 74–6.

34. J. J. ('Scelig') O'Kelly, NAI, BMH, WS 384, p. 15.

35. Denis F. Madden, BMH, WS 1103, p. 4.

36. *An Claidheamh Soluis*, November 1904.

37. Crowley, *Patrick Pearse*, p. 41.

38. Cited in Aidan Doyle, 'An Irishman's Diary', *Irish Times*, 27 June 2015, p. 17. The phrase was widely used in republican circles, including the pro-Fenian Henry Joy McCracken Literary Society of Belfast during the United Irishman centenaries. *The Northern Patriot*, February 1896. For use of the toast 'Ireland a Nation' in Buenos Aires, Argentina, see *Shan Van Vocht*, 7 June 1897, and *United Irishman*, 17 March 1902.

39. *United Irishman*, 24 May 1902.

40. O'Kelly, BMH, WS 1765, p. 26.

41. O'Kelly, BMH, WS 1765, p. 44.

42. *Irish Times*, 25 February 1905.

43. *Irish Times*, 24 March 1905.

44. *Irish Times*, 8 April 1905. Pearse seconded a Tom Kettle motion at the Catholic Graduates and Undergraduates Association AGM in the Gresham Hotel on Thursday, 16 November 1905. *Irish Times*, 20 November 1905.

45. *Irish Times*, 17 May 1905.

46. Piaras Béaslaí, 'Pearse at the Bar', in O'Kelly, BMH, WS 1765, p. 14.

47. *Irish Times*, 17 May 1905.

48. *Irish Times*, 19 May 1905.

49. Adhamhnán Ó Súilleabháin, *Domhnall Ua Buachalla: Rebellious Nationalist, Reluctant Governor* (Dublin: Irish Academic Press, 2015), pp. 33–4. Ua Buachalla, aka Donal 'Dan' Buckley, secured the teaching services of Revd Michael O'Hickey, Professor of Irish at Maynooth College. Patrick Colgan, BMH, WS 850, p. 1.

50. Colgan, BMH, WS 850, p. 2.

51. Cited in Ó Súilleabháin, *Domhnall Ua Buachalla*, pp. 34–5.

52. *Limerick Post*, 8 March 2014. See Seamus O'Buachalla, *Padraig Mac Piarais agus Éire lena Linn* (Dublin: Mercier, 1979), p. 47.

53. *Irish Times*, 12 January 1907.

54. See www.irishmusicdaily.com.

55. O Gaora, *On the Run*, p. 55.

56. O Gaora, *On the Run*, p. 49.

57. O Gaora, *On the Run*, p. 145.

58. O Gaora, *On the Run*, p. 57.

59. Dr Philip Murphy, BMH, WS 1197, pp. 1–2.

60. See 'Education, Sgoil Éanna', *Freeman's Journal*, 1 August 1908, and *Irish Independent*, 12 August 1908.

61. *Freeman's Journal*, 1 August 1908. See also *Irish Times*, 23 June 1909.

62. Patrick Pearse, 'By Way of Comment', *An Macaomh*, 1 (1) (1909): 7.

63. *An Macaomh*, 1 (1) (1909): 70.

64. Patrick Pearse, 'St Enda's College Doing National Work for Ireland', *Gaelic American*, 7 March 1914, p. 5.

65. Pax O'Faoláin, in Uinseann MacEoin, *Survivors: The Story of Ireland's Struggle as Told through Some of Her Outstanding Living People Recalling Events from the Days of Davitt, through James Connolly, Brugha, Collins, Liam Mellows and Rory O'Connor to the Present Time*, 2nd edn (Dublin: Argenta, 1987), p. 135.

66. O'Faoláin, in MacEoin, *Survivors*, p. 135.

67. Eamon Bulfin, BMH, WS 497, p. 1.

68. O'Kelly, BMH, WS 1765, pp. 98–9.

69. Frank de Burca, BMH, WS 694, p. 1. Dr de Burca, BMH, WS 105, p. 1. Dr de Burca, an employee of the British Excise Service, recruited IRB men from GAA clubs in London prior to his transfer to Belfast. When working in Kilkenny he inducted Thomas MacDonagh into the IRB (BMH, WS 105, pp. 1–2).

70. Patrick Pearse to Domhnall Ua Buachalla, August 1908, in Ó Súilleabháin, *Domhnall Ua Buachalla*, p. 39. See also O'Buachalla Collection, Kilmainham Gaol Museum, 2011/0550.

71. Desmond Ryan, BMH, WS 725, p. 1.

72. Pearse, 'St Enda's', *Gaelic American*, 7 March 1914, p. 7. Kevin Henehen, a Seattle youth of Galway parentage, was briefly enrolled in St Enda's. See Patrick Pearse to Mr Henehen, 17 October 1910, in O'Buachalla, *Letters of P. H. Pearse*, p. 471.

73. *Freeman's Journal*, 22 April 1909. The 'midsummer close' of the school on 22 June 1909 was marked by an even more elaborate play inspired by the story of Cuchulain: 'warriors, monks, hurlers, women, musicians and deerhounds took part in the presentation'. Eoin MacNeill distributed awards. *Irish Times*, 23 June 1909.

74. *Freeman's Journal*, 2 April 1910.

75. *Freeman's Journal*, 2 April 1910.

76. *Irish Independent*, 19 February 1910.

77. *Western People*, 24 July 1909.

78. *Irish Independent*, 19 February 1910.

79. *Freeman's Journal*, 20 October 1909. Revd Professor Tas of St Pieter's College, Brussels, visited St Enda's on 12 September 1912 to observe its bilingual methodology. *Irish Times*, 9 September 1912. International links were pursued in May 1913 when students performed a play at the Abbey Theatre written by Indian poet Rabindranath Tagore. Lennox Robinson produced the well-received performance, which was followed by a one-act morality play, *Rí*, written by Pearse. *Irish Times*, 22 April and 19 May 1913.

80. *Irish Independent*, 5 April 1910.

81. Crowley, *Patrick Pearse*, pp. 86–7.

82. Louise Gavan Duffy, BMH, WS 216, p. 1.

83. Patrick Pearse to D. O'Connor, 3 September 1912, in O'Buachalla, *Letters of P. H. Pearse*, p. 283.

84. Pearse to O'Connor, 3 September 1912.

85. O'Kelly, BMH, WS 1765, p. 26.

86. O'Kelly, BMH, WS 1765, pp. 26–7.

87. O'Kelly, BMH, WS 1765, pp. 26–7.

88. O'Kelly, BMH, WS 1765, p. 28.

89. Maeve McGarry, BMH, WS 826, p. 3.

90. McGarry, BMH, WS 826, p. 3.

91. Kitty O'Doherty, BMH, WS 355, p. 3.

92. Crowley, *Patrick Pearse*, pp. 94–5.

93. O'Kelly, BMH, WS 1765, p. 72.

94. Sighle Bean Uí Dhonnchadha, in MacEoin, *Survivors*, pp. 331–2.

95. Diary of Dick Humphreys in MacEoin, *Survivors*, p. 333. Clarke belonged to an IRB family from Meath with Kerry and Dublin associations. Jim Clarke of Ballybunion, originally Dowth, was a close friend of Austin Stack. His brother Phil Clarke knew James Connolly and was killed in 1916. 'Statement of James (Jim) Clarke', Typescript, Private Collection (Pierse/Buckley).

96. Humphreys Diary, p. 334.

97. Ruán O'Donnell, *Robert Emmet and the Rising of 1803* (Dublin: Irish Academic Press, 2003), pp. 117–18; and Joseph W. Hammond, 'Town Major Henry Charles Sirr', *Dublin Historical Record*, 4 (1) (1941): 14–75.

98. Humphreys Diary, p. 334.

99. Uí Dhonnachada, in MacEoin, *Survivors*, p. 338.

100. See *An Claidheamh Soluis*, July 1909, and Alfred White, BMH, WS 1207, p. 3.

101. Michael Lonergan, BMH, WS 140, p. 2.

102. Bulfin, BMH, WS 497, pp. 1–2.

103. Bulfin, BMH, WS 497, pp. 1–2. Bulfin claimed to have met Liam and Barney Mellows, Eamon Martin, Gerry and Paddy Holahan, Liam Ryan and Michael Lonergan in Colbert's Circle. He then 'introduced' St Enda's boys Frank de Burca, Fintan Murphy, Des Ryan, Joe Sweeney, Conor and Eunan McGinley 'and others' (BMH, WS 497, p. 1).

104. *Irish Times*, 15 April 1913.

105. Humphreys Diary, p. 334.

106. MacBride in MacEoin, *Survivors*, p. 108. See also Seán MacBride, *That Day's Struggle: A Memoir, 1904–1951*, ed. Caitriona Lawlor (Dublin: Curragh Press, 2005), p. 16.

107. Anthony J. Jordan, *Seán MacBride* (Dublin: Blackwater Press, 1993), p. 19; and MacBride in MacEoin, *Survivors*, p. 110.

Chapter 2

1. Ryan, BMH, WS 725, p. 2.

2. Ryan, *A Man Called Pearse*, p. 5.

3. Ryan, BMH, WS 725, p. 2.

4. *An Claidheamh Soluis*, 8 November 1913, p. 7.

5. *An Claidheamh Soluis*, 8 November 1913, p. 7.

6. Ryan, BMH, WS 725, p. 2.

7. Ryan, BMH, WS 725, p. 2.

8. McCartan, BMH, WS 766, p. 6. MacDiarmada had worked in Glasgow as a train conductor before returning to Ireland and joining the IRB. He was an 'organiser' in 1907. O'Kelly, BMH, WS 1765, p. 41. McCullough's uncle John was an associate of McGarrity in Philadelphia. McCullough, BMH, WS 915, p. 3.

9. McCartan, BMH, WS 766, pp. 24–5. See also Diarmuid Lynch, BMH, WS 4, p. 3.

10. McCartan, BMH, WS 766, p. 20.

11. Pat McCartan, BMH, WS 100, p. 3.

12. Thomas Barry, BMH, WS 1, p. 2.

13. McCartan, BMH, WS 766, pp. 20–1.

14. McCartan, BMH, WS 766, pp. 21–2.

15. McCartan, BMH, WS 100, pp. 6–7.

16. De Burca, BMH, WS 105, p. 2.

17. McCartan, BMH, WS 766, p. 25.

18. McCartan, BMH, WS 766, p. 25. O'Hegarty had been a mainstay of the Gaelic League in London, as well as the IRB, and was reputedly influential in cultivating the young Michael Collins when they were civil servants there. O'Kelly, BMH, WS 1765, p. 75.

19. O'Kelly, BMH, WS 1765, pp. 1–3.

20. Ceannt, BMH, WS 264, p. 5.

21. Ceannt, BMH, WS 264, p. 6.

22. See *Gaelic American*, 1 November 1913, p. 5.

23. O'Kelly, BMH, WS 925, p. 1.

24. Ruaidhri Henderson, 'Foreword', BMH, WS 1686.

25. Seamus de Burca, *The Soldier's Song: The Story of Peadar O Cearnaigh* (Dublin: P. J. Burke, 1957), p. 94.

26. De Burca, *Soldier's Song*, p. 94.

27. De Burca, *Soldier's Song*, p. 94.

28. *An Claidheamh Soluis*, 7 November 1913. See also Ceannt, BMH, WS 264, p. 16.

29. De Burca, *Soldier's Song*, pp. 94–5.

30. Bulfin, BMH, WS 497, p. 1.

31. Ryan, BMH, WS 725, p. 1.

32. Ryan, BMH, WS 725, p. 1.

33. Ryan, BMH, WS 725, p. 2.

34. See Chris Dooley, 'John Redmond's Finest Hour', *Irish Times*, 19 September 2015.

35. O'Kelly, BMH, WS 1765, p. 104.

36. Cited in *Irish Times*, 19 September 2015. See *An Barr Buadh*, 5 April 1912.

37. O'Kelly, BMH, WS 1765, p. 104.

38. Ryan, BMH, WS 725, p. 3.

39. Min Ryan, BMH, WS 399, p. 1.

40. Mortimer O'Connell, BMH, WS 804, pp. 10–11.

41. Ryan, BMH, WS 725, p. 3. According to Ryan, 'Dillon had an interview with Miss Pearse after the Rising and told her that he warned MacNeill that revolution was not his job and he ought to stay with the Irish [Parliamentary] Party crowd' (BMH, WS 725, p. 3).

42. *Irish Times*, 24 July 1911.

43. Bulfin, BMH, WS 497, p. 1.

44. Ryan, BMH, WS 725, p. 2. P. S. O'Hegarty had delayed the proposed induction of Michael Collins into the IRB in London 'for quite a long time' as there were concerns that he 'had been drinking too much'. Dr Brian A. Cusack, BMH, WS 736, p. 2.

45. *Irish Freedom*, June 1913. Pearse and Councillor J. T. O'Kelly were the main speakers at a Gaelic League rally in the Phoenix Park on 28 June 1913. *Irish Times*, 28 June 1913. His speech was militant in tone: 'Let people not think that the establishment of Home Rule in Dublin would make Ireland a nation. No, they had a lot to do before they built up an Irish nation.' *Irish Times*, 20 June 1913.

46. *Irish Freedom*, October 1913.

47. O'Kelly, BMH, WS 1765, p. 105.

48. Bulmer Hobson, BMH, WS 81, 'The Rising', p. 1.

49. The O'Rahilly, *The Secret History of the Irish Volunteers* (Dublin: Irish Publicity League, 1915), p. 3.

50. F. X. Martin (ed.), *The Irish Volunteers, 1913–1915: Recollections and Documents*, new edition (Dublin: Irish Academic Press, 2013), p. 39. Ryan, Campbell and Deakin soon

excused themselves from the committee (Martin, *The Irish Volunteers*).

51. McCullough, BMH, WS 915, p. 6.

52. O'Kelly, BMH, WS 1765, p. 105.

53. *Gaelic American*, 29 November 1913, p. 2.

54. *Gaelic American*, 29 November 1913, p. 2.

55. O'Connell, BMH, WS 804, p. 11.

56. Bulmer Hobson to the Editor, 14 November 1913, in *Gaelic American*, 29 November 1913, p. 2.

57. *Gaelic American*, 29 November 1913, p. 16.

58. *Freeman's Journal*, 21 November 1913.

59. See 'George Henry Moore and the Fenians', *Gaelic American*, 4 October 1913, p. 1.

60. *Nationality*, 17 July 1915, p. 4.

61. *Gaelic American*, 29 November 1913, p. 2.

62. *Gaelic American*, 29 November 1913, p. 8. See *The Hibernian*, 10 July 1915, p. 6.

63. *Gaelic American*, 29 November 1913, p. 8.

64. O'Kelly, BMH, WS 1765, p. 42; and P. S. Doyle, BMH, WS 155, 'Questionnaire'.

65. Information of Dick O'Carroll, Dublin, 8 July 2015.

66. *Gaelic American*, 13 December 1913, p. 1.

67. Tomas O Maoileoin in MacEoin, *Survivors*, p. 77.

68. O Maoileoin in MacEoin, *Survivors*, p. 78.

69. O Maoileoin in MacEoin, *Survivors*, p. 78. See also Tom Malone, *Alias Sean Forde: The Story of Commandant Tomas Malone, Vice OC East Limerick Flying Column, Irish Republican Army* (Dublin: Danesfort Publications, 2000), pp. 11–12. He was OC of the Tyrrellspass Section, Irish Volunteers, in April 1916. Peadar Bracken, BMH, WS 361, p. 7.

70. De Burca, BMH, WS 694, p. 1.

71. *Gaelic American*, 13 December 1913, p. 1.

72. Ryan, BMH, WS 725, p. 7.

73. Bulmer Hobson, BMH, WS 84, 'Padraig Pearse', 26 January 1948, p. 1.

74. Lynch, BMH, WS 4, p. 3.

75. De Burca, *Soldiers' Song*, p. 140. Kearney was Centre of the O'Leary Circle which also held meetings in 41 Parnell Square. Murray, BMH, WS 254, p. 1.

76. Charles Donnelly, BMH, WS 824, p. 1.

77. O'Kelly, BMH, WS 1765, pp. 54–5. See also Seamus Daly, BMH, WS 360, p. 4. The

Teeling Circle of the IRB contained Gaelic League members Bulmer Hobson, Pat McCartan, Diarmuid O'Hegarty, Michael O Foghludha and Seamus Deakin. Hobson, BMH, WS 100, p. 3. Liam Tannam, a 3rd Battalion Volunteer officer favoured by the IRB, was inducted into the Teeling Circle in July 1915. Tannam, BMH, WS 242, p. 5. In 1914 they met in the Dublin Typographical Association Office in Gardiner Street. Mortimer O'Connell, BMH, WS 804, p. 2.

78. Liam O'Carroll, BMH, WS 314, p. 1.

79. Michael Motherway, BMH, WS 1027, p. 3.

80. J. J. Walsh, BMH, WS 91, pp. 1–2.

81. Ceannt, BMH, WS 264, p. 10.

82. *Gaelic American*, 7 February 1914, p. 3. See also Liam de Róiste, BMH, WS 1698, p. 229. In late September 1915, Spellissy was accused of sending messages to the US Consul in Munich outside 'regular diplomatic channels'. Co. Limerick-born Thomas St John Gaffney was the American Consul-General and a man suspected of pro-German sympathies for hosting Casement. De Róiste, BMH, WS 1698, pp. 229–30. See also *Cork Examiner*, 29 September 1915.

83. Lonergan, BMH, WS 140, p. 2.

84. Bulfin, BMH, WS 497, p. 3.

85. See *Irish Times*, 8 June 1914.

86. De Burca, BMH, WS 694, pp. 1–2.

87. Donnelly, BMH, WS 824, p. 2.

88. De Burca, BMH, WS 694, p. 2. Michael Cremen, founder member of E Company, stated, 'P. H. Pearse was the Company Captain … Eamon Bulfin was a Lieutenant'. Michael Cremen, BMH, WS 563, p. 1. Ex-'University group' member Fintan Murphy moved back into St Enda's on 1 January 1916 and transferred from the Bermondsey Company (London) into E Company. Fintan Murphy, BMH, WS 370, p. 1.

89. Donnelly, BMH, WS 824, p. 1. Frank Sheridan and Peter Horan were joint treasurers (Donnelly, BMH, WS 824, p. 2). Liam Clarke received severe facial injuries when a 'tin can grenade', improperly activated by Paddy Sweeney, exploded in his hands in the GPO (Donnelly, BMH, WS 824, p. 5). Founding Second Lieutenant Eamon Bulfin was under Pearse as OC until Boland assumed the role. Clarke was First Lieutenant. Bulfin, BMH, WS 497, p. 3.

90. De Burca, BMH, WS 694, pp. 18–20.

91. O Gaora, *On the Run*, pp. 58–9.

92. James Gleeson, BMH, WS 1012, p. 1.

93. *Gaelic American*, 14 February 1914, p. 7.

94. Robert Brennan, BMH, WS 125.

95. *Gaelic American*, 14 February 1914, p. 2.

96. Michael Brennan, BMH, WS 1068, pp. 2–3.

97. Hobson, 'Rising', BMH, WS 81, p. 2. De Lacy was Centre of the Enniscorthy IRB. Seamus Doyle, BMH, WS 315, p. 1. It was understood that O'Connell had been in the US Army and was recruited to assist the Volunteers when in New York by Seán MacDiarmada. Charles Brennan-Whitmore, *Dublin Burning: The Easter Rising from behind the Barricades*, new edition (Dublin: Gill & Macmillan, 2013), p. xix.

98. Patrick Pearse to Mr Geary, 14 October 1913, Geary Papers, UL Special Collections. An itemised bill for educational materials used by Augustine Geary dated 20 November 1913 was submitted on paper bearing the obsolete Cullenswood House address. The Limerick student's annual report on 15 July 1914 claimed his conduct was 'excellent, and his character a fine manly one'. Geary Papers, UL Special Collections.

99. See Patrick Pearse, 'St Enda's College Doing National Work for Ireland', *Gaelic American*, 7 March 1914, p. 5.

100. *Gaelic American*, 7 March 1914, p. 5.

101. Ryan, BMH, WS 725, p. 6.

102. Ryan, BMH, WS 725, p. 6.

103. Hobson, BMH, WS 84, 'Padraig Pearse', 26 January 1948, p. 1.

104. Ryan, BMH, WS 725, p. 6.

105. *Gaelic American*, 28 February 1914, p. 2. Thomas P. Tuite, an Irish Fenian émigré who worked for Dr Thomas Addis Emmet, had presented a lecture to the Harlem Gaelic Society entitled 'Emmet's Life in Pictures' on 5 November 1913. *Gaelic American*, 15 November 1913.

106. *Gaelic American*, 28 February 1914, p. 2.

107. *Gaelic American*, 28 February 1914, p. 8.

108. *Gaelic American*, 24 January 1914, p. 8.

109. *Gaelic American*, 7 March 1914, p. 2.

110. *Gaelic American*, 7 March 1914, p. 7.

111. *Gaelic American*, 7 March 1914, p. 7.

112. *Gaelic American*, 31 January 1914, p. 5; *Gaelic American*, 28 February 1914, p. 5. Minturn fell ill and was replaced by Counsellor Alexander Rorke. *Gaelic American*, 14 March 1914, p. 1.

113. *Gaelic American*, 7 March 1914, p. 5.

114. *Gaelic American*, 14 March 1914, p. 1.

115. Hobson, BMH, WS 84, 'Pearse', 26 January 1948, p. 1.

116. *Gaelic American*, 14 March 1914, p. 2.

117. *Gaelic American*, 14 March 1914, p. 2.

118. *Gaelic American*, 14 March 1914, p. 2.

119. *Gaelic American*, 14 March 1914, p. 5.

120. See Patrick Pearse to Denis Spellissy, 4 March 1914, in Cohalan Papers, American Irish Historical Society, New York.

121. *Gaelic American*, 21 March 1914, p. 7.

122. *Gaelic American*, 28 March 1914, p. 11.

123. *Gaelic American*, 4 April 1914, p. 5.

124. John Kenny to the Editor, 17 March 1914. *Gaelic American*, 28 March 1914, p. 7.

125. Seumas MacManus to the Editor, *Gaelic American*, 28 March 1914, p. 7. MacManus was recovering from illness on a book tour that brought him to Walla Walla, Washington. *Gaelic American*, 14 March 1914, p. 2.

126. MacManus to the Editor, *Gaelic American*, 28 March 1914, p. 7.

127. *Gaelic American*, 18 April 1914, p. 8.

128. *Gaelic American*, 28 March 1914, p. 11.

129. *Gaelic American*, 11 April 1914, p. 5.

130. *Gaelic American*, 18 April 1914, p. 5.

131. *Gaelic American*, 25 April 1914, p. 5.

132. *Gaelic American*, 9 May 1914, p. 8.

133. Lonergan, BMH, WS 140, p. 2. In 1948, Lonergan was Executive Secretary of the American Irish Association of New York (BMH, WS 140, p. 2).

134. *Gaelic American*, 2 May 1914, p. 3.

135. *Gaelic American*, 9 May 1914, p. 8.

136. *Gaelic American*, 2 May 1914, p. 3.

137. *Gaelic American*, 16 May 1914, p. 3.

138. *Gaelic American*, 2 May 1914, p. 5.

139. *Gaelic American*, 9 May 1914, p. 8.

140. *Gaelic American*, 6 June 1914, p. 1 and 20 June 1914, p. 1.

141. Patrick Pearse to Daniel F. Cohalan, 19 August 1915, Cohalan Papers.

Chapter 3

1. O'Kelly, BMH, WS 384, p. 23.

2. *Freeman's Journal*, 9 April 1914.

3. *Gaelic American*, 27 June 1914, p. 7.

4. *Gaelic American*, 27 June 1914, p. 7.

5. *Gaelic American*, 4 October 1913, p. 1.

6. *Gaelic American*, 13 December 1913, p. 1.

7. O'Kelly, BMH, WS 1765, p. 117.

8. *Gaelic American*, 4 July 1914, p. 1.

9. Cited in Martin, *The Irish Volunteers*, p. 60.

10. Ryan, BMH, WS 725, p. 7.

11. *Gaelic American*, 4 July 1914, p. 4.

12. Sean Fitzgibbon, BMH, WS 130, p. 8.

13. *Gaelic American*, 18 July 1914, p. 2.

14. Ua Caomhanaigh, BMH, WS 889, p. 41. Michael O'Hanrahan was 'Executive Official' of the Armament Subcommittee tasked with obtaining weapons for the Volunteers. Casement's connections in London, including Alice Stopford Green, were responsive to fund-raising for this purpose. Darrell Figgis became an agent of the London group on the Continent. O'Kelly, BMH, WS 1765, pp. 128–9.

15. O'Kelly, BMH, WS 1765, p. 47.

16. Geraldine Dillon (née Plunkett), BMH, WS 358, p. 1.

17. *Gaelic American*, 18 July 1914, p. 8. For eyewitness assessment, see Madden, BMH, WS 1103, p. 6.

18. *Irish Independent*, 9 July 1914.

19. Murray, BMH, WS 254, p. 2.

20. Murray, BMH, WS 254, p. 2.

21. Murray, BMH, WS 254, p. 2.

22. Martin, *The Howth Gunrunning*, Part IV.

23. *Sunday Press*, 26 July 1964; and Martin, *The Howth Gunrunning*, p. 171.

24. Fitzgibbon, BMH, WS 130, p. 12. Michael Buckley is probably the 'M. Buckley' on a list of subscribers compiled by Pearse. Others were J. J. Walsh and John O'Connor. (Patrick Pearse), 'Subscribers', nd, MSS.

25. Patrick Pearse to Joe McGarrity, 14 August 1916, in Martin, *The Howth Gunrunning*, p. 196. See also Bulmer Hobson Papers, NLI, MS 13162.

26. O'Kelly, BMH, WS 1765, pp. 135–8.

27. Dillon, BMH, WS 388, p. 2.

28. Ua Caomhanaigh, BMH, WS 889, p. 41.

29. Ua Caomhanaigh, BMH, WS 889, pp. 41, 43.

30. O'Kelly, BMH, WS 1765, p. 77.

31. Brennan, BMH, WS 125.

32. Brennan, BMH, WS 125.

33. Ryan, BMH, WS 725, p. 7.

34. Ryan, BMH, WS 725, p. 7.

35. Hobson, BMH, WS 81, 'Rising', p. 10.

36. Ryan, BMH, WS 725, p. 7.

37. Joseph E. A. Connell Jnr. (ed.), *Dublin Rising 1916* (Dublin: Wordwell, 2015), p. 66.

38. Connolly, BMH, WS 523, pp. 5–6.

39. Cited in Ceannt, BMH, WS 264, p. 13.

40. *The Hibernian*, 17 July 1915, p. 5.

41. Motherway, BMH, 1027, p. 6.

42. Motherway, BMH, 1027, p. 6.

43. Sean Boylan, BMH, WS 212, p. 2.

44. Boylan, BMH, WS 212, p. 2.

45. Sean O'Keefe, BMH, WS 188, p. 2.

46. Liam Manahan, BMH, WS 456, p. 4.

47. Donnelly, BMH, WS 824, p. 2.

48. McCartan, BMH, WS 766, p. 32.

49. McCartan, BMH, WS 766, p. 32. See also De Róiste, BMH, WS 1698, p. 229.

50. Diarmuid Lynch, BMH, WS 4, 'Casement Pamphlet', pp. 1–3.

51. McCartan, BMH, WS 766, p. 35.

52. Hobson, BMH, WS 81, 'Rising', p. 3. See also *Irish Volunteer*, 31 October 1914.

53. Staines, BMH, WS 284, p. 4.

54. Donnelly, BMH, WS 824, p. 3.

55. Donnelly, BMH, WS 824, p. 3.

56. *Irish Times*, 14 November 1914.

57. *Irish Times*, 16 November 1914.

58. *Irish Times*, 21 November 1914.

59. Ryan, *A Man Called Pearse*, p. 2.

60. *Irish Times*, 29 April 1916.

61. Martin, *Irish Volunteers*, pp. 211–12.

62. Connolly, BMH, WS 523, p. 11.

63. Connolly, BMH, WS 523, p. 11.

64. Connolly, BMH, WS 523, p. 11.

65. Cleary, BMH, WS 972, p. 5.

66. O'Ceallaigh in de Burca, *Soldier's Song*, pp. 92–5.

67. Brien, 'Extremists', 21 June 1915, NAI, CSO/JD/2/16 (1). Frank Henderson recalled that 'C Company of the 2nd Battalion met ... at 25 Parnell Square, and it might be described as the City Company' (BMH, WS 249, p. 4).

68. Staines, BMH, WS 284, p. 2.

69. Simon Donnelly, BMH, WS 433, p. 8.

70. Henderson, BMH, WS 1686.

71. McCabe, BMH, WS 277, p. 2. Neil Kerr attended from Liverpool and Joe Gleeson from Scotland (McCabe, BMH, WS 277, p. 2). On 20 May 1915, the miracle plays *Isogán* and *The Master* were performed in the Irish Theatre, Hardwicke Street. Willie Pearse starred in *The Master* while St Enda's boys acted most other parts. *Irish Times*, 20 May 1915.

72. Lynch, BMH, WS 4, p. 4.

73. Lynch, BMH, WS 4, p. 4. Dick Connolly claimed that a January 1915 gathering in Clontarf advanced plans, raised in May and September 1914, to appoint a military council. He understood that its first co-opted members, Pearse, Ceannt and Plunkett, sat apart from the main body in an adjacent room divided by folding doors. When the partition was pulled back, Connolly was 'rather surprised when I saw Pearse there. It was the first time I knew he was in the IRB. He was sitting in the corner ... I was told this was the Military Committee.' Connolly, BMH, WS 523, p. 9.

74. *Irish Volunteer*, 5 June 1915. The house on Dawson Street was acquired in August/September 1914 when the original headquarters rented by Hobson at 41 Kildare Street was condemned by Dublin Corporation as 'unsafe'. Hobson, BMH, WS 81, 'Rising', p. 1.

75. Séamus Fitzgerald, BMH, WS 1737, p. 6.

76. Pearse, cited in James A. Gubbins, BMH, WS 765, p. 9.

77. *Irish Volunteer*, 5 June 1915.

78. Tadhg Moloney, 'The Day Patrick Pearse and His Allies Were Stoned in Limerick',

Limerick Leader, 23 May 2015. See also A. J. O'Halloran, 'Whit-Sunday Riots, 1915', *Limerick Chronicle*, 25 May 1940.

79. Brennan, BMH, WS 1068, p. 6. Cathal Brugha was also part of the Dublin contingent. Gubbins, BMH, WS 765, p. 11.

80. Kevin McCabe, BMH, WS 926, p. 4.

81. *Irish Volunteer*, 5 June 1915.

82. Brennan, BMH, WS 1068, p. 6.

83. Brennan, BMH, WS 1068, p. 6.

84. See back cover, 'A Newman', *Tracts for the Times No. 5: Ascendancy While You Wait* (Dublin, nd [1915]). Publications by Brian O'Higgins, The O'Rahilly and United Irishmen hero Myles Byrne were advertised. Whelan & Son also sold US .22 rifles whereas 'gunmaker' L. Keegan of Inns Quay traded in 'revolvers, rifles, [and] cartridges'. *The Hibernian*, 26 June 1915, p. 8. See also *Irish Volunteer*, 26 June 1915, p. 8.

85. *Nationality*, 26 June 1915, p. 6.

86. Patrick Pearse, *From a Hermitage*, Pamphlet (Dublin, 1915).

87. *Workers' Republic*, 3 July 1915, p. 1.

88. Brien, 'Extremists', 11 June 1915, NAI, CSO/JD/2/1 (2).

89. Superintendent Owen Brien, 'Movements of Dublin Extremists', 1, 2, 3, 7 and 10 June 1915, NAI, CSO/JD/2/1 (2). J. J. Walsh had been dismissed from the Postal Service in May 1915 arising from his anti-recruiting activities and role within the Cork City Volunteers. Barred from Cork, he opened a shop in Blessington Street, Dublin, on 1 July, which simplified contact with Clarke. Walsh, BMH, WS 91, p. 4. He was reputedly 'deported' to and from England. *Nationality*, 17 July 1915, p. 3. See also *The Hibernian*, 3 July 1915, p. 4.

90. James Stephens, *The Insurrection in Dublin* (Gerrards Cross: Colin Smythe, 1978), p. 91.

91. Patrick Pearse to Joe McGarrity, 26 June 1915, in O'Buachalla, *Letters of P. H. Pearse*, p. 342.

92. Brien, 'Extremists', 3 June 1915, NAI, CSO/JD/2/1 (2), and *Irish Volunteer*, 5 June 1915. Milroy was an early member of Sinn Féin and in 1906 promoted the party with Sean T. O'Kelly. O'Kelly, BMH, WS 1765, p. 29.

93. De Róiste, BMH, WS 1698, p. 200.

94. Brien, 'Extremists', 10 June 1915, NAI, CSO/JD/2/1 (2).

95. Brien, 'Extremists', 21 June 1915, NAI, CSO/JD/2/16 (2). Éamonn Ceannt, The O'Rahilly, T. J. Sheehan, Frank Fahy, Thomas Byrne, William Partridge, Peter Doyle, Bulmer Hobson, Countess Markievicz, J. J. Buggy, Sean T. O'Kelly, J. J. Walsh, John O'Mahoney, George Irvine, Patrick O'Malley (Galway), Barney Mellows and Joe

McGuinness were identified as attendees (Brien, 'Extremists', 21 June 1915, NAI, CSO/JD/2/16 [2]). G-Division Detective Sergeant Maguire spied on Na Fianna Éireann and Irish Volunteers in Glasgow in 1916. Seamus Reader, BMH, WS 1767, p. 21. Irvine was an IRB Centre. Kevin McCabe, BMH, WS 926, p. 1.

96. *Workers' Republic*, 26 June 1915, p. 8. The ICA noted the presence of Cumann na mBan, Na Fianna Éireann, 'Girl Guides' and 'Boy Scouts of Liberty Hall' (aka 'National Guard'). An unexpected development occurred when local units of the National Volunteers lined up and saluted the visitors (*Workers' Republic*, 26 June 1915, p. 8).

97. *Workers' Republic*, 26 June 1915, p. 8.

98. Henderson, BMH, WS 1686.

99. See Eoin MacNeill to the Editor, *Irish Press*, 28 and 31 May 1935.

100. *Irish Volunteer*, 26 June 1915, p. 4.

101. *Irish Volunteer*, 26 June 1915, p. 5. See also 'Field Training, Chapter X, Exercises in the Active Defence' (*Irish Volunteer*, 26 June 1915, p. 5).

102. Hobson, BMH, WS 81, 'Rising', p. 5.

103. O'Kelly, BMH, WS 1765, p. 78. MacDiarmada met with IRB figures Michael O Foghludha, Diarmuid Lynch, Thomas Ashe and Michael Cowley prior to his arrest on 18 June 1915. O'Kelly, BMH, WS 1765, p. 78.

104. Doyle, 'Irishman's Diary', *Irish Times*, 27 June 2015.

105. Doyle, 'Irishman's Diary', *Irish Times*, 27 June 2015.

106. Lynch, BMH, WS 4, p. 6.

107. O'Kelly, BMH, WS 1765, p. 81.

108. *An Claidheamh Soluis*, 7 November 1913.

109. *Gaelic American*, 25 July 1914, p. 7. Having watched a performance of the drama *Fionn*, Hyde reportedly 'paid tribute to the excellent work carried on at St Enda's' and praised Pearse as exemplifying 'the philosophy of all who were concerned with the creation of what might be called an Irish Ireland, as distinct from an imitation English Ireland' (*Gaelic American*, 25 July 1914, p. 7).

110. *Gaelic American*, 4 October 1913, p. 8.

111. *Gaelic American*, 25 October 1913, p. 8.

112. Connolly, BMH, WS 523, p. 10.

113. Brien, 'Extremists', 2 July 1915, NAI, CSO/JD/2/24 (1). For the Fenian Kickham, see R.V. Comerford, *Charles J. Kickham: A Study in Irish Nationalism and Literature* (Dublin: Wolfhound, 1979), pp. 54, 134.

114. Brien, 'Extremists', 2 July 1915, NAI, CSO/JD/2/26 (1). Regional leaders James

Leddin (Limerick), Austin Stack (Kerry) and Paddy Hughes (Louth) attended, as did Dublin area leaders, Bulmer Hobson, Thomas MacDonagh, Ned Daly, Piaras Béaslaí, Con Colbert, Éamonn Ceannt and The O'Rahilly. Brien, 'Extremists', 2 July 1915, NAI, CSO/JD/2/26 (1).

115. Comerford, *Charles J. Kickham*, pp. 134–5.

116. *Ná Bac Leis*, 3 July 1915, p. 1.

117. Brien, 'Extremists', 10 July 1915, NAI, CSO/JD/2/31 (2). Longford-born McGuinness had returned from living in the USA in 1906 and was a leading Sinn Féin member in Dublin. Brien, 'Extremists', 13 July 1915, NAI, CSO/JD/2/33 (1).

118. John MacDonagh, BMH, WS 532, p. 2.

119. Patrick Pearse, 'A Character Study', in Patrick Pearse, Thomas MacDonagh, Arthur Griffith, James Connolly and Brian O'Higgins, *Diarmuid Ó Donnabháin Rosa, 1831–1915: Souvenir of Public Funeral to Glasnevin Cemetery, Dublin, August 1st, 1915 with second edition* (Dublin: O'Donovan Rossa Funeral Committee, 1915), p. 5.

120. Pearse et al., *Diarmuid Ó Donnabháin Rosa, 1831–1915*.

121. De Róiste, BMH, WS 1698, p. 213.

122. *Weekly Irish Times*, 7 August 1915.

123. Patrick Ramsbottom, BMH, WS 1046, p. 4.

124. Ronan McGreevy, 'Rare Footage of Padraig Pearse to Be Shown in New Film', Irish Times, 29 August 2014. Available at www.irishtimes.com/news/ireland/irish-news/rare-footage-of-padraig-pearse-to-be-shown-in-new-film-1.1912117 (accessed 9 November 2015).

125. Ryan, BMH, WS 725, p. 5.

126. *Irish Republican News*, 25 July 2015.

Chapter 4

1. Ryan, BMH, WS 725, p. 5

2. Ryan, BMH, WS 725, p. 5.

3. Cremen, BMH, WS 563, p. 2.

4. De Róiste, BMH, WS 1698, p. 221. Corconian Liam de Róiste, a member of the Coiste Gnótha of the Gaelic League, had met O'Donovan Rossa in Ireland and found him 'a likeable man; humorous, simple with a fund of stories which he told in Irish or in simple country-idiom English'. De Róiste, BMH, WS 1698, p. 203. Millstreet Feis was a cover for a side meeting of the IRB and Volunteers to extend their influence into the Duhallow/Muskerry sector. See Jim Cronin, *Millstreet's Green and Gold* (Cork, 1984).

5. De Róiste, BMH, WS 1698, p. 221.

6. Gleeson, BMH, WS 1012, p. 1.

7. John J. O'Reilly, BMH, WS 1031, p. 1.

8. *Saoirse*, October 2013, p. 16.

9. Brennan-Whitmore, *Dublin Burning*, p. 8.

10. Staines, BMH, WS 284, p. 2.

11. Staines, BMH, WS 284, p. 2.

12. McCullough, BMH, WS 915, p. 9.

13. Henry Corr, BMH, WS 227, p. 1.

14. De Róiste, BMH, WS 1698, p. 237.

15. Manahan, BMH, WS 456, p. 6.

16. Brennan-Whitmore, *Dublin Burning*, p. 16.

17. Staines, BMH, WS 284, pp. 2–3.

18. Doyle, BMH, WS 155, 'Questionnaire'. Liam Tannam had the unenviable task of attempting to swear his Volunteer commander Éamon de Valera into the IRB: 'Dev laughed at him and took no notice. Tom MacDonagh swore in Dev eventually.' Doyle, BMH, WS 155, 'Questionnaire'.

19. Henderson, BMH, WS 249, p. 12.

20. Bracken, BMH, WS 361, p. 2.

21. Bracken, BMH, WS 361, p. 2. Bracken joined the Gaelic League as a schoolboy and moved into Cumann na nGael which was 'really a cover for the IRB'. Sworn into the IRB by 1867 veteran William Kennedy in 1904, the group met in Tullamore. On moving to Stradbally in 1906, Bracken started a Sinn Féin cumann but emigrated to Australia four years later. He returned in September 1914 to join the Tullamore Volunteers on the verge of the split. Bracken, BMH, WS 361, pp. 1–2. Pearse was also preoccupied with mundane student recruitment duties. See Patrick Pearse to Madam O'Boyle, 28 August 1915, http://historyofdonegal.com.

22. McCullough, BMH, WS 915, p. 12.

23. Lynch, BMH, WS 4, p. 6.

24. Reader, BMH, WS 1767, p. 1.

25. Reader, BMH, WS 1767, p. 1.

26. Reader, BMH, WS 1767, p. 4.

27. Reader, BMH, WS 1767, p. 18. At the November 1915 centennial commemoration of John Mitchel's birth, Pearse commented that Irish insurrections were always 'just too late', to which Connolly replied, 'Will this one also be too late?' Frank Robbins, BMH, WS 585, p. 37.

28. Lynch, BMH, WS 4, p. 8.

29. Lynch, BMH, WS 4, p. 8.

30. Lynch, BMH, WS 4, p. 8.

31. Henderson, BMH, WS 1686. Pearse briefed Pat McCartan that Tyrone/Antrim Volunteers were to 'concentrate at Bellcoo and hold the line of the Shannon' to prevent British forces 'crossing into Connacht' to confront German landings. Pearse claimed, 'Don't waste time dealing with police [barracks]' in Ulster. McCartan, BMH, WS 766, pp. 47–8.

32. *Irish Volunteer*, 3 July 1915.

33. Henderson, BMH, WS 1686, p. 3.

34. O'Brien, BMH, WS 1776, p. 53.

35. McCartan, BMH, WS 766, p. 37. Richard Connolly replaced P. S. O'Hegarty as London representative and attended his first Supreme Council meeting in Dublin in September 1913. Richard Connolly, BMH, WS 523, p. 3. For Gleeson, aka 'Redmond', in 1916, see Bulfin, BMH, WS 497, p. 7.

36. McCullough, BMH, WS 915, p. 13.

37. O'Brien, BMH, WS 1776, p. 75. McCullough, who related this account to O'Brien, was adamant that MacDiarmada had no part in the Connolly dialogue. O'Brien, BMH, WS 1776, p. 72. Pearse informed Des Ryan to the contrary. Ryan, BMH, WS 725, p. 6. Hobson, no longer at the centre of affairs, recollected Volunteer and IRB concern that 'Connolly, towards the end of 1915, decided to have a little insurrection', resulting in his being 'kidnapped'. Hobson, 'Rising', BMH, WS 81, p. 4.

38. McCartan, BMH, WS 766, p. 42.

39. McCullough, BMH, WS 915, p. 14.

40. McCullough, BMH, WS 915, p. 14.

41. O'Brien, BMH, WS 1776, pp. 68–9.

42. O'Brien, BMH, WS 1776, p. 62. In the Hermitage, Pearse asked Ryan for a loan of *Workers' Republic*, which he read 'very carefully' before remarking, 'That is dangerous enough.' According to Ryan, 'He told me that he had not been able to sleep for a week; the Citizen Army were threatening action and that he and Sean MacDermott had gone to Connolly, told him they were going to have a Rising, that he was ruining their plans and would he hold his hand. Finally Pearse persuaded Connolly. He said there seemed to be a terrible mental struggle going on in Connolly at the time and then with tears in his eyes he [Connolly] grasped Pearse's hand and said, "God grant, Pearse, that you were right," and Pearse said "God grant that I was." Pearse added to me, "Perhaps Connolly was right; he is a very great man."' Ryan, BMH, WS 725, p. 6.

43. O'Brien, BMH, WS 1776, pp. 62–3.

44. O'Brien, BMH, WS 1776, pp. 61–2. See also Dillon, BMH, WS 358, pp. 7–8.

45. Ryan, BMH, WS 725, p. 5.

46. O'Brien, BMH, WS 1776, p. 75.

47. Hobson, 'Rising', BMH, WS 81, p. 4.

48. Hobson, 'Rising', BMH, WS 81, p. 4.

49. Staines, BMH, WS 284, p. 4. Staines recalled, 'the feeling of those present at these meetings was that we should not let the war end without our generation making a gesture or a protest against the British rule and occupation of the country'. Staines, BMH, WS 284, p. 4.

50. Lynch, BMH, WS 4, p. 8.

51. Lynch, BMH, WS 4, p. 8. For earlier discussion of Limerick and IRB Liverpool–New York communications with Clan na Gael, see Piaras Béaslaí, 'How the Fight Began!' in *Dublin's Fighting Story, 1916–21: Told by the Men who Made It*, with an introduction by Diarmuid Ferriter (Cork: Mercier Press, 2009), p. 32. Shortly before execution, MacDiarmada told Wexford associates that a timber merchant had agreed to receive the weapons on Limerick City docks: 'a messenger was dispatched to Germany to make this new arrangement … [who] got as far as Berne but that was the last they had heard of him'. Doyle, BMH, WS 315, p. 16.

52. Cotton, BMH, WS 184, p. 7.

53. Cotton, BMH, WS 184, p. 6. Cotton's IRB duties led to dismissal from the Civil Service on 3 March 1915. Cotton, BMH, WS 184, p. 71. Tralee Ancient Order of Hibernians (IAA) sponsored Pearse's speech in the Rink. Michael Doyle, BMH, WS 1038, p. 3. See also Madden, BMH, WS 1103, pp. 7–8, and Patrick Garvey, BMH, WS 1011, p. 3. ICA member William Partridge had contact with Stack in Tralee, according to Castlegregory Volunteer Patrick O'Shea. In January 1916, O'Shea fell in with Pearse and Stack as they travelled by train from Cork to Dublin after a Munster GAA event: 'I went with him to O'Connell Bridge where he was met by Sean McDermott.' Patrick O'Shea, BMH, WS 1144, pp. 1–2. Partridge travelled to Kerry on Good Friday in connection with arrangements to move arms by rail across the province. Doyle, BMH, WS 155, p. 9. On Easter Saturday, Partridge assisted Tralee messenger William Mullins in meeting Pearse et al. in Liberty Hall. Pearse told him, 'there will be no change in the original plans.' William Mullins, BMH, WS 123, p. 4.

54. Donal J. O'Sullivan, *District Inspector John A. Kearney: The RIC man who Befriended Sir Roger Casement* (Victoria, BC: Trafford, 2005), pp. 74–5.

55. Daniel Kelly, BMH, WS 1004, p. 15.

56. *Enniscorthy Echo*, 11 March 1916.

57. *Enniscorthy Echo*, 11 March 1916.

58. *Enniscorthy Echo*, 11 March 1916. The Tricolour was also displayed at Bodenstown in June 1914. *Gaelic American*, 11 July 1914, p. 1.

59. *Enniscorthy Echo*, 11 March 1916. When addressing the March 1914 Emmet com-memoration in New York, he had claimed, 'When England thinks she has trampled out our battle in blood, some brave man rises and rallies us again; when England thinks she has purchased us with a bribe, some good man redeems us by a sacrifice.' *Gaelic American*, 14 March 1914, p. 2.

60. *Enniscorthy Echo*, 11 March 1916. Contrasting the London media's derogatory atti-tude towards Scottish nationalists with those of Ireland, a pro-republican print queried 'What has saved us? The life and death of Emmet; the intelligence of Davis; the vigour and majesty of James Stephens; the incomparable prose of revolt which Mitchel formed from the language of our enemy; and laid at the feet of our lady of distress.' *Nationality*, 26 June 1915, p. 3.

61. Brennan, BMH, WS 125. Seamus Doyle met Pearse after the concert. Pearse 'told me that the Insurrection was near at hand and arranged a code with me to signify that the orders for the Rising were to be put into force'. Doyle, BMH, WS 315, p. 6. See also Thomas Doyle, BMH, WS 1041.

62. De Burca, BMH, WS 694, p. 2.

63. De Burca, BMH, WS 694, p. 2. See also Ryan, BMH, WS 725, p. 9.

64. Daly, BMH, WS 360, pp. 17–18.

65. Brennan, BMH, WS 125.

66. MacDonagh, BMH, WS 532, pp. 3–4.

67. Murphy, BMH, WS 370, p. 1.

68. Norway to Gadsden, 25 April 1916, p. 36.

69. De Burca, BMH, WS 694, p. 3.

70. De Burca, BMH, WS 694, p. 4. Brennan was First Lieutenant of the Tullamore Vol-unteers and Second in Command to Pearse's associate Peadar Bracken. Having shot an RIC Sergeant, Bracken was on the run in Westmeath. Bracken, BMH, WS 361, pp. 2–6.

71. De Burca, BMH, WS 694, p. 4.

72. Desmond Ryan, in Patrick Pearse, *The Story of a Success: Being a Record of St Enda's College, September 1908 to Easter 1916*, ed. Desmond Ryan (Dublin and London: Maunsel & Company Ltd., 1917), p. 98.

73. Hobson, 'Rising', BMH, WS 81, p. 6.

74. Hobson, 'Rising', BMH, WS 81, p. 6.

75. Hobson, 'Rising', BMH, WS 81, p. 7.

76. O'Sullivan, BMH, WS 393, pp. 3–4.

77. O'Sullivan, BMH, WS 393, pp. 3–4.

78. Henderson, BMH, WS 249, p. 14.

79. Henderson, BMH, WS 249, p. 14. This was evidently a variant of Pearse's militant 'Be Prepared' lecture, one of the Saturday night series of which Liam O'Carroll was Secretary. Senior Dublin officers attended, and they were generally joined by Mac-Donagh, Clarke, De Valera, Connolly, Ceannt, Hobson and Ted Sheehan. O'Carroll, BMH, WS 314, p. 5. For another account, see Oscar Traynor, BMH, WS 340, p. 5. Traynor recalled there was 'dead silence' for a time after Pearse finished. O'Carroll, BMH, WS 314, p. 5.

80. McDowell, BMH, WS 173, p. 3; emphasis added. McDowell was uncertain in October 1948 whether the contingency on Easter manoeuvres formed part of the general address or had occurred in private conversation with Pease that preceded business. McDowell, BMH, WS 173, p. 3.

81. McDowell, BMH, WS 173, p. 6. Kevin O'Sheil, a non-IRB member due to paternal injunction, described Dr Pat McCartan as being 'long before Easter Week an avowed separatist, despising all manner of Constitutional Nationalism and relying purely on the sword for the liberation of Ireland'. Kevin O'Sheil, BMH, WS 1770, p. 649.

82. Walker, BMH, WS 139, p. 3. Michael O'Hanrahan was responsible for 'An Cumann Cosanta', an 'insurance scheme … for the protection of men who were victimised for being members of the Volunteers'. MacDonagh, meanwhile, organised a group of doctors willing to 'cooperate in the event of hostilities'. Henderson, BMH, WS 249, p. 22.

83. *Irish Volunteer*, 8 April 1916.

84. Vincent 'Vinny' Byrne, BMH, WS 423, p. 1.

85. Byrne, BMH, WS 423, p. 1. Hunter frequently 'took charge' when MacDonagh was absent on GHQ and Military Council business. Henderson, BMH, WS 249, p. 20.

86. Bulfin, BMH, WS 497, p. 3.

87. Cotton, BMH, WS 184, p. 5.

88. Thomas F. Byrne, BMH, WS 564, pp. 1–14. Byrne spent three months as an organiser attached with the Galtee Brigade in Tipperary in 1914. Their training officer had been mobilised with the Sherwood Foresters (Nottingham Regiment), which saw much action in Dublin during the Rising. When in the capital, Byrne was a daily visitor to Tom Clarke's shop. Byrne, BMH, WS 564, pp. 30–1. Leslie Price was at the special Volunteer social and mused in retrospect 'that those responsible for the Rising had it in mind that it was their last reunion'. Among the attendees were Clarke, MacDiarmada, Min Ryan, Diarmuid Hegarty and Eamon Price. Price, BMH, WS 1754, pp. 3–4.

89. Byrne, BMH, WS 423, p. 17.

90. See Brien, 'Extremists', 7 July 1915, NAI, CSO/JD/2/28.

91. Byrne, BMH, WS 423, p. 15.

92. Bracken, BMH, WS 361, p. 6.

93. Byrne, BMH, WS 423, p. 16.

94. Byrne, BMH, WS 423, p. 16.

95. Boylan, BMH, WS 212, p. 3. Gerard Byrne, a member of the IRB Mangan Circle and Volunteer 4th Battalion, was also briefed by Pearse in St Enda's in relation to the Kells district of Meath: 'He told me that he had pretty reliable information that the British were going to make a wholesale collection of arms in the country, and that they were going to resist. I was to see McDermott for final instructions'. Gerard Byrne, BMH, WS 143, p. 5.

96. Boylan, BMH, WS 212, p. 3.

97. Boylan, BMH, WS 212, p. 4. According to Boylan, 'I asked him on that day for permission to take my men into the city for the fighting when the Rising would start and to join up with the Dublin Brigade. Pearse took a map from the wall and placed it on the table and put his finger on it and said "Your task is communications, and under no circumstances must you go beyond that line". This was the village of Mulhuddart where he was pointing his finger on the map. I understood that I was to keep communication to and from the city open.' Boylan, BMH, WS 212, p. 4.

98. O'Kelly, BMH, WS 1765, p. 42.

99. Cited in Ryan, BMH, WS 725, p. 3.

100. Hobson, 'Rising', BMH, WS 81, p. 7.

101. Hobson, 'Rising', BMH, WS 81, p. 8. O'Connor, 'in the course of March', informed P. J. Little, Editor of *New Ireland*, 'about certain information that was coming from Dublin Castle in reference to measures to be taken to suppress the Volunteers. He gradually produced the text of what, it was contended, was a document on the files of Dublin Castle'. P. J. Little, BMH, WS 1769, p. 10.

102. Hobson, 'Rising', BMH, WS 81, p. 8.

103. Ryan, BMH, WS 725, p. 3.

104. Ryan, BMH, WS 725, p. 3.

105. Ryan, BMH, WS 725, p. 4.

106. Ryan, BMH, WS 725, p. 4.

107. O'Kelly, BMH, WS 925, p. 1.

108. Hobson, 'Rising', BMH, WS 81, p. 8.

109. Hobson, 'Rising', BMH, WS 81, p. 8.

110. McCullough, BMH, WS 915, p. 20.

111. McCullough, BMH, WS 915, p. 20. For Morrow and the *Irish Review* writers, see Geraldine Plunkett, 'Foreword', *The Poems of Joseph Mary Plunkett* (Dublin, n.d.), pp. viii–ix.

112. Donnelly, BMH, WS 824, p. 3.

113. Cremen, BMH, WS 563, p. 1.

114. De Burca, BMH, WS 694, p. 5. MacDiarmada's IRB contacts in England and Scotland assisted Barney Mellows and Nora Connolly O'Brien in springing Liam Mellows. Connolly O'Brien, BMH, WS 286, pp. 9–12.

115. De Burca, BMH, WS 694, p. 5. Ryan believed Mellows departed on 'Holy Thursday'. Ryan, BMH, WS 725, p. 8.

116. Gubbins, BMH, WS 765, p. 20.

117. Gubbins, BMH, WS 765, pp. 20–1. Pearse thought highly of Monteith.

118. Manahan, BMH, WS 456, p. 10.

119. Manahan, BMH, WS 456, p. 10.

120. Manahan, BMH, WS 456, p. 10. According to Manahan, 'some time prior to Easter Week, I was initiated as a member of the IRB. This was believed to be necessary, because the Volunteer leaders were making use of that organization'. Manahan, BMH, WS 456, p. 16.

121. De Burca, BMH, WS 105, p. 3.

122. McCullough, BMH, WS 915, p. 15. McCullough queried the strategy: 'I pointed out the length of the journey we had to take, the type of country and population we had to pass through and how sparsely armed my men were for such an undertaking. I suggested that we would have to attack the RIC barracks on our way through, to secure the arms we required. Connolly got quite cross at this suggestion and almost shouted at me "You will fire no shot in Ulster: you will proceed with all possible speed to join Mellows in Connaught, and," he added, "if we win through, we will then deal with Ulster" ... I looked at Pearse, to ascertain if he agreed with this and he nodded assent, with some remark like "Yes, that's an order".' McCullough, BMH, WS 915, p. 15.

123. John McGallogly, BMH, WS 244, p. 7. For Scottish Volunteer and IRB activity, see Reader, BMH, WS 1767, pp. 1–4.

124. Ryan, BMH, WS 725, p. 4.

125. *Irish Independent*, 18 April 1916.

126. De Róiste, BMH, WS 1698, p. 309. For Kelly's deposition, see *Irish Times*, 29 April 1916.

127. De Róiste, BMH, WS 1698, p. 308.

128. Monsignor Michael Curran, BMH, WS 687, p. 22. Sean T. O'Kelly repeated the

rumour to Curran on 9 April 1916 while giving the impression it was genuine and originated in Dublin Castle. On 19 April, MacNeill told him in 2 Dawson Street that it was real. Curran, BMH, WS 687, p. 23.

129. Curran, BMH, WS 687, p. 18.

130. Bracken, BMH, WS 361, p. 6.

131. Staines, BMH, WS 284, p. 7.

132. Doyle, BMH, WS 315, p. 7.

133. MacDonagh, BMH, WS 532, p. 4. MacDonagh discovered that an earlier delegate had reached Pierce McCann, warning him not to mobilise. McCann, an IRB member, died from influenza in 1919 shortly following a hunger strike in Gloucester Prison. MacDonagh, BMH, WS 532, pp. 2–4.

134. MacDonagh, BMH, WS 532, p. 6.

Chapter 5

1. O'Kelly, BMH, WS 925, p. 2.

2. Hobson, 'Rising', BMH, WS 81, p. 11.

3. Murphy, BMH, WS 370, p. 4.

4. Murphy, BMH, WS 370, p. 5.

5. Hobson, 'Rising', BMH, WS 81, pp. 12–13.

6. Ryan, BMH, WS 725, p. 7.

7. Dillon, BMH, WS 358, pp. 12–13.

8. Brennan, BMH, WS 125.

9. Boylan, BMH, WS 212, p. 4.

10. Boylan, BMH, WS 212, p. 4.

11. O'Sullivan, BMH, WS 393, p. 4.

12. O'Sullivan, BMH, WS 393, p. 4. O'Sullivan met Daly and went to Clarke's shop. All three met that evening in Fleming's Hotel, Gardiner Place. As Volunteer officers were then required to avoid sleeping at home or in regular haunts, Daly and O'Sullivan slept in the Four Courts Hotel. O'Sullivan, BMH, WS 393, p. 6.

13. Fr Eugene Nevin, BMH, WS 1605, p. 30.

14. Henderson, BMH, WS 249, p. 27.

15. Henderson, BMH, WS 1686.

16. Henderson, BMH, WS 1686.

17. Dillon, BMH, WS 358, p. 7. See also Gubbins, BMH, WS 765, p. 21.

18. O'Sullivan, *District Inspector John A. Kearney*, pp. 130–1. Donal Sheehan of Limerick, Charlie Monaghan of Belfast and Cornelius 'Con' Keating of Kerry perished in an operation involving MacDiarmada, Plunkett, Stack and Michael Collins (pp. 130–1). Driver Tommy McInerney survived. Dillon, BMH, WS 358, p. 7. Unavailable IRB man Dr Brian Cusack had been the first choice to bring Clarke's 'very special communication to John Devoy' from Liverpool. Cusack, BMH, WS 736, p. 5.

19. McCartan, BMH, WS 766, pp. 44–5.

20. O'Sullivan, *District Inspector John A. Kearney*, pp. 58–9.

21. Gubbins, BMH, WS 765, pp. 22–3.

22. Gubbins, BMH, WS 765, pp. 22–3.

23. Lynch, BMH, WS 192, p. 10.

24. Henderson, BMH, WS 1686.

25. Liam Ó Bríain, BMH, WS 6, p. 24.

26. Ryan, BMH, WS 399, p. 8.

27. Liam Ó Bríain, BMH, WS 7, p. 31.

28. Tannam, BMH, WS 242, p. 10.

29. McCabe, BMH, WS 277, p. 4.

30. McCabe, BMH, WS 277, p. 4. Thomas MacDonagh had given a similar strategic assessment to the officers of the 2nd Battalion, not least Frank and Leo Henderson and Oscar Traynor. MacDonagh claimed, 'It would be an all-Ireland Rising, that we would not win, but that we would keep fighting the British for so long that we would attract world-wide attention. He said the fight would start in the cities, that as far as we were concerned it would be in Dublin, that after about a week's time we would be driven out of the city and we would take to the country, where we would put up a great fight for some time, but that eventually we would have to capitulate.' McGallogly, BMH, WS 249, p. 13. MacDonagh had been invited to visit Dr O'Kelly's home on 22 April. Later that night he told his brother at a house in Lower Gardiner Street that 'the rising had been postponed'. MacDonagh, BMH, WS 532, p. 7.

31. McDowell, BMH, WS 137, p. 4. McCabe managed a modest turnout and acts of sabotage in the Keash/Mullinbreena/Tobercurry area but could not entice the RIC out of their barracks. He went on the run and evaded detection. McCabe, BMH, WS 277, pp. 5–6.

32. Connolly O'Brien, BMH, WS 286, p. 26. Numerous militant Scottish IRB and Volunteer members had relocated to Dublin. McGallogly, BMH, WS 244, pp. 1–2.

33. Boylan, BMH, WS 212, p. 4.

34. O'Sullivan, *District Inspector John A. Kearney*, p. 131.

35. Colm Ó Lochlainn, BMH, WS 751, pp. 6–7.

36. Hobson, 'Rising', BMH, WS 81, p. 14.

37. *Sunday Independent*, 23 April 1916.

38. Ryan, BMH, WS 399, p. 9. MacNeill remained in a back room and, according to his host, did not closely interact with those milling around the front of the house. Dr Seumus O Ceallaigh, BMH, WS 471, p. 6.

39. Ryan, BMH, WS 725, p. 10. See also Le Roux, *Patrick H. Pearse*, pp. 366–7.

40. Patrick Pearse to Seán T. O'Kelly, 22 April 1916, BMH, 95/2/1.

41. O'Kelly, BMH, WS 925, p. 3.

42. O'Kelly, BMH, WS 925, p. 3.

43. Gubbins, BMH, WS 765, p. 27.

44. Bulfin, BMH, WS 497, p. 4.

45. Keegan, BMH, WS 217, p. 3.

46. Keegan, BMH, WS 217, p. 3.

47. Keegan, BMH, WS 217, pp. 5–6. Plunkett had spent part of April 1916 in 'Miss Quinn's Nursing Home in Mountjoy Square'. Ryan, BMH, WS 725, p. 4. He was assisted on Easter Monday by Commandant W. J. Brennan-Whitmore and later his aide-de-camp, Michael Collins. W. J. Brennan-Whitmore, 'Easter Monday 1916', *An tÓglach*, 4 (1), 16 January 1926. No. 44 Mountjoy Street (aka 'Grianan na nGaedhal') was owned by a Myra McCarthy, aunt of Keating Branch Gaelic League member, IRB and Volunteer captain, Fionán Lynch. MacDiarmada used the address during Easter Week. BMH, WS 192, pp. 1, 10.

48. Keegan, BMH, WS 217, p. 7. Clarke spent Easter Saturday in Fleming's Hotel in Gardiner Street but returned to his family home at 31 Richmond Avenue the following night with Seán McGarry and Tommy O'Connor. *Irish Times*, 27 June 2015. Removal of furniture from 75 Parnell Street to 10 Richmond Avenue had been monitored the previous year. Brien, 'Extremists', 28 June 1915, NAI, CSO/JD/2/20 (1). When, in December 1916, most of the Volunteers and ICA interned in Britain were emancipated, Fleming's staged a homecoming Christmas breakfast hosted by proprietor John O'Mahoney. Caldwell, BMH, WS 638, p. 15.

49. Cremen, BMH, WS 563, p. 3.

50. Cremen, BMH, WS 563, p. 3. See also O'Kelly, BMH, WS 925, p. 3.

51. Connolly O'Brien, BMH, WS 286, p. 32.

52. Connolly O'Brien, BMH, WS 286, p. 33.

53. Connolly O'Brien, BMH, WS 286, p. 34.

54. Keegan, BMH, WS 217, pp. 14–15.

55. Keegan, BMH, WS 217, pp. 14–15.

56. Keegan, BMH, WS 217, pp. 14–15.

57. Keegan, BMH, WS 217, p. 19. Markievicz met Daly and O'Sullivan in Liberty Hall. She entered the room 'with a small automatic in her hand, and asked in a peremptory tone if anyone knew where Hobson was, or his woman [Gregan] … "I want to shoot him".' O'Sullivan, BMH, WS 393, p. 8.

58. Keegan, BMH, WS 217, p. 20.

59. Staines, BMH, WS 284, p. 8.

60. Bulfin, BMH, WS 497, p. 5.

61. Henderson, BMH, WS 1686.

62. Henderson, BMH, WS 1686. In the early 1900s, members of the Keating Branch were opposed to 'advanced' nationalist politics, despite the presence of republicans Cathal Brugha, Diarmuid Dennehy and Seamus Ua Caomhanaigh. Ua Caomhanaigh, BMH, WS 889, pp. 20–1.

63. Gubbins, BMH, WS 765, p. 27.

64. Gubbins, BMH, WS 765, p. 27. A member the Clonmel IRB and Ancient Order of Hibernians recalled, 'McCann was the Commander of the Volunteers in South Tipperary at this time and had gone to Dublin to get detailed instructions … He was County Centre of the IRB … [We] would do nothing until we heard from him'. William Myles, BMH, WS 795, p. 9.

65. Connolly O'Brien, BMH, WS 286, pp. 37–8.

66. MacDonagh, BMH, WS 532, p. 9.

67. Con Casey in MacEoin, *Survivors*, p. 371. See also Doyle, BMH, WS 1038, pp. 3–4.

68. McDowell, BMH, WS 173, p. 5.

69. McDowell, BMH, WS 173, p. 7.

70. McDowell, BMH, WS 173, p. 7. Liam Tannam of the County Dublin Board, Irish Volunteers, had been informed by Ceannt, 'in the event of conflicting orders I was to take the orders of my next superior officer who was a member of the IRB'. Tannam, BMH, WS 242, p. 7. At 3.15 p.m. on 23 April he received one from Mac-Neill via Fr MacMahon of St Mary's College, Rathmines, and a 'white-faced young fellow'. The letter confirmed 'every word' of the *Sunday Independent* notice was 'true' and had been issued 'to avert a frightful catastrophe'. Tannam, BMH, WS 242, p. 14.

71. McDowell, BMH, WS 173, p. 9. The decision was taken by Denis McCullough, James Smyth, Sam Heron, Herbert Moore Pim, Dr Pat McCartan, Sean Kelly and Peter Burns. Liam Gaynor, Archie Heron and Cathal McDowell were absent. McDowell, BMH, WS 173, p. 8. Volunteers in Coalisland Drill Hall had been contacted around

9 p.m. by two couriers sent by Dundalk-based Ulster OC, P. J. Burke. This specified 'there would be no fighting, that they had received a Demobilization Order'. Connolly O'Brien, BMH, WS 286, p. 27. Burke had previously apprised McCartan regarding the *Aud* and on Holy Thursday went to Dublin with him to see Clarke. McCartan, BMH, WS 766, p. 46. See also McCullough, BMH, WS 915, pp. 25–8. Dundalk IRB leader Paddy Hughes, a link to the Newry sector, received a message from Pearse stating, 'The butter will arrive on the 24th.' Paddy Rankin of Newry cycled to Dublin and fought in the GPO. John Southwell, BMH, WS 230, p. 9.

72. McDowell, BMH, WS 173, p. 5.

73. Corr, BMH, WS 227, p. 2.

74. Fr Patrick Murphy, BMH, WS 1216, p. 1.

75. Brennan, BMH, WS 125. Min Ryan had carried a message from MacDiarmada to Sinnott on Holy Thursday to which he responded, 'That will be all right.' Ryan, BMH, WS 399, p. 7.

76. Bracken, BMH, WS 361, pp. 7, 13.

77. Bracken, BMH, WS 361, pp. 7, 13.

78. Brady, BMH, WS 676, pp. 18–19.

79. De Burca, BMH, WS 105, p. 3.

80. Byrne, BMH, WS 564, p. 17. See also Thomas Harris, BMH, WS 320, pp. 5–6. Harris spoke to Byrne's adjutant O'Kelly who had dismissed MacNeill's orders as 'he was not a member of the IRB'. BMH, WS 320, pp. 5–6.

81. De Burca, BMH, WS 694, p. 5.

82. De Burca, BMH, WS 694, p. 7.

83. Ryan, BMH, WS 725, p. 10.

84. Ryan, BMH, WS 725, p. 10. Seán MacDiarmada told Joseph Murray that MacNeill's actions made him 'so annoyed and upset that his mind refused to act'. Murray, BMH, WS 254, p. 2.

85. Ryan, BMH, WS 725, p. 9.

86. Kelly, BMH, WS 1004, p. 17.

87. Kelly, BMH, WS 1004, p. 17.

88. Staines, BMH, WS 284, pp. 9–10.

89. Leon Ó Broin, *Dublin Castle and the 1916 Rising* (Dublin: Helicon, 1966), pp. 31, 84–5.

90. O'Kelly, BMH, WS 925, p. 4.

91. O'Kelly, BMH, WS 925, p. 4. O'Kelly was uncertain of chronology in February

1954, but the 'big breakfast' could not have followed the Sunday disclosure of Mac-Neill's notice given that they soon vacated the house and could not have been fed any time after Monday morning. BMH, WS 925, pp. 3–4.

92. O'Kelly, BMH, WS 925, p. 5.

93. Fr Aloysius, BMH, WS 200, p. 3.

94. Ryan, BMH, WS 725, p. 11. Eily O'Hanrahan, sister of Michael, returned to Enniscorthy with a third note from Pearse to Seamus Doyle in as many days: 'We start at noon today. Carry out your orders.' Doyle, BMH, WS 315, p. 10.

95. Connolly O'Brien, BMH, WS 286, p. 39.

96. Connolly O'Brien in MacEoin, *Survivors*, p. 200.

97. Connolly O'Brien in MacEoin, *Survivors*, p. 200. Ina Connolly married Archie Heron, 'a Protestant radical from Portadown', who joined the IRB. Connolly O'Brien in MacEoin, *Survivors*, p. 203. See also Lorcan Collins, *James Connolly* (Dublin: The O'Brien Press, 2012), p. 271. He had been given rank in the Volunteers 'a short time' prior to Easter 1916. McDowell, BMH, WS 173, p. 4. Heron knew the Connollys from joint 'Betsy Grey' Sluagh/Na Fianna Éireann activities in Belfast. Connolly O'Brien, BMH, WS 286, p. 4.

98. Elizabeth and Nell Corr, BMH, WS 179, p. 6.

99. Connolly O'Brien, BMH, WS 286, p. 41. This concerned the seizure of two motorboats at Maghery Ferry to embark men at Crumlin on the Antrim shore of Lough Neagh. McCullough, BMH, WS 915, p. 17.

100. Connolly O'Brien, BMH, WS 286, p. 40.

101. McCartan, BMH, WS 766, p. 49.

102. Nora Connolly O'Brien, in MacEoin, *Survivors*, p. 200.

103. Connolly O'Brien, BMH, WS 286, p. 43.

104. A. J. O'Halloran, 'The Irish Volunteers in Limerick City', in *Limerick's Fighting Story, 1916–21* (Cork: Mercier Press, 2009), p. 47. Margaret McGarry carried the Military Council orders to Limerick on 24 April 1916 where she found 'considerable differences of opinion ... They complained of the contradictory messages which they had received'. Cited in O'Brien, BMH, WS 1766, p. 5. She and Volunteer son Milo learned from John Daly that Colivet's men were in Killonan and of The O'Rahilly's mission the previous day. Milo McGarry, BMH, WS 356, p. 2. Maeve McGarry recalled: 'near one o'clock on Easter Sunday night, there was a knock and mother [Margaret] knew the meaning of it and said to herself as she went down the stairs, "This is the call." She opened the door and admitted Miss Marie Perolz and Charlie Wyse-Power. They came into the dining room and told her they had a despatch for her from Pearse. They gave her instructions about what she was to do next morning.

She was to take the despatch to Limerick to Daly's house, where she was to contact Colivet. If he questioned her, she was to give the password (Sarsfield).' Maeve McGarry, BMH, WS 826, p. 4. See also Brennan, BMH, WS 1068, p. 8.

105. Gubbins, BMH, WS 765, pp. 27–8.

106. De Róiste, BMH, WS 1698, p. 313.

107. Peg Duggan, BMH, WS 1576, p. 4. See also O'Doherty, BMH, WS 355, p. 9.

108. Riobárd Langford, BMH, WS 16, p. 4.

109. Langford, BMH, WS 16, p. 2.

110. Samuel P. O'Reilly, 'New York Easter Commemoration Oration', n.d., MS (Private Collection, Holt Moore Family, New York).

111. Samuel P. O'Reilly, 'A New Yorker's Story of the Irish Rebellion', *New York Journal-American*, 10 April 1966.

112. S. P. O'Reilly to Mary Holt Moore, n.d. (Private Collection, Holt Moore Family, New York).

113. Staines, BMH, WS 284, p. 1.

114. Quoted in O'Reilly, 'A New Yorker's Story of the Irish Rebellion'.

115. Quoted in O'Reilly, 'A New Yorker's Story of the Irish Rebellion'. For Daly's speech, see Desmond Ryan, *The Rising: The Complete Story of Easter Week* (Dublin: Golden Eagle Books, 1957), p. 203. Ryan, writing as 'Granuale', countered anti-Volunteer statements issued by Sean O'Casey and Michael Mullen in the *Irish Worker* in 1914 prior to Connolly's return from Belfast. O'Brien, BMH, WS 1776, p. 52.

116. Diarmuid Lynch, 'Easter Week, 1916', p. 2. In 1936–7, Lynch compiled a report on the GPO garrison which was reviewed by 'a general meeting' of the veterans in 1937. The proposed 'GPO Roll' publication did not materialise. Diarmuid Lynch to Ruaidhri Henderson, 5 June 1945, in Henderson, BMH, WS 1686.

117. Ui Dhonnachada in MacEoin, *Survivors*, p. 338.

118. Ui Dhonnachada in MacEoin, *Survivors*, p. 338.

119. De Burca, BMH, WS 694, p. 7.

120. De Burca, BMH, WS 694, p. 7.

121. Cremen, BMH, WS 563, p. 4.

122. Donnelly, BMH, WS 824, p. 4; Cremen, BMH, WS 563, p. 4.

123. De Burca, BMH, WS 694, p. 8. Donnelly's cyclist unit was harassed by 'separation women' near Jacob's Factory and heard gunfire exchanged by the ICA and British near Portobello Barracks. Donnelly, BMH, WS 824, p. 4.

124. Caldwell, BMH, WS 638, p. 6.

125. Joe Good, *Inside the GPO: A First Hand Account* (Dublin: The O'Brien Press, 2015), p. 45. Good recalled, 'It was hard to realise that this tall, scholarly man, somewhat stout (with a bad figure resulting from a sedentary life), and a cast in one eye, was our major revolutionary leader. He gave us a lecture on street and home fighting. There is no doubt he was an excellent teacher, for his precepts were later carried out to the letter. Pearse spoke slowly with careful, very measured, cadences. I didn't know then that he was struggling with an habitual stutter.' Good, *Inside the GPO*, pp. 45–6.

126. Bracken, BMH, WS 361, pp. 7–8.

127. Caldwell, BMH, WS 638, p. 4. McGallogly, BMH, WS 244, pp. 2–4; Staines, BMH, WS 284, p. 10.

128. Lynch, 'Easter Week, 1916', p. 1.

129. Brennan-Whitmore, 'Easter Monday 1916', *An tÓglach*, 4 (1), 16 January 1926, p. 4; Brennan-Whitmore, *Dublin Burning*, pp. 39–40; and Staines, BMH, WS 284, p. 10.

130. Lynch, 'Easter Week, 1916', p. 1.

131. M. J. Staines and M. W. O'Reilly, 'The Defence of the GPO', *An tÓglach*, 4 (2), 23 January 1926, p. 3. A dispatch rider claimed unreliably that 'the first shot was fired at 12 sharp by Commandant Patrick Pearse from the GPO'. Reynolds, BMH, WS 350, p. 10. He averred Pearse commended him the following day for maintaining contact with other battalions. Reynolds, BMH, WS 350, p. 12. Later missions included delivering a message from Pearse to W. T. Cosgrave in the South Dublin Union. Reynolds, BMH, WS 350, p. 13.

132. Staines, BMH, WS 284, p. 12.

133. Lynch, 'Easter Week, 1916', p. 1.

134. Brennan-Whitmore, 'Easter Monday 1916', p. 5.

135. Brennan-Whitmore, *Dublin Burning*, p. 49.

136. Cremen, BMH, WS 563, p. 4. Cremen was uncertain whether 'I' or 'we' had been uttered by Connolly. Bulfin raised one of the flags while Joe Gleeson of the IRB attended to the second. Bulfin, BMH, WS 497, p. 7. See also Ryan, *A Man Called Pearse*, p. 129.

Chapter 6

1. Brennan-Whitmore, *Dublin Burning*, p. 50.

2. Lynch, 'Easter Week, 1916', p. 2.

3. O'Brien, BMH, WS 1776, p. 70.

4. Donnelly, BMH, WS 824, p. 6.

5. *Poblacht na hÉireann*, 1916.

6. *Gaelic American*, 7 March 1914, p. 7.

7. Lynch, 'Easter Week, 1916', p. 5. In a written appeal for St Enda's funding in New York, Pearse invited subscriptions from 'Irishmen and Irishwomen'. *Gaelic American*, 7 March 1914, p. 5.

8. Shelley, BMH, WS 870, p. 3.

9. Curran, BMH, WS 687, p. 42.

10. Curran, BMH, WS 687, p. 42.

11. O'Kelly, BMH, WS 925, p. 6.

12. Ryan, BMH, WS 399, p. 13.

13. Lynch, 'Easter Week, 1916', p. 3.

14. Lynch, 'Easter Week, 1916', p. 5.

15. Lynch, 'Easter Week, 1916', p. 5.

16. Ua Caomhanaigh, BMH, WS 889, p. 45.

17. Murray, BMH, WS 252, p. 2.

18. Rowan, BMH, WS 871, p. 3. See also McGallogly, BMH, WS 244, p. 59.

19. Sir Arthur Irwin to Dorothy Irwin, 25 April 1916, in *Irish Times*, 15 March 2014.

20. Norway to G[adsden], 1 May 1916, in Keith Jeffrey (ed.), *The Sinn Féin Rebellion as They Saw It* (Dublin: Irish Academic Press, 1999), p. 65. Connolly, according to MacDiarmada, was responsible for neutralising state communications in 'the Telephone Exchange, Dublin Castle and the north city'. Lynch, 'Easter Week, 1916', p. 2. Lynch believed that Connolly, around 4.15 p.m., sent men who had evacuated Liberty Hall to reinforce City Hall. On moving through Temple Bar they were warned of British possession of the Telephone Exchange and came under fire. Lynch, 'Easter Week, 1916', p. 5.

21. Lynch, 'Easter Week, 1916', p. 3.

22. Staines, BMH, WS 284, p. 14. Bulfin had no orders regarding Dublin Castle. Bulfin, BMH, WS 497, pp. 5–6.

23. Lynch, 'Easter Week, 1916', p. 5.

24. Lynch, 'Easter Week, 1916', p. 5.

25. Walsh, BMH, WS 91, p. 4. Walsh claimed to have mobilised twenty Hibernian Rifles using a listing provided by Scollan. He wrongly believed they belonged to various Irish Volunteer companies and were first referred to as Hibernian Rifles upon arrival in the GPO. Walsh, BMH, WS 91, p. 4. Leading AOH-IAA man Sean Milroy fought in 1916 and, when cut off, was rescued on 26 April by a sally led by James Connolly. Henderson, BMH, WS 249, p. 48.

26. Thomas Leahy, BMH, WS 660, p. 10.

27. Jeremiah Joseph O'Leary, BMH, WS 1108, p. 17.

28. Ryan, BMH, WS 399, p. 13.

29. Lynch, 'Easter Week, 1916', pp. 4–5.

30. Byrne, BMH, WS 564, p. 18. Byrne claimed responsibility for protecting the RIC men from O'Kelly but noted that the local sergeant later credited 'Donal Buckley' (Domhnall Ua Buachalla). Byrne, BMH, WS 564, p. 19. Thomas Harris recalled, 'Donal Buckley had just arrived from Dublin and had the information that the rising was on in the city.' Harris, BMH, WS 320, p. 8. A small group of IRB-directed Volunteers sabotaged rail and telecommunications in the Colt Wood area of Laois on Easter Sunday, having deployed before MacNeill's orders arrived. Ramsbottom, BMH, WS 1045, p. 6.

31. Colgan, BMH, WS 850, p. 8.

32. Byrne, BMH, WS 564, p. 19.

33. De Burca, BMH, WS 694, p. 11.

34. De Burca, BMH, WS 694, p. 11.

35. Gregan, BMH, WS 685, p. 10.

36. Charles MacAuley, BMH, WS 735, p. 5.

37. MacAuley, BMH, WS 735, p. 7.

38. Lynch, 'Easter Week, 1916', p. 6.

39. Colgan, BMH, WS 850, p. 16.

40. Lynch, 'Easter Week, 1916', p. 6. See also Byrne, BMH, WS 564, p. 20.

41. Byrne, BMH, WS 564, p. 21.

42. Murray, BMH, WS 254, p. 2.

43. O'Reilly, 'A New Yorker's Story of the Irish Rebellion'. See also Helen Litton, *Edward Daly* (Dublin: The O'Brien Press, 2013), pp. 117–19.

44. Lynch, 'Easter Week, 1916', p. 7. Staines reported Walsh's incautious actions to Pearse, who stated, probably rhetorically, that he 'must cease or be shot'. Staines, BMH, WS 284, p. 13. Cork City Volunteers heard rumours on Easter Sunday that 'Padraig Mac Piarais had assumed chief command. Bulmer Hobson has been arrested by the Citizen Army … Eoin MacNeill has "ratted".' De Róiste, BMH, WS 1698, p. 315.

45. Cleary, BMH, WS 972, p. 6. In mid-November 1917, the republican core marched in Dungarvan as part of a Sinn Féin rally addressed by Count Plunkett. Cleary was standard-bearer of a Tricolour that 'bore initials of IRA … the first national flag to bear those initials outside Dublin'. Cleary, BMH, WS 972, p. 10.

46. *Irish War News*, 25 April 1916.

47. Lynch, 'Easter Week, 1916', p. 8.

48. 'Explanatory Note' in Lynch, 'Easter Week, 1916', p. 10.

49. Lynch, 'Easter Week, 1916', p. 5.

50. See O'Donnell, *Robert Emmet and the Rising of 1803*, Appendix II.

51. Patrick Pearse, 'The Provisional Government to the Citizens of Dublin', 25 April 1916. For text, see Irish Times, *1916 Rebellion Handbook*, new edition (Dublin: Irish Times Books, 1998), p. 45.

52. Lynch, 'Easter Week, 1916', p. 7. Dick McKee of G Company, 2nd Battalion, was supposed to have 'seized Trinity College' while others occupied the Bank of Ireland, but this did not occur. Henderson, BMH, WS 249, p. 26.

53. Henderson, BMH, WS 249, pp. 41–2.

54. Charles Saurin, 'Hotel Metropole Garrison' in *An tÓglach*, 13 March 1926. See also Henderson, BMH, WS 429, p. 28, and Seamus Daly, BMH, WS 360, p. 35.

55. Lynch, 'Easter Week, 1916', pp. 8–9.

56. Uí Dhonnchadha, in MacEoin, *Survivors*, p. 339.

57. Uí Dhonnchadha, in MacEoin, *Survivors*, p. 339.

58. Lynch, 'Easter Week, 1916', p. 9.

59. Lynch, 'Easter Week, 1916', p. 10.

60. Ryan, BMH, WS 399, p. 17.

61. Henderson, BMH, WS 249, pp. 45–6.

62. Lynch, 'Easter Week, 1916', p. 9.

63. Lynch, 'Easter Week, 1916', p. 9.

64. Henderson, BMH, WS 249, p. 47.

65. *Irish Times*, 29 April 1916.

66. Lynch, 'Easter Week, 1916', p. 2.

67. Bucknill, 'Letters', BMH, WS 1019. The flag flown from Boland's had been 'obtained at St Enda's – the only flag De Valera had'. Diarmuid Lynch, 'The National Flag, 1916', BMH, WS 120, p. 4.

68. Bracken, BMH, WS 361, p. 9. See Staines and O'Reilly, 'The Defence of the GPO', p. 4. Jeweller Myles R. Hopkins was a financial backer of the *Sinn Féin* weekly into 1915 when it lapsed. O'Kelly, BMH, WS 1765, p. 100. Diarmuid O'Leary, Managing Director at Hopkins & Hopkins, was an IRB man involved in the Kilcoole gun-running in August 1914. O'Kelly, BMH, WS 1765, p. 137.

69. Ryan, BMH, WS 399, pp. 17–18.

70. Rowan, BMH, WS 871, p. 4.

71. Henderson, 'Easter Week Rising: A Tabulated Summary of Events in Dublin from April 24th to April 29th 1916', BMH, WS 1686, p. 6. See also Thomas Walsh and James Walsh, BMH, WS 198, p. 18.

72. Walsh and Walsh, BMH, WS 198, p. 18.

73. Rowan, BMH, WS 871, pp. 4–5.

74. Henderson, 'Tabulated Summary', BMH, WS 1686, p. 7.

75. Lynch, 'Easter Week, 1916', p. 11.

76. Price, BMH, WS 1754, p. 9.

77. Price, BMH, WS 1754, p. 9.

78. Lynch, 'Easter Week, 1916', p. 11.

79. Caldwell, BMH, WS 638, p. 8.

80. Michael Staines, 'Criticism of Broadcast', BMH, WS 943, p. 3.

81. Lynch, 'Easter Week, 1916', p. 11. The firm Hopkins & Hopkins were 'manufacturing jewellers' well disposed towards the Irish Volunteers. *Ná Bac Leis*, 26 June 1915, p. 3. The Dublin Bread Company restaurants also advertised in the militant press. *The Hibernian*, 3 July 1915, p. 7. A British Army corporal guarding prisoners in the Custom House after the Rising admitted 'going around the city seeing the positions held by the rebels' when in plainclothes on 25 April. O'Brien, BMH, WS 1776, p. 10.

82. Donnelly, BMH, WS 824, p. 8.

83. Lynch, 'Easter Week, 1916', p. 12.

84. De Burca, BMH, WS 694, p. 14.

85. Ryan, BMH, WS 724, p. 11.

86. Ryan, BMH, WS 724, p. 12. Carney, according to Ryan, was 'Connolly's grim and hero-worshipping secretary' (BMH, WS 724, p. 12). Brennan-Whitmore, who did not know Pearse well and was generally posted outside the GPO, noted, 'Moving slowly about, he never sought to interfere with anyone or anything. His mind was obviously up in the clouds and at time he conveyed an impression of futility, as it he would be utterly helpless in a sudden and unexpected emergency. At the same time his mere presence was a tonic to everyone. There was a mystic atmosphere about his personality which inspired confidence and an urge to achive great things. He was not just respected by the little garrison, he was almost worshipped.' Brennan-Whitmore, *Dublin Burning*, p. 60. Pearse subsequently referred Brennan-Whitmore to Connolly to receive orders that placed him in command of an outpost. *Dublin Burning*, p. 63.

87. Ryan, BMH, WS 724, p. 17. Clarke reputedly used the exact words 'wiped out' in conversation with Min Ryan which may indicate prior conversations with Pearse.

Ryan, BMH, WS 399, p. 16.

88. Gregan, BMH, WS 685, p. 11.

89. Ryan, BMH, WS 399, p. 19.

90. Ryan, BMH, WS 399, p. 19.

91. Ryan, BMH, WS 399, p. 19.

92. Ryan, BMH, WS 399, p. 19.

93. Ryan, BMH, WS 399, p. 19.

94. Quoted in O'Reilly, 'A New Yorker's Story of the Irish Rebellion'.

95. Good, *Inside the GPO*, p. 81.

96. Good, *Inside the GPO*, p. 81.

97. Desmond FitzGerald, 'Inside the GPO', *Irish Times*, 7 April 1966.

98. FitzGerald, 'Inside the GPO'.

99. *Irish Times*, 29 April 1916.

100. P. J. Brennan to Sean Nunan, 15 September 1951, in Sir Alfred Bucknill, BMH, WS 1019.

101. Bucknill, BMH, WS 1019, p. 3.

102. F. H. Boland to Sean Nunan, 5 February 1953, in Bucknill, BMH, WS 1019.

103. McGallogly, BMH, WS 244, p. 11. McGallogly was processed following capture with Tom Clarke and Eamonn Duggan. All three withheld comment when invited to respond to the charges. Clarke praised the silent Scot afterwards, saying he had 'acted wisely'. He was court-martialled with Willie Pearse, J. J. Walsh and Sean McGarry. McGallogly, BMH, WS 244, pp. 11–12.

104. O'Reilly, BMH, WS 1031, p. 9.

105. Murphy, BMH, WS 1216, p. 2.

106. Lynch, 'Easter Week, 1916', p. 12.

107. Lynch, 'Easter Week, 1916', p. 13. Materials used to build armoured vehicles were provided by Guinness Brewery in St James's Gate. According to Mary Norway, on 28 April, engineers 'made three splendid armoured cars by putting great long boilers six feet in diameter on to their large motor lorries. Holes are bored down the sides to let in air, and they are painted grey. The driver sits inside too. They each carry twenty-two men or a ton of food in absolute security.' Cited in Jeffrey, *The Sinn Féin Rebellion*, p. 57. Eight hundred Guinness workers were allegedly 'told to go and enlist' in 1914. 'Anti-Conscript' to the Editor, *Workers' Republic*, 26 June 1915.

108. Ryan, BMH, WS 724, p. 18.

109. Shelley, BMH, WS 870, pp. 4–5.

110. Lynch, 'Easter Week, 1916', p. 14. See Staines and O'Reilly, 'The Defence of the GPO', p. 5.

111. Good, *Inside the GPO*, p. 89.

112. Good, *Inside the GPO*, p. 89.

113. Good, *Inside the GPO*, p. 89.

114. Quoted in Connolly O'Brien, BMH, WS 286, p. 48. William O'Brien conversed with James Connolly on the street and through windows and formed the impression that his friend was 'in charge of everything'. O'Brien, BMH, WS 1766, p. 77.

115. O'Brien, BMH, WS 1766, p. 4.

116. De Burca, BMH, WS 694, p. 15.

117. De Burca, BMH, WS 694, p. 15. A suggestion that possession of the Pillar might frustrate rebel activities was investigated by Pearse, who sent Slattery, a trained engineer, to examine the position. Cremen, BMH, WS 563, p. 6.

118. De Burca, BMH, WS 694, p. 17.

119. Bucknill, 'Letters of an English Soldier in Ireland', BMH, WS 1019, p. 6.

120. Lynch, 'Easter Week, 1916', p. 14.

121. Lynch, 'Easter Week, 1916', p. 16.

122. De Burca, BMH, WS 694, p. 18.

123. Ua Caomhanaigh, BMH, WS 889, p. 55.

124. Ryan, BMH, WS 724, p. 20.

125. James Connolly to 'Soldiers', 28 April 1916, in Bucknill, BMH, WS 1019.

126. James Connolly, 'Army of the Irish Republic', 28 April 1916, in Bucknill, BMH, WS 1019.

127. Diary of Sergeant Samuel Henry Lomas, *Irish Times*, 8 March 2014.

128. Bucknill, 'Letters', BMH, WS 1019.

129. Ua Caomhanaigh, BMH, WS 889, p. 52.

Chapter 7

1. Gavan Duffy, BMH, WS 216, p. 8.

2. Lynch, 'Easter Week, 1916', p. 15.

3. Ryan, BMH, WS 724, p. 20.

4. Harris, BMH, WS 320, p. 11.

5. Lynch, 'Easter Week, 1916', p. 15.

6. Lynch, 'Easter Week, 1916', p. 15.

7. Lynch, 'Easter Week, 1916', p. 16.

8. Lynch, 'Easter Week, 1916', p. 16.

9. Murphy, 'The Evacuation and Surrender', BMH, WS 370, p. 8.

10. O'Reilly, 'Oration', MS (Private Collection, Holt Moore Family).

11. Quoted in Lynch, 'Easter Week, 1916', p. 16. The full text of the speech was written in the form of a manifesto headed: 'Headquarters, Army of the Irish Republic, General Post Office, Dublin, 28th April, 1916, 9.30 am'. See *Rebellion Handbook*, p. 47.

12. Ua Caomhanaigh, BMH, WS 889, p. 56. See also Staines, BMH, WS 284, p. 17.

13. O'Sullivan, BMH, WS 393, p. 12.

14. Lynch, 'Easter Week, 1916', p. 17.

15. De Burca, BMH, WS 694, p. 18.

16. Caldwell, BMH, WS 638, p. 9.

17. Ua Caomhanaigh, BMH, WS 889, pp. 56–7. See also McGallogly, BMH, WS 244, p. 54.

18. Tannam, BMH, WS 242, p. 36.

19. Tannam, BMH, WS 242, p. 36.

20. Tannam, BMH, WS 242, p. 36.

21. Lynch, 'Easter Week, 1916', p. 17.

22. Caldwell, BMH, WS 638, p. 10. McLaughlin had been promoted by Connolly. Members of Pearse's Company recalled the retreat: 'There was no panic whatsoever. We marched out in two-deep, each man holding his rifle, pointing upwards … When we reached the side door leading into Henry Street Commandant Pearse was standing in the small hallway watching and waiting until the last man had passed out of the building'. De Burca, BMH, WS 694, p. 19.

23. Bucknill, 'Letters', BMH, WS 1019, p. 5.

24. O'Reilly, 'A New Yorker's Story of the Irish Rebellion'. See also Combri Group, HQ16: The Citizen's Plan for Dublin, Part 1 (Dublin, 2012), p. 2. Available online at www.gaelicadventure.org/pdfs/h16.pdf (accessed 3 November 2015).

25. De Burca, BMH, WS 694, p. 19.

26. Staines and O'Reilly, 'The Defence of the GPO', p. 6.

27. Ua Caomhanaigh, BMH, WS 889, p. 57.

28. Cremen, BMH, WS 563, p. 6.

29. Bracken, BMH, WS 361, p. 11. Some accounts list the Henry Place spur leading directly to Moore Street as Henry Lane. Bracken, BMH, WS 361, p. 11. See also Staines, BMH, WS 284, p. 17.

30. De Burca, BMH, WS 694, p. 20. See also Bulfin, BMH, WS 497, p. 10. Tannam specified that the whitewashed building was being fired upon by the British military. Tannam, BMH, WS 242, p. 36.

31. Bulfin, BMH, WS 497, p. 11.

32. De Burca, BMH, WS 694, p. 20.

33. Leahy, BMH, WS 660, p. 14.

34. Traynor, BMH, WS 340, p. 24.

35. Combri Group, *HQ 16*, p. 3.

36. De Burca, BMH, WS 694, p. 21.

37. Ua Caomhanaigh, BMH, WS 889, p. 58.

38. Ua Caomhanaigh, BMH, WS 889, p. 59.

39. Ua Caomhanaigh, BMH, WS 889, p. 59. After the surrender, a Royal Irish Regiment soldier confided that he had been a Volunteer. 'He said we should have waited till they came back from France and they would have been in the fight'. Ua Caomhanaigh, BMH, WS 889, p. 62.

40. Lynch, 'Easter Week, 1916', p. 17. Caldwell was among those who accessed the house at Moore Street corner. He recalled 'a number of houses running down Moore Street had been bored through to provide a line of retreat'. Caldwell, BMH, WS 638, p. 10.

41. Donnelly, BMH, WS 824, p. 8.

42. Good, *Inside the GPO*, p. 107.

43. Ua Caomhanaigh, BMH, WS 889, p. 59. Staines 'heard Connolly compliment McLoughlin and promote him Commandant'. Staines, BMH, WS 284, p. 17. O'Sullivan recalled that McLoughlin 'aggressively informed us that he had been appointed Commandant by Pearse'. O'Sullivan, BMH, WS 393, p. 12.

44. Lynch, 'Easter Week, 1916', p. 18.

45. Lynch, 'Easter Week, 1916', p. 18.

46. Tannam, BMH, WS 242, p. 41.

47. Cremen, BMH, WS 563, p. 8.

48. Cremen, BMH, WS 563, p. 8.

49. De Burca, BMH, WS 694, p. 22.

50. De Burca, BMH, WS 694, p. 22. The postponement was probably the six-hour delay referenced by Des Ryan. Ryan, BMH, WS 724, p. 22. When court-martialled, Hibernian Rifles officer J. J. Walsh claimed to have 'held no official position in the Volunteers'. McGallogly, BMH, WS 244, p. 12.

51. Bracken, BMH, WS 361, p. 12. Liam Tannam recalled that Sean McLoughlin's

detailed local knowledge gave rise to the plan to reach the Williams & Woods Factory 'across Parnell Street into Kings Inn Street'. Sixteen men with fixed bayonets under George Plunkett were evidently those who gathered in the yard of Kelly's Fish Shop. They were to 'suddenly emerge into … O'Rahilly Parade, turn left and then right and charge the barricade held by the British at the Parnell Street end of Moore Street'. Tannam, BMH, WS 242, p. 39. See also Bulfin, BMH, WS 497, p. 12.

52. Patrick Pearse to Margaret Pearse, 1 May 1916, in Bucknill, BMH, WS 1019.

53. Pearse to Pearse, 1 May 1916.

54. John Twamley, BMH, WS 629, p. 6.

55. Bulfin, BMH, WS 497, p. 12.

56. Ua Caomhanaigh, BMH, WS 889, p. 60.

57. Dorothy Macardle, *The Irish Republic* (London: Victor Gollancz, 1937), p. 182.

58. Good, *Inside the GPO*, p. 111.

59. Good, *Inside the GPO*, p. 111.

60. Brigadier General W. H. M. Lowe to Patrick Pearse, 29 April 1916, in Connell, *Dublin Rising 1916*, p. 55.

61. Pearse to Pearse, 1 May 1916.

62. Good, *Inside the GPO*, pp. 111–12.

63. *Irish Times*, 2 May 1916.

64. Ryan, BMH, WS 724, p. 22.

65. Ryan, BMH, WS 724, p. 22.

66. Ryan, BMH, WS 724, p. 22.

67. Cremen, BMH, WS 563, p. 8.

68. O'Reilly, 'A New Yorker's Story of the Irish Rebellion'.

69. De Burca, BMH, WS 694, p. 24.

70. Caldwell, BMH, WS 638, p. 11.

71. O'Reilly, 'A New Yorker's Story of the Irish Rebellion'. O'Reilly was held in Knutsford Prison and Frongoch until liberated in late 1916. Sergeant Lomas noted the events of 2 p.m., 29 April: 'Orders are passed for us to stand by as a white flag was approaching the end of Moore Street. This was found to be from Sean O'Connelly [sic] asking for terms of surrender. Instructions were sent back up the street for O'Connelly to come down and interview the General in command of our troops. This was done, O'Connelly being carried down on a stretcher, as he was wounded in the leg. Whilst standing by, we came across the dead body of O'Reilly [The O'Rahilly].' Lomas Diary, *Irish Times*, 8 March 2014. MacDiarmada 'spoke with emotion of the fight against

fearful odds by the Dublin Brigade'. De Burca, BMH, WS 694, p. 24.

72. Sam O'Reilly, Miscellaneous MSS notes, Private Collection, Holt Moore Family.

73. Caldwell, BMH, WS 838, p. 11.

74. Pearse to Pearse, 1 May 1916.

75. Cited in Ó Broin, *Dublin Castle and the 1916 Rising*, p. 113.

76. Patrick Pearse, Orders, 29 April 1916, in Fr Augustine, OFM, CAP, BMH, WS 920.

77. Bucknill, 'Letters of an English Soldier in Ireland', BMH, WS 1019.

78. Pearse to Pearse, 1 May 1916.

79. Caldwell, BMH, WS 638, p. 12.

80. Ryan, BMH, WS 724, p. 24.

81. De Burca, BMH, WS 694, p. 25. See also 'Scelig' (J. J. O'Kelly), 'The GPO', in *Dublin's Fighting Story, 1916–21: Told by the Men who Made It*, with an introduction by Diarmuid Ferriter (Cork: Mercier Press, 2009), p. 207; and Cremen, BMH, WS 563, p. 8. Lea Wilson was serving as an RIC district inspector when IRA counter-intelligence officers Frank Thornton and Liam Tobin shot him dead with the assistance of Wexford's Joe McMahon. Whelan, BMH, WS 1294, p. 14.

82. John Shouldice, BMH, WS 162, p. 1.

83. Augustine, BMH, WS 920. See also Aloysius, BMH, WS 200, p. 6.

84. Augustine, BMH, WS 920. According to Fr Columbus Murphy, Pearse was deep in thought when he arrived into Arbour Hill but then recognised his Capuchin garb and offered his hand, saying, 'Oh, Father, the loss of life, the destruction! But, please God, it won't be in vain.' Quoted in *Irish Times*, 27 June 2015. Fr Columbus was escorted to the Four Courts by Lieutenant J. R. Hempseed of the 5th Battalion, South Staffordshire Regiment. *Irish Times*, 8 May 1916.

85. MacDonagh, BMH, WS 532, p. 13.

86. Byrne, BMH, WS 423, p. 2.

87. Seán Etchingham, cited in Murphy, BMH, WS 1216, p. 8. Gorey Volunteer James Gleeson saw the delegates pass through the town under RIC/British escort on their way to meet Pearse in Dublin on 30 April 1916. Gleeson, BMH, WS 1012, p. 3. See also Whelan, BMH, WS 1294, p. 7.

88. Etchingham, cited in Fr Murphy, BMH, WS 1216, p. 8. Mauser rifles, probably part of the batch run into Kilcoole in August 1914, were used in the Rising and subsequently by F Company of the 4th Battalion. The unit trained in the grounds of St Enda's, Rathfarnham. George Joseph Dwyer, BMH, WS 678, pp. 1–2.

89. Doyle, BMH, WS 315, p. 14.

90. Doyle, BMH, WS 315, p. 14.

91. Whelan, BMH, WS 1294, p. 7.

92. *Irish Times*, 1 May 1916.

93. Bucknill, 'Letters', BMH, WS 1019, n.p.

94. Boland to Nunan, 5 February 1953.

95. O'Brien, BMH, WS 1776, p. 15.

96. O'Brien, BMH, WS 1776, p. 15.

97. Bucknill, 'Letters', BMH, WS 1019, n.p.

98. Gerald Doyle, BMH, WS 1511, pp. 20–1.

99. Doyle, BMH, WS 1511, pp. 20–1.

100. Thomas Pugh, BMH, WS 397, p. 8.

101. Bucknill, 'Letters', WS 1019, p. 3.

102. Bucknill, 'Letters', WS 1019, p. 3.

103. Pearse to Pearse, 1 May 1916. MacDiarmada had told Denis McCullough on 17 April 1916 of the possible arrival of a vessel in Dublin 'with German officers to lead the Rising' but doubted that his friend really expected any such aid. McCullough, BMH, WS 915, p. 21.

104. Boland to Nunan, 5 February 1953.

105. Pearse, 2 May 1916, NLI, MS 17, 306, p. 2.

106. Barton, *From Behind a Closed Door*, p. 110.

107. Pearse, 2 May 1916, NLI, MS 17, 306, p. 1. On the eve of execution, Pearse wrote his final poem, 'The Wayfarer'. See Mairéad Ashe Fitzgerald (ed.), *A Terrible Beauty: Poetry of 1916* (Dublin: The O'Brien Press, 2015), p. 33.

108. Pearse to Pearse, 1 May 1916.

109. Augustine, BMH, WS 920.

110. Bucknill, 'Letters', BMH, WS 1019.

111. Bucknill, 'Letters', BMH, WS 1019.

112. *Irish Times*, 16 May 1916.

113. Aloysius, BMH, WS 200, p. 12.

114. Barton, *From Behind a Closed Door*, p. 114.

115. Lomas Diary, *Irish Times*, 8 March 2014. For Maconchy, see Charles Townshend, *Easter 1916: The Irish Rebellion* (London: Allen Lane, 2005), pp. 197–8.

116. Boland to Nunan, 5 February 1953.

117. See Shane Kenna, *Thomas MacDonagh* (Dublin: The O'Brien Press, 2014), pp. 167–8.

118. Patrick Pearse to Margaret Pearse, 3 May 1916, in O'Buachalla, *Letters of P. H. Pearse*, p. 382. One of the last poems written by Pearse, 'Renunciation', ended: 'I have turned my face / To this road before me, / To the deed that I see / And the death I shall die.' Pearse, *Plays, Stories, Poems*, p. 325.

119. Bucknill, 'Letters', BMH, WS 1019.

120. *Irish Times*, 27 June 2015.

121. Curran, BMH, WS 687, p. 72.

122. Curran, BMH, WS 687, p. 77.

123. Cited in Ó Broin, *Dublin Castle and the 1916 Rising*, p. 131.

124. Cited in Ó Broin, *Dublin Castle and the 1916 Rising*, p. 131.

125. *Irish Times*, 31 May 1916 and 17 July 1917. See also *Wolfe Tone Annual, 1946, Laochra na Casca, Soldiers of 1916* (Dublin, 1946), pp. 72–4.

126. Staines, BMH, WS 284, p. 20.

127. Doyle, BMH, WS 1511, p. 23.

128. Callender, BMH, WS 923, p. 26.

129. Aloysius, BMH, WS 200, p. 12.

130. Nevin, BMH, WS 1605, p. 49.

131. Nevin, BMH, WS 1605, p. 49.

132. Ryan, BMH, WS 725, p. 3.

133. Aloysius, BMH, WS 200, p. 16.

134. Ó Broin, *Dublin Castle and the 1916 Rising*, p. 131.

135. Mrs T. M. Sullivan, BMH, WS 653, Chapter 13.

136. Hobson, BMH, WS 81, 'Rising', p. 10.

137. Hobson, 26 January 1948, BMH, WS 84, 'Pearse', p. 2.

138. *Irish Volunteer*, 19 December 1914.

Index

and the IRB   105, 107, 130,
135–8, 190
and Irish Volunteers   104,
107–8, 115–17, 127, 132,
146, 158
plans for Easter Rising   161,
166–7, 172–3, 175, 179,
181, 183, 185, 196
travels to USA   100
MacDonagh, John   144,
162, 167
MacDonagh, Thomas   34, 40,
56, 61, 69, 99, 104, 107–8
in Easter Rising   244, 265,
268, 272
execution   273–7
and the IRB   138
and Irish Volunteers   111,
113, 115, 119, 121, 127–8,
138, 147
plans for Easter
Rising   160–1, 166–8,
178, 180–1, 183, 193
McDonnell, Mick   150
MacDonnell, Thomas   36
McDowell, Cathal   147–8,
176, 185–6
McElligot, Jimmy   214
McGallogly, John   161
McGarrity, Joe   51, 53, 75, 82,
85, 94, 100, 112, 171, 190
McGarry, Maeve   43
McGarry, Margaret   43
McGarry, Milo   43
McGarry, Sean   200
McGinley, Con and
Eunan   71
McGinley, Conor   166
Mac Giolla Bhríde,
Niall   29–30
Mac Giollarnáth, Seán   44
McGuinness, Joe   119
McGuire, Judge John C.   85
McKee, Dick   128
Macken, Francis   248
McLoughlin, John
(Sean)   251, 256
MacManus, Seumas   41–2, 81
McManus, Terence
Bellew   119
MacNeill, Eoin   21–2, 24, 27,
62–4, 69, 74, 87, 89
countermanding order   175,
177–88, 190, 192, 198–9,
204, 214–15, 217, 222
and Gaelic League   117

and Irish Volunteers   95,
97–9, 103, 106, 109, 111,
115–16, 118–19, 125–7,
130–1, 146, 155–6
opposed to Easter
Rising   162, 166–7, 171,
173, 174, 231, 278
MacNeill, James   146
MacNeill, John see MacNeill,
Eoin
McNulty family   139
McNulty, Seamus   189–90
Maconchy, Brigadier E.
W.   273
MacSwiney, Mary   195
MacSwiney, Terence   69, 108,
111, 124, 195
McTigue, John J.   76
Madden, Denis F.   25
Mahaffy, J. P.   102, 103
Mallin, Michael   114, 132,
136, 268
Malone, Michael 'Mick'   226
Malone, Seamus   187
Malone, Tom   66
Manahan, Liam   100, 127,
160, 161
Manchester Martyrs   65, 68–9
Mannix, Daniel   23
Markievicz, Countess
Constance   47, 52, 111,
131–2, 136, 182, 192, 259
Martin, Eamon   56, 89
Martyn, Edward   27
Maxwell, General Sir
John   224–5, 233–4, 262,
268, 270, 275–6, 278
Maynooth   213–15
Mellows, Liam   56, 66, 70, 72,
95, 96, 113, 127, 129
escape from Reading
Gaol   159
and Irish Volunteers   127,
129, 144, 157
Mendicity Institute   268
Metropole Hotel   226
Milligan, Alice   40
Minturn, Judge James F.   78
Mitchel, John   80, 141
Moloney, Helena   54, 137
Monteith, Robert   107, 128,
160, 185
Moore, Colonel Maurice   40
Moore, John   154
Moore Street   253–5, 258
Moran, D. P.   27

Morrissey, Fr Edward   275
Morrogh-Ryan family   154
Morrow, Jack   157
Motherway, Michael   69
Mullin, James   22
Mullins, Willie   185
Murphy, Charlie   99
Murphy, Dr Philip   34
Murphy, Fintan   144, 166, 247
Murphy, Fr Columbus   266,
272
Murphy, Fr Patrick   187, 235
Murray, Eamon   131
Murray, Joseph   93, 208, 216

N

Nevin, Fr Eugene   169, 277
New Ireland Literary Society–2
Nolan, Major Thomas   76
Nugent, John D.   90–1, 95

O

O Baun, Tomás   131
Ó Braonáin, Séamus   145
Ó Bríain, Liam   173
O'Brien, Conor   94
O'Brien, James   210
O'Brien, Liam   178, 187
O'Brien, William   25, 69, 119,
134, 137–8, 204, 238, 268
O'Callaghan, Michael   73
O'Carroll, Liam   68
O'Carroll, Richard 'Dick'   66,
119
O'Casey, Sean   134
Ó Conaire, Pádraic   56
O'Connell, J. J.   74, 104, 111,
116, 123, 127, 151
opposed to Easter
Rising   160, 166–7, 169,
186
O'Connell, Mortimer   59, 64
O'Connor, James   119
O'Connor, Rory   155
O'Connor, Seamus   68, 127
O'Connor, Thomas   42, 55
O'Doherty, Joe   187
O'Doherty, Kitty (née
Gibbons)   43
O'Donovan Rossa,
Jeremiah   117–21, 124
O'Donovan Rossa, Mary
J.   118–20
O'Duffy, Eimar   74, 151,
166, 224